CW00662772

FREEDOM TO CHOOSE

FREEDOM TO CHOOSE

Cork & Party Politics in Ireland 1918–1932

Micheál Martin

The Collins Press

FIRST PUBLISHED IN 2009 BY
The Collins Press
West Link Park
Doughcloyne
Wilton
Cork

British Library Cataloguing in Publication Data

Martin, Micheal
    Freedom to choose : the formation of Irish political
    parties, 1918-1932
    1. Political parties - Ireland - History - 20th century
    2. Ireland - Politics and government - 1910-1921 3.
Ireland
    - Politics and government - 1922-1949
    I. Title
    324.2'417
ISBN-13: 9781848890015

Typesetting by The Collins Press
Typeset in Sabon 11 on 13 pt
Printed in Malta by Gutenberg Press Limited

CONTENTS

INTRODUCTION

From an early age, I have been interested in politics and the political process. When I went to further my studies at University College Cork, I began to think further about what motivates people to get involved in public service. This book is based on a dissertation which in part, aimed to address this question by focussing on the challenges that faced the early years of the state. In particular, I wanted to explore the circumstances in which people became involved in consolidating the Irish state and how their activities balanced issues which were of concern to the country at large with those which were of more local and regional interest. This is what my book is about. It is about the path towards the foundation of an independent Ireland and how this was perceived and influenced by local factors in Cork: how the sense of locality, family and friendship outside of Dublin interacted with what was being debated for the country in Dáil Eireann.

The period covered by this book was one of deeply held feelings. It was one of powerful ideologies, nationalism and socialism being among the more potent, while in more organised forms, Catholicism, the Gaelic League and the Gaelic Athletic Association were also powerful forces within the Ireland of the day. The manner in which all these influences emerged in Cork powerfully underlined the influence which *place* could have on these movements and direct how they might be developed. My purpose here is to examine this combination of ideas, how they were organised in Cork city and how in this process, this one place helped to bring stability to the newly independent Irish state.

The Anglo-Irish Treaty (1921) and the Civil War (1922–23) had brought about the break-up of Sinn Féin and as a result, a significant realignment of contemporary political interests. The supporters of the old Irish Parliamentary Party which had suffered a major electoral defeat in 1918, played a vital role in this realignment. So did the later split within Sinn Féin. Both political movements are central to this study. The support bases of the two main post-Treaty parties are also considered, as are the fortunes of the Labour Party. In Cork, Labour made a considerable impact on the 'pact election' of 1922 and although it failed to make an electoral breakthrough in that year, its relationship with Sinn Féin remained an important feature of Cork politics. Moreover, the election is crucial to understanding why Labour did not emerge as a major party at this time of political realignment.

The major parties during the 1920s were Cumann na nGaedhael and Fianna Fáil. As such, they form the focus of this study. For the Cork City constituency, it is clear that within Cumann na nGaedhael, several groups were competing for control of the party. Beyond this, there were additional tensions between the party leadership and the rank-and-file and these partly explain why the party went into decline as the 1920s unfolded. Although Fianna Fáil did not emerge as a distinctive political party until 1926, its base as an anti-Treaty party was more disparate. From the beginning, it also commanded the most stable pattern of partisan loyalty of all political parties. Furthermore, the development of Fianna Fáil as a highly organised, disciplined and national party was unusual in that it took place in the context of a society that was still dominated by a rural culture. The party considerably broadened its original anti-Treaty base, not least in Cork city, and by the end of the decade, it had absorbed a cross-section of the community, including the city's business interests.

The culture of early twentieth-century Cork politics contradicts the argument that stable democratic systems can take root only in the context of economic and social development, that party systems are rooted in social cleavages and that clientelistic politics are inconsistent with stable party loyalties and national political parties.[1] It also vindicates the view that 'democracy may not be a political impossibility in the underdeveloped world' and that despite the political disagreements of the second and third decades of the twentieth century, Ireland was not typical of the political landscape of contemporary Europe.[2] One of my arguments is that for the period under review, the Irish system deviates from the more familiar model of party-political development in that the major political parties in Ireland can claim to have 'stable heterogenous support bases'.[3]

Also running through this book are the implications of proportional representation (PR). It has often been argued that PR inevitably results in a multi-party system, fragmentation of public opinion, a weak parliament and an unstable government. My analysis of Cork during the 1920s does not bear this out. If anything, it suggests that the two main political parties remained strong. Moreover, the late Basil Chubb, long the doyen of political science in Ireland, argued several years ago that PR encouraged clientelistic politics in the sense that political representatives had to adopt the role of social brokers, mediating on behalf of their constituents with various public agencies.[4] In the early years of the system, Irish public representatives undoubtedly engaged in brokerage politics to a considerable extent although it should also be added that, in a variety of ways, much of this culture was already ingrained in rural Ireland.

Some analysts suggest that clientelistic politics are incompatible with a stable party system and party allegiances. Nonetheless, Sinn Féin TDs engaged in clientelistic politics from the foundation of their party and this did not prevent them from establishing and developing a strong partisan allegiance. The same can be said of Cumann na nGaedhael and Fianna Fáil during the 1920s. Indeed, as I will argue later, the irony is that there is a clear link between the demise of the third Sinn Féin party and the inability of its parliamentary representatives to provide a 'parish-pump' type service for their constituents.

During the early years of the state, the stability of party politics was also influenced by other factors. These included the relative underdevelopment of the economy, the scars of a civil war which destroyed political consensus and threatened the legitimacy of the new state, the partition of the island and the fact that as a result, the very boundaries of the state would remain a source of bitterness and conflict; the fact that there existed within both parts of the island distinct and entrenched minorities which either questioned or refused to accept the legitimacy of both jurisdictions and finally, the fact that the political leaders of the new Free State had no practical experience in state-building. Brian Farrell argued over thirty years ago that the emergence of a democratic and stable political system in Ireland against this background owed a great deal to the fact that Ireland had had an 'Irish Parliamentary Tradition' which proved to be resilient enough 'to encompass, neutralise and institutionalise the dispute [the Civil War] within the structures of a competitive political party system'.[5]

However, this view of things needs to be modified, if
only because it does not deal with the type of political
system that emerged from this 'tradition' or why it
emerged in the format that it did. It also does not highlight the fact that this 'tradition' was essentially elitist
and exclusive, with which large numbers did not identify.
Such people had to wait until the Representation of the
People Act (1918) extended the suffrage to all men over
twenty-one and women over thirty.[6]

The political system of the new state was also greatly
influenced by Ireland's predominantly rural culture and
the high value it placed on loyalty to persons and causes.
Moreover, as the urban/rural divide became blurred and
the population of rural Ireland declined during the
course of the twentieth century, the values of 'the
countryman' continued to exercise a considerable
influence over the direction of political life.[7] It also
promoted the belief that the best representatives were
locals who were rooted in their own communities.
Indeed, since the foundation of the state, there has been
an upward trend in the number of TDs living in or
adjacent to their constituencies. This ensured that the
new system would be dominated by clientelism and, as
Basil Chubb saw it, partly explains why so many
deputies played 'only a minimal part in the formation of
policy and legislation, an activity that most of them
consider to be primarily the function of their parliamentary leaders'.[8] However, this is not to suggest that outside
of the Dáil, people were not interested in the great
questions of the nation as well as in the ways in which
these impacted on their own communities. This study is
about that interaction and the processes and organisations which were formed to pursue them. It will also
discuss how these were reflected in the electoral contests
of the period, including the 1918 general election and the

1920 local elections which set the scene for so much that happened thereafter.

This book is based on an MA thesis by research which I submitted to University College Cork (UCC) in 1987. In giving colour to my study, my major primary source was, without question, the Liam de Róiste diaries, available in the Cork Archive Institute. The diaries, which run from 1903 to mid-1928 are very detailed and provide a unique and fascinating insight into Cork politics during the early years of the last century. The importance of the information which de Róiste provides here is enhanced by the sense of reflection which the author offers on the events and people which surrounded him at this time. The *Cork Examiner* corroborated and supplemented the material available in the de Róiste diaries. Because the paper treated in a very comprehensive manner all the general elections and local government elections of the period and gave extensive coverage to political affairs in general, it was also indispensable to this study.

The Archives Department in UCD also contain a number of important collections which have been central to this study. These include the papers of Mary MacSwiney which are invaluable, especially on the splits within the third Sinn Féin party and the formation of Fianna Fáil, and the papers of Ernest Blythe and Richard Mulcahy which give crucial insights into the development of Cumann na nGaedhael, especially during its period in government. UCD also holds the papers of Cumann na nGaedhael which were essential, especially for the later chapters. I also consulted the papers of Fianna Fáil which, like those of Cumann na nGaedhael, contain details of meetings of the National Executives, parliamentary parties and other committees of the two parties. At the time, these papers were kept at party headquarters but have since been moved to UCD, as have the papers of Éamon de Valera. I regret that I did not have the opportunity to consult the de Valera papers although I sense from a look at the relevant calendars that there is little in them that would change my interpretation of Cork politics during these years.

The secondary sources for this type of study have been growing in recent years. While I have tried to keep up with these since I did my original research, some gaps remain. Nonetheless, I think that the work of the historians and political scientists which I cite has stood the test of time. In particular, I was influenced by the work of Max Bart, R. K. Carty, Basil Chubb, Tim Pat Coogan, Brian Farrell, Michael Gallagher, Tom Garvin, Dermot Keogh, Michael Laffan, Joseph Lee, John A. Murphy, Peter Pyne, Brian Reynolds and Paul Martin Sacks.

I am also grateful to UCC for the opportunity to study there, to the staff of the Library, to my lecturers in the History Department and in particular, to Professor Dermot Keogh who guided and supervised me in writing my thesis. I am also grateful to those who keep the sources which the student needs for a study of this sort and for the kindness which they offered me as both a student and later, when I decided to do further research to turn my thesis into a book. These include the Directors and staff of the National Library of Ireland, the Library of UCC, now known as the Boole Library, Fianna Fáil Headquarters, the Archives Department at UCD, the Cork Archives Institute and in particular, its then Director, Patricia McCarthy, for her patience and kindness, and the staff of the Cork City Library who were always helpful in every way.

Although I had always wanted to publish my thesis, my commitments and duties as a public representative made this a long-term objective. I am glad that I can now realise this aim and in doing so, I wish to acknowledge the advice of Neil Collins, Tom Garvin, Michael Laffan and Eda Sagarra who read earlier drafts. In particular, I would also like to thank Maurice Bric as well as my research assistant, Anne Dolan, who helped me to shape a thesis into a book.

I also thank my wife, Mary, whose love and support I will never be able to repay, as well as Mary's parents, Tony and Mary, for their invaluable support. I especially remember my late uncles Buddy and Tom who always placed a high value on scholarship. My greatest debt is to my parents, Paddy and Lana, who have always supported my academic endeavours, as well as my brothers and sisters. My parents also provided me with an atmosphere conducive to learning at home. Hopefully, their progressive influence on me has borne fruit. Finally, I dedicate this book to my children, Micheál Aodh, Aoibhe, Cillian and Léana, in the hope that they will always enjoy the world of knowledge and learning.

1
1918–1921: NEW ERA IN ELECTORAL POLITICS

With the surrender of Germany on 11 November 1918, the First World War ended and a general election was called. The 1918 general election in Ireland was held with a vastly increased electorate. The Representation of the People Act (1918) meant that in Ireland as a whole, the number on the register increased dramatically from 701,475 to 1,936,673.[1] Of these, it has been estimated that two out of every three were entitled to vote for the first time. Although this encouraged an air of unpredictability about the outcome of the election, many felt that the organisationally revamped Sinn Féin party stood to gain most from the newly enfranchised, notably from the younger members of the electorate. In Westminister, the House of Commons was dissolved on 25 November 1918 and polling day was set for the following 14 December. As a result of the Redistribution of Seats (Ireland) Act of 1918, new parliamentary divisions had been drawn up for the country's counties and boroughs. Two boroughs were disenfranchised and two new university seats created. Every constituency returned one MP, except for Cork City and Dublin University, which returned two by a system of proportional representation.[2]

In nationalist Ireland, the major electoral battle would be fought between Sinn Féin and the Irish

Parliamentary Party. The post-1916 Sinn Féin organisation was determined to pursue a policy of complete
separation from England.[3] The party's Ard-Fheis was
held in Dublin's Mansion House in October 1917 and
this ratified and consolidated the party which had
developed during the previous six months. Although for
many it was almost as vague as nationalism or
separatism, what was once the 'Sinn Féin movement'
had been transformed into an organised political force.
Liam de Róiste had clear views on this which were not
without influence. De Róiste was well known in Cork,
being one of the original founders and by now president
of the Sinn Féin Executive in the city, a prominent
member of the Gaelic League, a co-founder of the city's
Irish Volunteers, and one of the founders of the Cork
Industrial Development Association. In his view, the
election of Éamon de Valera as President of Sinn Féin
meant 'that the military organisation [the Volunteers]
had become, as I may say, subordinate in policy to the
civil organisation [Sinn Féin]'. In de Róiste's view, this
should also be reflected at local level. In June 1917, he
had already stated that the Sinn Féin Executive in Cork
'claims the right to direct and control the organisation in
Cork City and county, as the best means of preventing a
break up of the forces [that are] here making for Irish
independence'.[4]

By October 1917, de Valera had succeeded in uniting
the various strands within Sinn Féin by producing a
formula which papered over potentially divisive cracks.
Moderates, pacifists, dual monarchists and republicans
were placated by the formula that 'Sinn Féin aims at
securing the international recognition of Ireland as an
independent Irish Republic. Having achieved that status
the Irish people may by Referendum freely choose their
own form of Government'.[5] This formula, and the

success with which it was implemented, was to be of crucial importance to the development of Irish party politics. Irish independence was the primary political objective. Issues such as class politics, workers' rights and welfare policies were deferred but on the understanding that they could be dealt with once independence was achieved. The constitutional relationship between Ireland and Britain was, and remained, the dominant issue. The formula was unanimously adopted at the Ard-Fheis and prevented the emergence of splits. It also cemented the party and consolidated its growth. While the party's growth was further facilitated by the threat of conscription which hung over the country in 1918, the 1,200 clubs that had been represented at the Mansion House had become 1,500 *cumainn* (branches) by November 1918.[6]

In the Cork City Borough constituency, 'national' issues also predominated. No major local or sectional issue arose. From August 1918 onwards, Sinn Féin leaders were discussing candidates for the constituency and were paying particular attention to the Labour Party's attitude to the election. De Róiste's diaries provide evidence that consultations and correspondence between Sinn Féin and Labour was taking place as late as 1 November when a special Trade Union Congress decided by 96 votes to 23 to withdraw Labour candidates from the coming election.[7] The Labour Party leader, Thomas Johnson, justified the National Executive's recommendation to Congress on the grounds that 'the democratic demand for self-determination to which the Irish Labour Party and its candidates give their unqualified adherence will thereby obtain the freest chance of expression at the polls'. He believed that the demand for Irish independence should be put to the Paris Peace Conference with as much unanimity as possible. He maintained that Labour's ultimate aim was the creation of a 'workers republic' which would be very different from those 'Republics of Europe and America where political democracy is but a cloak for capitalist oligarchy'.[8]

In a diary entry on 21 August 1918, de Róiste recorded that a representative of the Transport Union had asked him to arrange a meeting with some men of the Sinn Féin Comhairle Ceanntair (District Council) to discuss candidates for the municipal and local elections in the county. Reflecting on this development, de Róiste wrote that 'there is a break away from the official trades organisations' and suggested that there was a move 'to overthrow the men who have been ruling the Trades Organisations and amalgamated societies for so long in Ireland'.[9]

De Róiste and Cork's Sinn Féin Executive consulted with Cathal O'Shannon (who was on both national executives) and asked him to stand. But while de Róiste was awaiting a reply from O'Shannon, the Sinn Féin Executive in Cork unanimously selected J. J. Walsh as well as de Róiste himself *in absentia*.[10] De Róiste was surprised at this decision and stated that it would not have happened had he been present. His diary entries of 4–5 September reveal that at earlier meetings he had indicated he was unwilling to stand and had put forward the names of O'Shannon along with Professors Stockley and O'Rahilly of University College Cork. In addition to Walsh, other names mentioned included Terence MacSwiney, Tomás MacCurtain, Donal O'Callaghan and Diarmuid Lynch. According to de Róiste, the qualities that Sinn Féin looked for in candidates were 'intellectual capacity of candidates' capabilities, appeal to the mass of the people, likelihood of success, labour interests, *Aimsir na Cásca* [the period of the Easter Rebellion] and so on'.[11]

4

De Róiste was particularly anxious to avoid a rift between Sinn Féin and the Transport Union as he regarded the latter as the most progressive section of the Labour movement. He believed that while many of them strongly believed that socialism should be the prime objective, many others were strongly pro-Sinn Féin. However, he was also aware that there was a definite section of the Labour movement which was hostile to Sinn Féin and which would do all that it could to organise Labour as a means of defeating Sinn Féin. Summing up the dilemma which was facing both parties, de Róiste wondered on 6 September 'which is the stronger in the mind of the mass of the people – labour interests, trade interests or national and political interests? Most men say national and political interests'. He himself had no doubts and reflected the predominant view within Sinn Féin that 'the pure national idea in fact should be the issue not any sectional idea or interest however great'. The fundamental issue as far as de Róiste was concerned was attendance at Westminster. If Labour or the Transport Union nominated a candidate who would attend Parliament in London, Sinn Féin would have to oppose such a candidate. However, if a person who had been selected by the Transport Union was prepared to abstain from attending at Westminster, then de Róiste reflected the policy of the party's Standing Committee that:

> he ought to be supported by Sinn Féin and that a Sinn Féin candidate ought to retire in his favour. Such a man would combine the national idea and the labour idea (and no matter how the middle or upper classes feel or reactionary labour men feel, the forward labour movements are going to play a big part in the destinies of all countries in the near future).[12]

Although an official announcement from the Standing Committee of Sinn Féin confirming the candidatures of Walsh and de Róiste appeared in the *Cork Examiner* on 15 September, consultations between the two sides continued until November. It appears that O'Shannon and certain elements in the Transport Union were not keen on de Róiste's candidature. They believed him to be a 'Griffithite', a suspicion which reflected the widespread distrust in radical circles of Griffith's monarchist views. Furthermore, the outgoing 'All for Ireland League' MP, William O'Brien, in a letter to Seán T. O'Kelly, had scathing comments to make on Sinn Féin nominees:

> Let me once more impress upon you that your candidates are – rightly or wrongly – despised by the average thinking man in Cork. You would do more wisely by running De Valera, who would carry Walsh at the next General Election.[13]

While the long-term implications of the Labour Party decision not to contest the 1918 general election remains a matter for speculation, it enabled Sinn Féin to appeal, unhindered, to the working classes on the issue of abstention from Westminster. Brian Farrell, writing on the development of the Irish Labour Party, attributes Labour's failure to come to the centre stage of Irish political life to its decision not to participate in the 1918 general election.[14] However, it is difficult to uphold such a contention. As can be gleaned from de Róiste's diaries and indeed, from the experience of the local government elections of 1920, Labour was far from a homogeneous body during this period. There was a considerable rift between the Transport Union section and the Official Trades Council. The former were pro-Sinn Féin and believed that the national issue was paramount while the latter wanted to go it alone. In that context, it is difficult to see how Labour could have put up a credible electoral performance. It must also be acknowledged that the electorate was being presented with a national issue of the most fundamental kind: whether the newly elected public representatives would attend Westminster or, alternatively, set up their own parliament in Ireland. Given this reality, one could argue that the issue of capital versus labour would never have managed to displace the focus on the so-called 'national question'. Finally, the relatively good performance of the Labour Party in the general election of June 1922 seemed to indicate that its decision not to contest the 1918 election was not the critical factor responsible for the party's ultimate failure to play a central role in the political development of the modern Irish state.

On the other hand, it must be accepted that the victory of the 'national issue' over all other issues in 1918 foreshadowed much of what was to follow during the first decade of the Free State. In any event, de Róiste suggests that there were many in Sinn Féin who were not hostile to some of Labour's policies, particularly in relation to improving the conditions of the working man and the creation of a welfare state. At the first meeting of Dáil Éireann in 1919, for example, a socio-economic policy document, which later became known as the Democratic Programme of the First Dáil, was read and adopted.[15] In terms of political ideology, the Programme could be described as being left of centre.[16] In addition, in the 1920 local government elections in Cork city, Sinn Féin candidates had no qualms about standing with the Transport Union on the same platforms. They ran a joint ticket. Certain sections of the Labour movement were absorbed into the Sinn Féin movement during this period when national issues predominated. Moreover, Labour lost personnel and activists to Sinn Féin between 1918 and 1922 and never got them back.

We also learn from de Róiste's diaries that abortive attempts were made to establish a unified stance between the old Irish Parliamentary Party and Sinn Féin and that Bishop Cohalan of Cork intervened to facilitate such a development. In a letter of 2 November to de Róiste, Bishop Cohalan wrote that:

> There is another matter of much more importance, and at present this is confidential for yourself. A number of prominent nationalists always associated with Parliamentarianism are elected and to try to approach the Peace Conference with one voice. That would suppose a compromise. The propositions would be:
>
> (1) All candidates at election to pledge themselves to at least temporary abstention from Parliament. (The meaning of 'temporary' abstention will be understood from proposition 3.)
>
> (2) There should be a united and solemn appeal to the Peace Conference for the right to decide our destiny by self-determination.
>
> (3) The question of going to Parliament after the Peace Conference – in case neither sovereign independence nor a Home Rule Parliament is given to be decided afterwards, say by referendum. Could a contested election be avoided on these terms? Of course there should be some tribunal to decide how many of the old Parliamentarians would be allowed to survive; and how many Sinn Féin candidates.

In reply, de Róiste suggested that Sinn Féin wanted a united voice for the Paris Peace Conference and to avoid contested elections, but that no compromise on abstention from Westminster was likely. However, he was not in favour of a tribunal to decide candidates and maintained that Sinn Féin throughout the country would accept neither dictation nor authoritarianism, a reaction perhaps against the machine methods of older parties to force candidates on constituencies. For himself, de Róiste declared that he would be in favour of meeting 'Party men' and offered to get the views of the Sinn Féin Executive on the matter to see if a meeting could be arranged. However, having read a letter of John Dillon in that day's *Cork Examiner* in which the Irish Parliamentary Party leader virulently attacked Sinn Féin and accused it of conspiring with the Germans, de Róiste added in a postscript to his letter to the Bishop that if Dillon's letter represented the attitude of his party and its supporters, there was a poor hope that an agreement could be reached.[17]

Before corresponding with de Róiste, Bishop Cohalan, in a speech to the Catholic Young Men's Society, had suggested that all parties should get together on how to present Ireland's case before the Peace Conference.[18] Subsequently, at a meeting of supporters of the Irish Parliamentary Party, held on 10 November in Cork, a resolution was passed which appealed for 'unity' at the election. It also declared that Ireland was as entitled to self-determination as much as Czechoslovakia or Yugoslavia. De Róiste's reaction was cynical, as revealed by his caustic comment that the 'desire on some of the Dillonite followers to save themselves, rather than a real desire to do the best for the country is unfortunately only too apparent'.[19]

In an entry dated 1 December, de Róiste outlined a scenario as to why the attempts at unity floundered.

According to his sources, he had learned that at about the time Bishop Cohalan had written to him regarding a possible agreement, the chief 'Party men', Coroner Murphy, John J. Horgan and a Mr MacCabe, together with the Bishop himself, had advised against a contest. As far as de Róiste could gather, the Sinn Féin idea that Ireland should attempt to obtain the Peace Conference's approval for self-determination had been ridiculed by John Dillon. A meeting to decide the matter was held on 20 November in the Hibernian Hall on Cork city's Morrison's Island. Coroner Murphy presided and spoke strongly against contesting Cork in opposition to Sinn Féin. He finally resigned his position as chairman of the United Irish League in Cork and left the meeting. Horgan and MacCabe and some others did likewise. However, according to de Róiste, '"the Die Hards" remaining determined to go on, not that they felt they would win but [they wanted] to fight Sinn Féin anyhow, in the hope of keeping their organisation going till the next election'.[20] Obviously some members of the Irish Parliamentary Party in Cork had seen the writing on the wall. The intervention of Bishop Cohalan was also significant. He was to play an important and often controversial role in Cork during this period.

There was also a demand for a unified approach from the business sector. In the *Cork Examiner* of 2 November 1918, 157 merchants and traders signed a declaration entitled 'Some Suggestions for Ireland's Future Settlement'. This declaration expressed the view that Ireland had suffered enough and that a unified approach was necessary to solve her political problems. Thus, it suggested that it 'behoves us to clearly state our opinion that it would be better for us to sink our differences and unite for the general benefit of our whole country, irrespective of politics or creed'. It also suggested that the government should make a generous temporary grant to help bring together the various 'contending opinions in the country and which would also be used for development purposes'. In its editorial on the same day, the paper welcomed the declaration in enthusiastic fashion, claiming that it would have 'great weight on political opinion'. It appealed to all concerned to spare no effort to bring all interests together to settle the Irish question:

> We believe that a further Convention, not selected by any outside power, not necessarily taken from the ranks of elected men, but delegates from such a body as is represented by the names we publish today [in the businessmen's declaration], with a number nominated by Mr Dillon and by Mr De Valera and by the various Labour bodies, may find a solution that has so far eluded a very earnest effort of able Irishmen.

The call for unity was echoed by John J. Horgan who, in a letter to the *Cork Examiner* on the same day, felt that there was no reason why all parties should not agree to establish a national body representing nationalist Ireland to pursue the claim of national self-determination. He saw very little difference between the programmes of Sinn Féin and the Nationalist Party:

> Both have formulated their electoral programmes. The one asks for an Irish Republic, the other for the establishment of national self-government including full and complete executive legislative and fiscal powers. Both agree that we should appeal to the Peace Conference. The only real difference is a difference as to method . . . of attending the Imperial Parliament.

Horgan felt that permanent abstention from Westminster would lead to certain failure while attendance there would provide Ireland with a forum to address the world.[21]

Sinn Féin, however, did not respond very enthusiastically to the calls for unity which were articulated by certain business, church and media leaders of Cork city. John Dillon was unenthusiastic as well and considered that Sinn Féin's demands that nationalists should both agree to a policy of absolute independence and separatism from England, and recognise the principle of abstention from parliament, were unacceptable to him and his party.[22]

In Cork city six candidates were eventually proposed. Sinn Féin nominated de Róiste and Walsh while the Irish Parliamentary Party selected Major Maurice Talbot-Crosbie and R. L. O'Sullivan. The Unionist Party which supported the maintenance of the legislative union between Great Britain and Ireland, also fielded two candidates, Daniel Williams and Thomas Farrington. Of the six candidates, it appeared that Walsh was in the best position to get elected, having fought in the GPO in Dublin in 1916. His death sentence had been commuted to penal servitude and he was eventually released under the general amnesty of January 1922. He was also a member of Cork Corporation and had for many years been chairman of the Cork County Board of the GAA.[23] De Róiste, commenting on his chances against Walsh, wrote that he had 'fought in 1916, he was in prison and I have never yet been in court, been prosecuted, been in prison'. He went on: 'In fact it is a little curious, perhaps, that of all the candidates chosen so far, I am the only one who has not been in prison at present, or who is not on the run'.[24] One can clearly discern here the beginning of a phenomenon that was to last for a considerable time in

Irish electoral politics: the electoral value of having fought in the 1916 Rising and subsequently in the War of Independence, or of having been imprisoned during this period. On the other hand, the Nationalist candidates had a very different background. Talbot-Crosbie had fought in the Great War while O'Sullivan was a well-known Cork city barrister.

The Representation of the People Act (1918) meant that the electorate in Cork had increased from 12,000 to 50,000 approximately. Sinn Féin took every opportunity to make the most of it, especially the extension of the female vote. In Cork city, in particular, although most of the activists themselves could not vote as the franchise was restricted to women over thirty, Cumann na mBan formed a vital, and often overlooked, component of Sinn Féin's electoral machine by registering first-time voters far in advance of their opponents.[25] However, despite the activities of Cumann na mBan, the Act provided for an unpredictable electorate. In an editorial of 25 November 1918, the day on which Parliament was dissolved, the *Cork Examiner* commented that:

> No election ever held presents greater difficulty to those who theorise on its probable result, simply because no one can accurately estimate the voting proclivities of the new electorate, and no one could be daring enough to assert in advance how the majority of the millions of female voters will poll.

Sinn Féin's candidates in Cork reiterated their demand for complete separation from Great Britain. In particular, they tried to appeal to Labour interests. J. J. Walsh, speaking at a meeting in Blarney, said that it was a special pleasure for him to address men 'who were essentially and almost unanimously trade unionists and see how trade unionism had acted in that great fight for national liberty'. He continued by saying that Labour had said:

> 'Our nation first and then ourselves.' They said as Sinn Féin said in Easter Week: 'We are but the instruments of this country, the motherland above and before everything, the motherland free, then and not till then can we afford to discuss the smaller issues.' That was the stand Labour took.[26]

Clearly, Walsh felt that he was indebted to Labour for its decision to abstain from contesting the election. However his reference to 'the smaller issues' was not calculated to entice the more ideological Labour supporter.

Reporting on the campaign, the *Cork Examiner* observed that attendance at, or abstention from, Westminster until Ireland's own parliament would be established was perhaps the main difference between Nationalist and Sinn Féin candidates. Both parties received considerable coverage from the *Cork Examiner* with perhaps the Irish Parliamentary Party receiving a slightly larger share of attention. The paper eventually came out in support of the Irish Parliamentary Party and on the day before polling, it declared in an editorial that 'Irish abstention from Parliament means the silencing of Ireland's voice, and a triumph for Lloyd George, in which Sir Edward Carson will gladly share'. On polling day, the paper was even more emphatic:

> The Irish people on the one hand are invited to support a practical policy of Dominion Self-Government, which is the country's one chance of national salvation, and on the other, they are asked to seek a mirage Republic. Today they will be called upon to make their choice in the polling booths and

to say whether they prefer a policy of rainbow-
chasing or one which prefers practical tangible
advantages in the present.[27]

The campaign in Cork does not merit F. S. L. Lyons'
description as 'a bitter and ugly one with no holds barred
on either side'.[28] In the weeks before the election, the
Cork Examiner reported that the conduct of the campaign
was little short of exemplary. Its readers were informed
that both the Nationalist and Sinn Féin candidates had
called on Dr Cohalan and that he had expressed his
sincere pleasure at the splendid way in which the election
campaign was being conducted on all sides and the hope
that it would continue in such a manner until polling
day.[29] De Róiste's view of events confirms this, recording
that the election had 'showed much of my own spirit,
friendliness, toleration, absence of abuse and personalities, no clouding of issues, yet good humour and respect
for opponents' opinions and argument'.[30] However, as
Michael Laffan has concluded, others did not share de
Róiste's experience. Although

> several of the defeated Nationalist candidates
> commented on the good nature of the campaign and
> the fairness of the results . . . the election was
> marked nonetheless by widespread violence and
> personation. Speakers were stoned and meetings
> were disrupted. In East Cork, the police divided the
> population into two neat categories: 'the community
> generally is engaged in either intimidation or being
> intimidated'.

Dillon warned an audience in Ballaghdereen that
Claremen were on the way to bully the Mayo electors. In
Wexford many people were injured as rival mobs
bludgeoned each other with sticks. Fr O'Flanagan was

howled down by Redmondites and the meeting ended with a police baton charge.[31]

As early as 8 December de Róiste was predicting an easy victory for Sinn Féin. He based his assessment on the attendances at rallies and feedback from canvassers. According to de Róiste, most of those who opposed Sinn Féin were 'some ex-servicemen, their followers, policemen, ex-policemen and their wives – the "ignorant old ladies" of unionist persuasion, [and] anti democratic shopkeepers and middle-class people; timid people who fear revolutionaries'.[32] It is very difficult, of course, to corroborate this and de Róiste's comment must be considered as being general in nature. Undoubtedly many ex-servicemen supported the Nationalist Party, as would members of the RIC, whose position would have been endangered by a Sinn Féin victory (as, of course, it subsequently was). And it is nothing new to learn that middle-class people and some tradespeople were wary of a radical change in the status quo. As Peter Hart has observed:

> each side looked on the other as a mob of armed hoodlums, and themselves as the upholders of decency. Both saw the 'rabble' and corner-boys as being on the other side. British . . . soldiers and many local Protestants regarded all civilians as 'Shinners'. Everyone appealed to more or less the same labels and categories to place the IRA and mark its social boundaries.

The results in Cork mirrored that of the country as a whole with the two Sinn Féin candidates topping the poll. The following was the result of the first count:

J. J. Walsh (SF)	20,801
Liam de Róiste (SF)	20,506

Maurice Talbot-Crosbie (Nat.)	7,480
R. L. O'Sullivan (Nat)	7,162
Daniel Williams (U)	2,519
Thomas Farrington (U)	2,254[33]

Commenting on the result, on 30 December, the *Cork Examiner* stated in an editorial that:

> Ireland has taken a course, however, for good or ill that completely breaks away from all her past. Maddened with the treachery of the 'predominant partner', growing tired of a party that she entrusted to do her work for over 35 years, to our thinking she has thrown discretion to the wind, and at a very critical moment trusted her affairs to men of little experience.

The editorial was certainly accurate in the sense that the 1918 general election was a watershed. A new type of public representative had come upon the scene with new ideas and attitudes, dedicated to the concept of an 'Irish Ireland' not only in cultural terms but in economic terms as well. The economic ideas of Arthur Griffith had taken root against the background of the cultural revival of the late nineteenth and early twentieth centuries and these were to have a major influence on the development of the modern Irish party political system. More important still, the idea of complete separation from Britain had now been endorsed by the Irish electorate. The attempts to realise this ideal was to dominate Irish politics thereafter. The immediate consequences of the election were obvious. Before the election the Irish Parliamentary Party had 78 seats, Sinn Féin 7, and Unionists 18. After the election, Sinn Féin had 73 seats, Nationalists 6, and Unionists 26. Politically the result meant that Sinn Féin was now the main voice of Irish nationalism. Moreover, it was a voice with which, sooner or later, the British government would have to deal.

The newly elected members of Sinn Féin assembled in the Mansion House in Dublin on 21 January 1919 and held the inaugural session of Dáil Éireann. Invitations were sent to all the Irish MPs who had been elected in 1918. In the event, Unionists and members of the Irish Parliamentary Party refused to attend. Many of the Sinn Féin deputies were either in jail or in hiding. As a result, no more than twenty-seven of those who had been elected were present at this inaugural meeting. Cathal Brugha acted as provisional President. At this meeting, a provisional constitution was adopted and a Declaration of Independence read. The Dáil then appointed three delegates to the Peace Conference: Éamon de Valera, Arthur Griffith and Count Plunkett. A 'Message to the Free Nations of the World' was read in Irish, French and English, and adopted. Finally, a socio-economic policy document, the Democratic Programme, was read and adopted.[34]

The second session of Dáil Éireann which was held on 1 April 1919 was a much larger affair. Partly because the British government had released the Sinn Féin internees in the interim, fifty-two members attended. At this meeting de Valera was elected President and nominated his cabinet. Arthur Griffith was appointed Deputy President and Minister for Home Affairs while Michael Collins was given the important portfolio of Finance. Two months later de Valera embarked on a prolonged tour of the United States, where he succeeded in raising a considerable amount of finance and gaining moral support from the American public.[35]

The First Dáil had considerable success in two major areas: the administration of justice and local government. Sinn Féin courts were set up all over the country to arbitrate on local grievances. The authority of the Dáil courts was upheld and their decisions enforced by a body of Republican police. Their impact can be gauged from the fact that by the time of the truce in 1921 over 900 parish courts and 70 district courts were in operation.[36] In the area of local government, the councils controlled by a Sinn Féin majority declared their allegiance to Dáil Éireann, thereby severing their connection with the British administration and incurring considerable financial losses in doing so. However, it is true that the work of the Dáil was severely hampered by the War of Independence. The ambush at Soloheadbeg, County Tipperary, where two RIC constables were shot dead while escorting a cartload of gelignite on 21 January 1919, is generally regarded as marking the start of the conflict. The first phase of the war lasted until the spring of 1920 and consisted largely of attacks by the Irish Volunteers (or, as they were officially known after August 1919, the Irish Republican Army) on RIC barracks, police huts and patrols.[37]

The next major electoral challenge for Sinn Féin were the municipal and urban elections of January 1920. These gave Sinn Féin an opportunity to confirm the 1918 general election results and to win an endorsement of its national policy. In order to accomplish this, Dáil deputies were encouraged to stand as candidates, thereby setting a precedent for the future. Secondly, Sinn Féin fought the election on the national issue as opposed to local municipal concerns with the result that the election also became a virtual vote of confidence in Sinn Féin's national policy.

In Cork city, Sinn Féin deputies Terence MacSwiney (who represented the Mid-Cork constituency in the Dáil), J. J. Walsh and de Róiste (both city deputies) were selected to stand. Privately, de Róiste expressed his unhappiness at being nominated. He disliked the idea of becoming involved in 'local petty affairs' or indeed in the type of grass-roots brokerage which was associated with this level of political representation. Above all, de Róiste did not feel that he could devote enough time and attention to local affairs while at the same time endeavouring to make a living and serving as an efficient and effective national political representative. The only argument that he could personally accept in favour of standing was the concept of civic duty or 'local patriotism', something which he had always advocated. The major factor which eventually led to de Róiste's candidature was Sinn Féin's difficulty to attract the right sort of candidate. Referring to his failure to avoid being a candidate, de Róiste said 'but all my efforts prove unavailing – and indeed there has been much trouble in getting men of the right kind to stand: men nationally sound.'[38] Quite clearly, therefore, a person's stand on the national issue was the primary factor which was taken into account when Sinn Féin set about selecting its candidates.

The selection process itself, according to de Róiste's diaries, proved to be a stormy business, with many disputes in the *cumainn*, resignations and even expulsions of some members. There were two opposing views within the *cumainn*. On the one hand it was proposed that certain members of public boards who had supported Sinn Féin in the past should be accepted as Sinn Féin candidates for the election; on the other it was argued that a clean sweep should be made and a new set of people selected. De Róiste himself favoured the 'clean sweep' idea and his account of the debate shows that this eventually prevailed. However, in some electoral divisions, he did not favour the methods that were being used. It appears that the IRA, the military wing of the movement, was heavily involved in the selection process. De Róiste commented on this as follows:

> To effect 'the clean sweep' in the Central Electoral area, actions very like what is called 'wire pulling' have occurred. One *cumann* was swamped and dissolved by the young men of the *óglaigh* [Volunteers] – who often express contempt for Sinn Féin as a 'mere political organisation' – in order to prevent the names of certain persons being even considered.[39]

Such tensions were nothing new. Since 1917, as Peter Hart has observed, 'the city's Sinn Féin clubs and committees were the scene for fierce battles over delegate and candidate selection between militant Volunteer and less "advanced" factions'. The veto which had been sought by the Volunteer leaders over Sinn Féin candidates in 1920 recalled the pact convention and the election of 1918 and would be echoed again in 1921 although, as Hart has again suggested, 'never with complete success, as de Róiste's political survival showed'.[40]

One could speculate here that younger members of Sinn Féin and the IRA were showing political ambition and were determined to avail of the opportunities which were presented by the local elections for their own personal advancement.[41] Secondly, de Róiste's comment quoted above confirms that strained relations between the political and military wings of Sinn Féin were evident at this stage. Studies on the topic indicate that internal friction of this type was a prominent and recurring feature of the Sinn Féin movement.[42]

Another interesting feature of the 1920 local elections in Cork was that Sinn Féin combined with the

Transport Union to form a single electoral ticket.[43] The party campaigned on a single platform, articulated the same policies, and acted as a unified party in contesting the election. This factor is significant in the context of the evolution of both the Sinn Féin and Labour parties. Sinn Féin once again absorbed Labour personnel and candidates in an electoral contest. The Labour movement was split, with the Cork and District United Trades and Labour Council nominating only twelve candidates. One can only speculate on the influence on Sinn Féin members of the presence of members of the Transport Union on the same electoral platform but the point must be made that the Sinn Féin leadership was obviously not averse to left-wing politics in general and must have had a fundamental empathy with their colleagues in the Labour movement.

The Sinn Féin and Transport Union alliance had the greatest strength in the number of nominated candidates, with fifty candidates competing for fifty-six seats. The Nationalist Party (the old Irish Parliamentary Party) nominated thirty-three candidates while twenty-two represented the Commercial Party (for which, see below). Thirty-seven candidates went forward as Independents. Among the Nationalists and Independents were people who were nominated on behalf of the Irish National Federation of Discharged Soldiers and Sailors (usually referred as the Ex-Servicemen's Association).[44] In the run-up to the election, Sinn Féin and the Transport Union were the most active in canvassing support and had well-organised campaigns. On 12 January 1920 the *Cork Examiner* reported that:

> the Sinn Féin and Transport Workers are the only party so far that have been in any way active in this direction [canvassing]. Their organisation is far

advanced and conducted on the well-defined lines so evidenced in elections throughout the country which claimed the attention of Sinn Féin.

Sinn Féin's attempt to present the national issue as paramount was countered by the Nationalist candidates who attacked the party's separatist policy by highlighting its implications for local issues such as housing and employment. In particular, they doubted the capacity of a Sinn Féin-dominated council to secure funds from Westminster for a public housing programme. At a public meeting which was held under the auspices of the Ex-Servicemen's Association in the City Hall, the outgoing Lord Mayor, William F. O'Connor, outlined a view of the approaching election. Referring to the manifesto issued on behalf of the Association's candidates, O'Connor stated that their chief aim was to secure better housing for the people of the city. He questioned the capacity of Sinn Féin to fulfil its declared aim to provide decent housing, especially in view of the fact that the outgoing Corporation had failed to provide such a scheme even though the central government had contributed 27s 6d for every £1 rent charged to the tenants. The Corporation had found the scheme unworkable because in its view, it was impossible for the authority to build houses that would be let for 6s or 7s a week. O'Connor thus wondered how the 'Republicans' could build houses without a government grant when the outgoing Corporation had failed to do so. On behalf of his party, however, he promised that they would secure better housing grants from the government and that unlike their opponents, they would support the establishment of a 'profiteering committee' to deal with dishonest traders who 'fleeced the people'. As they saw it, the essential difference between themselves and the

Republicans was that 'they would recognise the Government and get as much as they could in the matter of housing, and without Government aid not a house would be built in the lifetime of the new Corporation'.[45]

For its part, Sinn Féin made no apologies for declaring the 'national issue' to be paramount in these particular elections. At a meeting to support Sinn Féin and the Transport Union candidates, de Róiste gave a lengthy speech outlining Sinn Féin's attitude to the elections. He acknowledged that under more normal circumstances, a case could be made for parliamentary representatives to stay out of local politics. He admitted that if he followed his own wishes, he would not have been a candidate in a municipal election. However, he argued that one had to put one's personal feelings aside and irrespective of whether it was right or wrong for TDs to contest local elections, de Róiste felt that they had to be involved at all levels given the state of affairs in the country at that time. He declared that the reason he had consented to stand for the City Council of Cork was because he 'knew' that the national issue at that moment was paramount and added that the men of the Transport Union in the city and throughout Ireland recognised that as well. De Róiste argued that questions relating to rates and contracts were 'great questions in other times at a local election but in Ireland at the present time the question of questions was the national one'.[46]

De Róiste was somewhat vague on Sinn Féin's policies on municipal affairs but in relation to industrial matters, he claimed that Sinn Féin and the workers of Cork knew something about commerce and industry and mentioned the opening of a direct trade between Ireland and America through the Moore & MacCormack Shipping Company as evidence of this. The Dowdall brothers, who were prominent in both the commercial and public life of the city, were the shipping agents in Cork for the company. De Róiste and the Dowdalls, along with J. L. Fawsitt (the consul representing Dáil Éireann in America) were the principal figures behind the enterprise and were also members of Cork's Industrial Development Association, a body founded in 1903 with the aim of developing native industry and fostering and promoting Irish products.[47]

The Commercial (or Ratepayers) Party did not formally canvass as a party. Rather, it represented a collection of individuals who were active under one loosely defined umbrella. Indeed, some candidates were listed on the tickets of both the Nationalists and Commercial Party. These included William Desmond, Denis Buckley and the outgoing Lord Mayor, W. F. O'Connor. Others on the Commercial ticket included Unionists such as the outgoing Alderman Richard Beamish (later to become a Cumann na nGaedhael TD) and Thomas Farrington who had stood as a Unionist candidate in the 1918 general election. The Commercial candidates took out individual as well as joint advertisements in the *Cork Examiner*. Their focus was on fostering the general commercial life of the city. Improved housing was also a priority. Beamish, in a lengthy advertisement stressed the importance of the housing question, particularly in relation to production in the economy:

> The adequate housing of the labourer is all-important if real efficiency in production is to be expected, as the best efforts of men cannot be secured when they are herded together in unsanitary surroundings and inadequately paid.

The development of the cattle trade of Cork was also of vital economic importance to the city. Beamish was confident in this area, given that Cork's credit position was sufficient to secure adequate funds to carry them out.[48]

The Nationalist candidates also placed advertisements in the *Cork Examiner*. The official Labour Party candidates received little publicity. Neither they nor the Sinn Féin and Transport Union candidates had any newspaper advertisements at all, indicating no doubt a lack of funds. However, according to the *Cork Examiner*, the combined forces of Sinn Féin and the Transport Union organised the best campaign. Commenting on the freshness of their slate of candidates, a *Cork Examiner* reporter wrote:

> But if they have no past record in municipal affairs on which to claim the suffrages of the electors, they have had sufficient enthusiasm to make an exhaustive canvass of all the electoral areas of the city and though the other parties also visited the voters during the last fortnight on behalf of the candidates, it cannot be said that they set about their work with the energy that characterised the Sinn Féin and Transport Workers' canvassers.

These comments are significant, insofar as they indicated the continued politicisation of the Sinn Féin rank-and-file. They also indicated that Sinn Féin personnel were highly organised, efficient and effective campaigners. In addition, the political knowledge and electoral training which had been gained by members of Sinn Féin during this period was of value to them when they established new political parties after 1922 and no doubt contributed significantly to the formation of a stable parliamentary democracy. Furthermore the *Cork Examiner* could praise the general good humour that prevailed among the rival candidates. The election itself was devoid of ugly incidents and it was carried out in a civilised and orderly fashion. Michael Laffan gives an explanation:

In Cork the RIC had traditionally escorted the returning officers, their clerks and their ballot boxes to the counting centres, but this responsibility was now taken over by Volunteers riding bicycles.[49]

The editorials of the *Cork Examiner* on the elections did not favour any one party or policy. They expressed the view that people should vote for individuals rather than parties, provided that they were efficient. In an editorial at the beginning of the campaign, the paper bemoaned the apathy of the electorate despite the fact that there had been no elections in six years. The apparent lack of interest was due to the uncertainty and confusion prevailing among the electorate about the workings of Proportional Representation (PR), which had been introduced in Ireland in 1919. The editorial presented an excellent analysis of the workings of the system and pointed out the danger of large parties running too many candidates. It also highlighted the fact that the 'man out on his own', or the influential man representing a small but reliable party, had a good chance of securing election, provided that his friends and supporters stuck by him. However, the *Cork Examiner* conceded that the introduction of party and personal considerations complicated the situation somewhat. The average voter had not yet mastered the complexities of the PR system and many of the candidates were in a similar position.[50]

The major theme of subsequent editorials was that a monopoly of ability, honesty and independence was not the exclusive property of any one class and that the operation of PR would lead to a broader representation of all classes on the new council. In an editorial on 6 January, the paper suggested that 'what would probably be an ideally perfect representative assembly would be based on

27

honesty and ability, with a leaven of independents to play the part of impartial critics'. The same editorial accepted the principle behind PR and acknowledged that it was only fair that all who paid rates should be entitled to be represented in the administration of municipal affairs. In an editorial on 13 January, the paper expressed the view that the elector's personal knowledge of the candidates should prove a more accurate estimate of their qualifications for public office than that supplied by any ticket or tag. It would be best for the city (for capital and labour alike) if the best available, irrespective of class or previous experience, were selected. It concluded by once again observing the friendly nature of the campaign and the healthy rivalry of the respective candidates – all committed to the improvement of their city.[51] Finally, in its editorial on polling day, 15 January, the paper declared that PR was on trial and that the election marked a new era in municipal elections. If all classes succeeded in gaining representation, such a result would be equitable since all classes contributed to the payment of rates. Furthermore, it warned the electorate not to be 'put off' by the novelty of the system.[52]

In any event, the new electorate proved more than capable of handling the new electoral system, only 2.97 per cent spoiling their votes. According to the *Cork Examiner*, 68.04 per cent voted and the first-preference vote given to the combined ticket of Sinn Féin and the Transport Union was just 649 less than the combined vote of the other parties. Despite the warnings given to the parties by the *Cork Examiner*, the running of full tickets did not result in any unnecessary loss of seats by either Sinn Féin or the Nationalist Party. There was a strong correlation between the number of seats won and the parties' first-preference votes, as is illustrated in Table 1.[53]

Table 1: *Election to Cork Corporation, January 1920: Destination of First Preference Votes and Seats*

First Pref	Votes	% of Vote	No. of Seats	% of Total
Sinn Féin &				
Transport Union	8,822	48.23	30	53.57
Nationalists	4,439	24.27	14	25
Labour	960	5.25	3	5.36
Commercial	1,565	8.54	4	7.4
Ex-Servicemen's				
Association	937	5.12	3	5.36
Independents	1,570	8.58	2	3.57
Number of Registered Voters:		27,587		
Number who Voted:		18,763		
Spoiled Votes:		470		
Valid Poll:		18,293		

Transfers in Sinn Féin and the Transport Union bloc were solid, unlike those of other parties. Clearly therefore, despite the use of PR, stable party loyalties were emerging at this stage within the new electorate, albeit in relation to the largest political party. Sinn Féin's national policy transcended local matters for nearly half the electorate in Cork. The Central Ward provides a good example of the solidarity of Sinn Féin supporters. J. J. Walsh topped the poll here with a surplus of 270 votes. Of this surplus, 82 per cent transferred back to the remaining Sinn Féin and the Transport Union candidates. In the same area, Richard Beamish of the Commercial Party was also elected on the second count with a surplus of 195 votes. However, his surplus transferred in every direction. Only 37.44 per cent went back to his fellow Commercial Party candidates. Nationalist candidates received 24.1 per cent of Beamish's surplus while Sinn Féin received 17 per cent. The Nationalist candidate, Danny Gamble, was also elected on the first count. His transfers did not transfer solidly to his party either, Sinn Féin receiving 11 per cent, Labour 9 per cent, Independents 37 per cent, and his fellow party candidates only 30 per cent.[54]

Sinn Féin's total first preference vote of 48 per cent (even though this figure includes the Transport Union's share) represented a significant drop on the party's 1918 general election total of 68 per cent. This reflected a national trend. It can be attributed to a number of factors, including, for example, the sheer number of candidates (160 in all), each with their own personal support bases and appeal, as well as the number of strong local personalities standing as candidates, including Richard Beamish in the Central Ward, Sir Edward Fitzgerald in the South Ward No. 2 area and John Cronin, an Independent candidate who was elected on the first count in the South Ward No. 1 area. However, it must be said that a considerable section of the electorate did not see the local elections in the same light as Sinn Féin did. As the *Cork Examiner* put it on Saturday 17 January, the result:

> would appear to demonstrate the fact that the political element was not the only one which influenced the electors in making their choice and that the sharp line of demarcation which formerly existed has been blunted by other considerations to which the personal, or appreciation of past services or other causes may have contributed.

Neither was voting uniform throughout the city, as Table 2 illustrates.

Table 2: *Election to Cork Corporation, January 1920: Parties' Share of Votes by Ward*

Ward	SF & ITGWU	Nat.	Com.	Lab.	Ex-Serv	Ind.
Central	37.38	27.22	17.51	6.30	2.33	9.22
North-East	44.18	30.32	15.73	—	4.27	5.49
North-West No.1	50.00	18.00	4.27	13.70	7.63	4.00
North-West No.2	54.92	29.50	8.50	—	14.68	—
North-West No.3	63.00	5.20	—	8.63	12.89	9.32
South Ward No.1	51.83	21.07	4.04	3.70	—	19.34
South Ward No. 2	47.67	36.01	6.54	3.14	2.62	3.22

Sinn Féin received its lowest vote in the Central and North-East Wards – areas where, incidentally, the Commercial Party polled its highest votes. In the Central Ward, the party had a strong candidate in Alderman Richard Beamish, owner of the Beamish & Crawford Brewery. In the North-East Ward, Sir John Harley Scott and J. T. Mulligan took two seats for the Commercial Party. Scott, according to de Róiste, was of a Unionist disposition and was a member of the previous City Council.[55]

Although the *Cork Examiner* provides very comprehensive information on the election as a whole, it does not indicate the Transport Union element of the Sinn Féin ticket. Therefore, it is not possible to establish with any degree of accuracy which candidates belonged to the Transport Union and which to Sinn Féin candidates (with the exception, of course, of the better-known personalities). However, one can tentatively establish that of the thirty successful candidates, at least twenty were members of Sinn Féin, at least six were members of the Transport Union and the remaining four were probably members of the Transport Union. The *Cork Examiner* lists the occupations of the various Sinn Féin and Transport Union candidates (although it does not do this for the other candidates) and this helps to establish the party identity of some of them. The 1924 mayoral election of Seán French also provides clues. The newspaper report of this election mentions 'the nine Labour members' and indeed some of the councillors speaking from an official Labour Party perspective at this meeting stood on a joint Sinn Féin–Transport Union ticket in 1920.[56] Of the thirty Sinn Féin and Transport Union candidates elected, three were TDs, four were self-employed (two manufacturers, one chemist and one merchant), two were university professors, two were accountants, four were clerks, three were described as 'organisers' (possibly in the trade union movement) and the remainder were tradesmen or manual workers. One woman, a Miss Sutton, was elected to the Council as a representative of Sinn Féin and the Transport Union.[57]

Official Labour did particularly badly in these elections. Commenting on the performance of Labour in its various shades, de Róiste noted in his diary that 'Labour, official or otherwise has done very badly. These elections clearly show that the appeal to a war between the classes is not a very moving one in Ireland'.58 However, the point could be made here that the issues in the election were not specifically related to class politics at all. The Sinn Féin and Transport Union ticket was a broadly based one embracing working class, tradesmen, professionals, self-employed, shop-owners and small manufacturers. Its policy platform was national in character, seeking both recognition of Dáil Éireann as the legitimate parliament of Ireland and every means to achieve this, including control of local councils. The Nationalist Party, in combination with the Ex-Servicemen's Association, was similarly broadly based. The Commercial Party obviously had a restricted policy platform but strong personalities helped to broaden its appeal while official Labour had only twelve candidates in the field, thereby ensuring that it was in no position to mount a serious challenge to Sinn Féin. Given that there were to be no more local elections in Cork for nearly a decade, Labour's failure to gain more seats in 1920 obviously affected its capacity to produce quality candidates in subsequent elections in the early years of the Free State. Invariably, membership of local councils was an effective launching-pad to Dáil Éireann. Out of fifty-six candidates who were elected, Labour interests could claim only nine.

It could be argued that Sinn Féin benefited from its alliance with the Transport Union in electoral terms. Of course, the benefit was that it did not have to fight this election on socio-economic issues. In addition, it could appeal with credibility to the working class. Also, the profiles of the Sinn Féin candidates themselves indicate that the majority of them were either working class or lower middle class. They were certainly not doctrinaire capitalists – judging from their campaign speeches – and the point must be made that Sinn Féin, being essentially a 'catch-all' type of political movement, foreshadowed the emergence in the post-independence era of parties with similar occupational profiles and political attitudes. Sinn Féin successfully absorbed certain Labour interests via the 'national issue', which was to have far-reaching consequences for the development of the Irish Labour party. The role of municipal elections as a launching-pad for future political careers is graphically illustrated by the fact that ten of the successful candidates of 1920 were to stand in future Dáil general elections. Of these, eight served as members of the Dáil from 1918 at various times before 1932.[59]

De Róiste seems to have been relatively happy with Sinn Féin's performance although he reveals that in a number of areas, Sinn Féin was hoping to do better, such as in his own South Ward No. 2 (City Hall) where the party gained three seats. It had expected four. In the North West No. 2, where the party was hoping to win four seats, it won three. De Róiste described the successful Commercial candidates as men who stood on their own appeal and held a variety of political views, some of which even supported those of Sinn Féin.[60]

The *Cork Examiner*, in its editorial of 19 January, expressed satisfaction that the claims which had been made in favour of PR had been vindicated. 'As far as may be judged', it reported, 'the Irish election results fully justify the Proportional Representation Society's claim that the majority of the electors shall rule and [that] all considerable minorities shall be heard'. It expatiated at some length on the use of PR and concluded with the significant point that the elections had 'exploded' several fallacies that had been raised in opposition to the system. People did not find the system confusing and the counting officials had no difficulty in dealing with it.[61] In any event, the PR system had resulted in a broadly based and representative City Council, with five different groupings, including Independents. Those who voted for Sinn Féin voted solidly for that party down the line, indicating a strong party allegiance.

In its final editorial on the municipal elections, the *Cork Examiner* expressed the hope that the new Corporation, irrespective of party or other classification, would take a broad outlook and serve the city's interest by helping to make the most of their opportunities in 'contributing to its commercial and industrial uplift-ment'.[62] However, Sinn Féin was determined to use its majority on the Council to promote its policies. The first step in this direction was the election of a Lord Mayor.

The Sinn Féin candidate for the mayoralty was Alderman Tomás MacCurtain. The first meeting of the new Corporation was held on 30 January and MacCurtain was elected unanimously to the post. The non-Sinn Féin representatives felt that as Sinn Féin had won the majority of the seats, it was entitled to have its nominee elected. The new Lord Mayor, addressing the meeting, promised to assist every party and representa-tive who had the interest of the country at heart. He said that Sinn Féin was very pleased with the results of the municipal elections and that they 'were also pleased that certain minorities were represented in the Council because they recognised that in every stable community they had minorities that were entitled to representation in the government of the affairs of the country'. In an effort to demonstrate the party's commitment to 'efficiency', the Lord Mayor accepted a £100 reduction in his salary. Sinn Féin also opposed nominating anybody to the office of High Sheriff because in the words of Alderman Barry, no self-respecting Irishman would take the oaths required for the position. Under Lord Mayor's business, de Róiste proposed a motion pledging allegiance to Dáil Éireann and stressed the primacy of the national question:

> Any Irishman who claimed allegiance to Ireland and Ireland alone, any Irishman who called himself an Irish nationalist, any Irishman who in the past called himself a Home Ruler must choose to-day between two governments, the Government set up by the Irish people or the Government that rules by force alone.

Richard Beamish opposed this, believing that the Corporation should steer clear of all political matters:

> The majority were entitled to do as their party decided. He did not agree with their action in regard to the Shrievality [office of High Sheriff]. He strongly indicted British jealousy of Irish industrial development and added that while he had to bow to the will of the majority he would express his opinion.

The motion was carried on a majority, with some members of the Commercial and Nationalist parties opposing. A new era had emerged in local politics and this was symbolised by the hoisting of the tricolour over the City Hall and the frequent use of Irish during the inaugural meeting. The *Cork Examiner*, in its editorial on the morning after the meeting, welcomed the spirit of toleration which had characterised the meeting. It also praised the Lord Mayor's speech which exhibited a 'tolerant spirit and a grasp of affairs essential in the occupant of the Municipal Chair'.[63]

The new Lord Mayor was barely two months in office when he was murdered by unidentified members of the British forces in the early hours of 20 March 1920. This event marked the beginning of a new reign of terror which lasted throughout the year and from which the people and city of Cork suffered greatly. At about 1.30 a.m., Mrs MacCurtain heard a knock at the door of the house and within seconds, a group of men with blackened faces burst in, rushed up the stairs and shot the Lord Mayor at his bedroom door. In addition, as reported in the *Cork Examiner* that day, a large party of military, fully armed and led by an officer, later entered the house and thoroughly searched every room, including the room where MacCurtain lay dead.[64]

On the following morning, the *Cork Examiner* broke the news to a shocked public, publishing a picture of the dead Lord Mayor and praised him as 'a man of high character and personally was liked by a great many who differed with him politically. His tragic death will create a profound sensation throughout the country'. It also rallied public opinion behind Sinn Féin. On 22 March the *Cork Examiner* reflected the extent to which this crime was condemned in Cork:

> Representative public bodies in Cork City, trade and labour organisations, the branches of the Gaelic League in various districts, the judges of the Assize, the magistracy, in fact all sorts and conditions of men are unanimous in expressing their condemnation and abhorrence of the black crime for which Cork mourns today.

Bishop Cohalan also strongly condemned the murder as well as the fact that the military had raided the Lord Mayor's house after the shooting. During the weekend before the funeral, Cork virtually closed down. Thousands of young men and women wore the tricolour crossed with black, some business houses draped their windows, the theatres and places of amusement closed and concerts, lectures and other fixtures were cancelled. The funeral itself was a huge public event, with crowds following the funeral route, beginning in Roman Street, and out the Western Road to St Finbarr's Cemetery. The *Cork Examiner*'s comment on the funeral indicates the crucial nature of this entire episode, that 'by a demonstration of sympathy unequalled in the history of the city, Cork had paid its tribute of affection and respect to its Lord Mayor who now lies beneath the sod'.[65]

A coroner's jury returned a verdict of murder finding that the Lord Mayor had been 'wilfully murdered under circumstances of most callous brutality, that the murder was organised and carried out by the Royal Irish Constabulary, officially directed by the British government'. The jury returned a verdict of 'wilful murder' against Lloyd George, the viceroy, Lord French and the Chief Secretary, Ian MacPherson, as well as against three inspectors of the RIC (including Cork's District Inspector Swanzy) and some unknown members of the same force.[66]

Tomás MacCurtain's place as Lord Mayor was immediately taken by Terence MacSwiney, TD, who had represented the Mid-Cork Constituency since 1918. MacSwiney was a student of the Irish language and the author of many plays, poems and articles. He was commandant of the Cork No. 1 Brigade of the IRA. In his inaugural speech as Lord Mayor, he made the memorable comment that 'this contest of ours is not on our side one of rivalry or vengeance, but one of endurance – it is not those who can inflict the most, but those that can suffer most will conquer'. On 12 August 1920, while presiding at a meeting at the City Hall in Cork, the Lord Mayor was arrested. He was court-martialled on the charge of 'being in possession of documents the publication of which would be likely to cause disaffection to His Majesty'.[67] As a protest against the continuing arrests of public representatives, he went on hunger strike. Ten men arrested with him made the same declaration. They were imprisoned in Cork. The Lord Mayor, on the third day of his hunger strike, was put on board a warship and sent to London to be imprisoned in Brixton jail. His prolonged hunger strike drew worldwide attention to the Irish problem and foreign pressmen came to Ireland and to Brixton to gather information on the subject.[68]

On 17 October, one of the hunger strikers in Cork prison, Michael Fitzgerald, died. The removal of his body from Ss Peter and Paul's Church, off Patrick Street, was a particularly tense affair. As the cortège was about to leave the church, an officer arrived with revolver in hand, backed up by troops. He announced that he had orders to fire if more than 100 people followed the coffin and indicated that, if necessary, he would disperse the crowd with force. The thousands who had gathered to pay their respects dispersed quietly but the incident dramatically illustrated the absolute polarisation between the government and the governed.[69]

On 25 October Terence MacSwiney, on the seventy-fourth day of his hunger strike, died. His death was followed a few hours later by that of Joseph Murphy, another of the prisoners in Cork jail. The reaction of the *Cork Examiner* to the deaths of these two hunger strikers illustrated the degree to which the paper had swung behind Sinn Féin. This was primarily due to the government's policy of reprisals and repression. In its issue of 26 October, an entire page was dedicated to the dead Lord Mayor and included a pictorial as well as a written tribute. Pictures of MacSwiney with his family, at his first official function, of his schooldays and other events in his life, were all shown for a number of days after his death. In a simple statement, the paper declared that 'by the death of Lord Mayor MacSwiney Ireland has lost another of her most patriotic and noble-spirited sons and Cork its leading citizen'.[70] In its editorial in the same issue, MacSwiney was hailed as the devoted champion of Ireland's liberty and noted the fact that the entire world followed with the most profound sympathy 'his heroic fight against overwhelming odds'. As far as the *Cork Examiner* was concerned, MacSwiney had died 'to win liberty for a small nation – he has made the supreme sacrifice to hasten the coming of Irish freedom. Such sacrifices as his cannot be in vain . . . Terence MacSwiney has passed away but the cause of Irish freedom still lives. It can never die'.[71]

Such sentiments are understandable given the circumstances of the time and the nature of British government policy. Nonetheless, the terminology used was a far cry from the days when the *Cork Examiner* had warned the Cork electorate in 1918 not to follow a 'policy of rainbow-chasing', as it had described Sinn Féin's policy. The paper had always supported the Irish Parliamentary Party and its editorial policy before 1918 had made no secret of this. Indeed, in 1906, George Crosbie, a director of the paper, had stood as a Nationalist candidate in the general election of that year. But now its endorsement of MacSwiney's struggle was a graphic illustration of the degree to which the British authorities had alienated moderate nationalist opinion in Ireland and had forced it behind the Sinn Féin movement. Sinn Féin was now the dominant political force and the stance adopted by various elites reflected this. For example, Bishop Cohalan, who had visited

MacSwiney in Brixton Prison, wrote a letter to the *Cork Examiner* on the day MacSwiney's body arrived in Cork from England, welcoming home the 'hallowed remains'. It is worth quoting for its intensity and latent anger:

> For the moment it might appear that he had died in defeat. This might be conceded if there were questions merely of the individual, but it is not true when the issue of the nation is considered. Was Lord Edward Fitzgerald's death in vain? Was Robert Emmet's death in vain? Did Pearse and other martyrs in the cause of Irish Freedom die in vain? We are the weaker nation in the combat. Sometimes we tire of the conflict. Any special questions such as the questions of the land, of local government, of housing, of education, for a time engage our whole attention. But periodically the memory of the martyr's death will remind a young generation of the fundamental question of the freedom of Ireland. Terence MacSwiney takes his place among the martyrs in the sacred cause of the freedom of Ireland. We bow in respect before his heroic sacrifice. We pray that God may have mercy on his soul.

Bishop Cohalan was, it should be remembered, a moderate nationalist and had been a supporter of the Irish Parliamentary Party before 1918. However, since that time he had been 'extremely sensitive and sympathetic to Dáil Éireann' and was particularly critical of the government's policy.[72]

Some days before MacSwiney's death, the Catholic hierarchy had issued a strong statement on the state of the country. The bishops declared that oppression was rampant and that terrorism and partiality were the characteristics of the government which had reduced Ireland to a state of anarchy. The statement alleged that 'the flogging and massacring of civilians was rife and all perpetrated by the forces of the Crown which had established a reign of frightfulness which for murdering the innocent and destroying their property had only a parallel in the horrors of the Turkish atrocities'. The hierarchy stressed that it detested crime from whatever side it came but felt that the government's policy of reprisals was 'the vengeance of savages wreaked on whole towns or countryside without any proof of complicity in the crime'. The *Cork Examiner*'s editorial on the same day endorsed the hierarchy's stance and expressed the hope that the British people would take note of the considered views of the Irish hierarchy.[73]

The funeral of MacSwiney which took place on 31 October was a powerful demonstration of the nationalist cause. By the order of the Dáil, the day was observed as a day of public mourning throughout Ireland. In Cork city businesses closed down and thousands attended the funeral. The entire episode proved to be a major international embarrassment to the British authorities and only added to their already considerable difficulties in Ireland.

Cork was to see even more violence and atrocity. On 28 November, the IRA ambushed a party of Auxiliaries at Kilmichael in west Cork, killing eighteen. Three Volunteers were also killed. This was a major blow to the Auxiliaries and was followed by another ambush on 11 December at Dillon's Cross on the city's northside when a lorry carrying a number of RIC men and Auxiliaries was attacked as it drove towards the city. One Auxiliary was killed and eight were wounded. That night, homes in the Dillon's Cross area were burnt and the city centre was burnt to the ground by a band of drunken Black and Tans and Auxiliaries. The cost of the damage estimated at between £2–3 million. Most of the shops in Patrick Street were destroyed. The City Hall and adjoining Free Library lay in ruins.[74] Two members of the fire brigade were wounded by gunfire while at work. A British Labour commission, which was investigating the situation in Ireland at the time, reported on the burning of Cork and concluded:

> that during the greater part of the time that outbreaks of fire took place the Curfew regulations were in operation. The fires appear to have been an organised attempt to destroy the most valuable premises in the city.

The commission clearly laid the blame for the rampage on the Black and Tans and its revelations shocked moderate opinion in England.[75]

On the following morning Bishop Cohalan preached in the North Cathedral and stated that the city 'had suffered as much damage at the hands of the servants of the government as Dublin suffered during 1916'. He went on to excommunicate members of both the IRA and the British army. Cork had suffered an appalling level of violence and oppression during 1920 and Cohalan's decree must be placed in this context.[76]

One can only speculate on the significance of 'the reign of terror' in Cork during 1920 and 1921 and of the impact the deaths of MacCurtain and MacSwiney as well as the degree to which they influenced the future electoral behaviour of its citizens. However, that they rallied public opinion behind Sinn Féin cannot be questioned and the 'no contest' general election of 1921 graphically illustrates this. Erhard Rumpf and A. C. Hepburn have advanced the view that areas which had the greatest level of military activity during the War of

Independence were also the areas which experienced the greater military and political activity against the Anglo-Irish Treaty of 1921.[77] This was not the case in Cork. The general elections of 1922 and 1923 resulted in an overwhelming victory for the pro-Treaty candidates. One could suggest that Cork had endured so much violence and suffering during the War of Independence that the majority of its citizens had no appetite for a further round of hostilities and that they demonstrated this through the ballot box. The divide which resulted from the Anglo-Irish Treaty will be dealt with in greater detail in the next chapter. Certainly the de Róiste diaries, the *Cork Examiner* and the Catholic Church's political stance all support the contention that Cork was grateful for the respite which came in the form of a truce on 11 July 1921.

Another long-term electoral impact of the War of Independence was that it brought Sinn Féin to a dominant position in the city. It was they who were now effectively organising daily life. Even grief was structured. Funerals, particularly those of the two lord mayors, were massive political demonstrations organised by Sinn Féin personnel. Despite John Dillon's optimism in May 1921 when he forecast growing support and a bright future for his party, the Irish Parliamentary Party was by now virtually a thing of the past.[78] The identity of the Labour Party had also been submerged and many of its members, particularly those who were also members of the Transport Union, were indistinguishable from Sinn Féin. This fact became obvious in May 1921 when no one challenged Sinn Féin in the elections called under Lloyd George's Government of Ireland Act (1920). Although the unity of the Sinn Féin movement was eventually shattered by the Anglo-Irish Treaty and the subsequent Civil War, the dominant role played by its members during the War of Independence period guaranteed a long political career for many of them in the new Free State, irrespective of which side they took. It was perhaps the major factor responsible for the emergence of a 'two-and-a-half' party political system by 1932.

The Government of Ireland Act (1920) established two governments and parliaments in Dublin and Belfast with similar powers and characteristics. It also effected the partition of Ireland. Elections for the two parliaments were held in May 1921. In Northern Ireland, the Unionists won forty out of fifty-two seats. The remaining twelve seats were divided evenly between Sinn Féin and the old Nationalist party in accordance with a pre-election agreement.[79]

In Cork, the City Borough constituency was enlarged from a two-seater to a four-seater. Sinn Féin nominated four candidates, J. J. Walsh, de Róiste (both outgoing), Mary MacSwiney (sister of the deceased Lord Mayor of Cork, Terence MacSwiney) and the incumbent Lord Mayor, Donal O'Callaghan. De Róiste was soon to find that efforts were being made by members of the IRA to prevent his candidature. On 3 May 1921, he recorded how a member of the Standing Committee of Sinn Féin in Cork had called to inform him that 'the Oglaig [sic] objected to me as a candidate at the coming elections under the Partition Act'. De Róiste wrote to de Valera concerning the matter and discovered that the objection had definitely not come from Dublin. Apparently the objections to de Róiste were based on the misconception that he had supported the peace proposals which had been made some months earlier and that Dublin had forbidden his nomination.[80] However, a diary entry for 5 May reveals another reason: his lack of military activity. He felt that there was a basis for such a complaint:

Sé an gearán is mó a chuirtear am taov, deirtear liom
anois, ná ná bim 'gníomharach' mo dhóthain. Tá
bun leis an ngearán san admhuighim, acht tá taov
eile ar an scéal san. Tuigim féin an scéal san go
maith. Ni huigean lucht na ngearán an chúis.

[The greatest complaint made of me, it is said to me
now, is that I am not 'active' enough. There is I admit
a basis to that complaint, but there is another side
to the story. I understand that story well. Those who
complain do not understand the reason].[81]

The Standing Committee and Executive of Sinn Féin
eventually overruled the objections of the representatives
of the IRA and insisted on de Róiste's name being
included. Their minds may have been made up by the
strength of de Valera's resolve that it was:

a mistaken policy to appear at the present time to be
forcing out everybody who ventures to disagree with
our attitude . . . it will look very bad to have him
thrown out by a Convention which, under the
present circumstances, will scarcely be regarded as
sufficiently wide in its constitution.[82]

The episode is significant in that it illustrates a continuing
strain in relations between the military and political
wings of Sinn Féin and a distrust of politicians on the part
of the military men. As early as 20 October 1917, de
Róiste's diary records that:

every man who is not a Volunteer or in the good
graces of the Volunteers is to be pushed aside from
responsible positions in Sinn Féin. How far this is
general I know not, but it is a fair summary of the

local [Cork city] situation . . . we can only 'wait and see' those of us who are 'out of it' – pushed aside, practically scorned, certainly belittled.[83]

Along similar lines, he later also confided to his diary that 'public life is a queer game! I hear even criticisms of myself because I am not in prison! I know in my own soul that it is the mercy of God alone that has saved me from so many of the dangers and evils that surround us'. Less than two weeks after writing this entry, de Róiste himself narrowly avoided death. Black and Tans entered his home in the early morning of 15 May and shot dead a priest, Fr O'Callaghan, who was lodging there at that time. De Róiste immediately telegrammed the news of the murder to Pope Benedict XV and asked him to protest to the British government. In an interesting entry on 20 May, de Róiste also recorded that he had:

> heard last night that the correspondence that passed between the Sinn Féin Executive in Cork and the Volunteers regarding my nomination last week was with other correspondence captured by the Crown forces the other day. Had I been killed on Sunday morning this would have been brought up to show I was a 'moderate Sinn Féiner' and the 'extremists' were my murderers. That lie at least has been frustrated.[84]

The fact that there was ongoing correspondence between the Sinn Féin Executive on the one hand and the Volunteers on the other, indicates the degree of influence the military men were exerting on purely political and civil matters within the Sinn Féin movement. Todd Andrews would later talk along similar lines when he suggested that the members of the Free

State Dáil were adopting the 'menial status of mere politicians'. Tom Garvin refers to this disdain as a 'culture that had been accustomed to a distrust and even contempt for electoral politics ever since the fall of Parnell in 1891'.[85]

Before the nominations for the election, John Dillon had issued a public statement explaining the reasons behind the Irish Parliamentary Party's decision not to oppose Sinn Féin in the southern constituencies. First of all, Dillon felt that to oppose Sinn Féin would inevitably result in very bitter feelings being aroused, with consequent disorder and bloodshed. This is something for which he did not want to take responsibility. Secondly, given the circumstances of the time, Dillon felt that it would be extremely difficult to put before the people a clear issue upon which to vote. In his statement, he reiterated his irreconcilable opposition to the programme and methods of Sinn Féin. However, he also condemned the government's policy of repression which made it:

> practically impossible for any Nationalist Irishman to fight Sinn Féin at the election. To oppose and condemn Sinn Féin at this election would lay one open to the charge however unjust that charge might be, of supporting the Black and Tans, the Auxiliary Police, and the whole policy of Greenwood and Company.[86]

As a result, on 13 May 1921, the four Sinn Féin candidates – J. J. Walsh, de Róiste, Mary MacSwiney and Donal O'Callaghan – were elected unopposed. As Walsh was in prison, and O'Callaghan and MacSwiney were in America, de Róiste was the only candidate who was present at the election. In his speech thanking the returning officer, de Róiste, clearly understanding the historic nature of this election, declared that there was no basis left in Ireland at that time for a contest:

> This unopposed return we accept, and the world must accept, as evidence of the unanimity and solidarity of the Irish people in their adherence to the principle of Ireland's sovereign independence, in their allegiance to Dáil Éireann as the constitutional authority in this country and their abhorrence of and protest against the partition of their country by the English government.

The *Cork Examiner*, commenting on the formal election, mistakenly saw it as the 'death-knell' of partition:

> No matter what may be the outcome of the elections in the North-Eastern six-county area, where contests are to take place, 26 Irish counties out of 32 have, it may be said, already spurned and rejected the scheme of partition which the Prime Minister offered as a panacea for Irish grievances.[87]

Although the election result had no effect on the actual partition arrangement, it graphically demonstrated that the Government of Ireland Act was a dead letter in the twenty-six counties and that its rejection there, combined with increasing hostility in Britain and elsewhere towards the government's heavy-handed approach to Ireland, had brought about a significant change in policy. Lloyd George decided that a peaceful settlement had to be secured in Ireland, as opposed to inflicting a total military defeat on the IRA. As a result of prolonged negotiations, a truce between the British forces and the IRA came into effect on 11 July 1921. From the Truce emerged negotiations towards an

agreement which led to the signing of the Anglo-Irish
Treaty on 6 December 1921, an event which was to
have a paramount influence on the development of
modern Ireland.

2
1921–1923: THE YEARS OF
CONFRONTATION & UPHEAVAL

The signing of the Anglo-Irish Treaty on 6 December 1921 provoked an immediate cabinet crisis in Ireland with Éamon de Valera, Austin Stack and Cathal Brugha rejecting the Treaty while Arthur Griffith, Michael Collins, W. T. Cosgrave and Robert Barton supported it. This split foreshadowed a similar division in Dáil Éireann. The Dáil met on 14 December 1921 to debate the Treaty. Speakers in favour argued that the Treaty was the best that could be achieved and in the words of Michael Collins, gave 'not the ultimate freedom that all nations desire and develop to, but the freedom to achieve it.'[1] Collins' 'stepping stone' idea is of vital importance with regard to the development of Irish politics in the 1920s and 1930s and in particular, to the development of Fianna Fáil which later incorporated this idea into its own political programme. Other pro-Treaty speakers, including Griffith and Kevin O'Higgins, argued that there was nothing dishonourable in accepting Commonwealth status. Anti-Treaty speakers claimed that the Treaty was a sell-out of the Irish Republic which had been declared in 1916 and ratified by the Dáil in 1919. They also asserted that in no circumstances could they accept Dominion status or swear an 'oath of allegiance' to the British king.[2] It was the oath that proved to be a major stumbling block to acceptance of the Treaty. Later on, it provoked a further split in Sinn Féin and was to remain a major issue in Irish politics for several years.

The four Cork deputies also had differing views. Both J. J. Walsh and de Róiste favoured the Treaty while Mary MacSwiney and Donal O'Callaghan, the Lord Mayor, did not. Walsh endorsed Collins' 'stepping stone' idea but used more colourful language to do so. He supported the Treaty on the basis that it would provide the best preparation for resuming hostilities later on, that 'we are entrenching here, we wait for reinforcements and we wait for supplies and at an opportune moment we march on'.[3] In his memoirs, Walsh was less voluble. In 1944, he recalled that he had voted for the Treaty because he had seen no hope of doing better.[4]

De Róiste's diary over the period of the debate records the advantages and disadvantages of the Treaty. In an entry on 26 December 1921, he listed his objections as follows:

> Its wording in many clauses; the Governor General; the mention of King George in the proposed oath; the presumption of Dominion status, with 'loyalty' to the king; some of the arrangements regarding 'Ulster'; the 'maintenance parties' on our coasts; arrangements regarding cables and wireless stations.

However, he found the arguments in its favour more persuasive:

> The separate nationality of Ireland is distinctly admitted now; the sovereignty of the Irish people is almost entirely admitted internally, partially in external matters; Ireland gets a place in the League of Nations; gets a separate voice in moulding British Empire policy (am not enamoured with that: it may

be for good, but it may also be for Imperialism – which is bad); the British army evacuates most of the country; the right of Ireland to a separate army is admitted, the right to a navy is admitted; a demo-cratic republican form of government can be established; complete and absolute control over judicature, law, police, education, fiscal policy, social organisation, trade, industry, commerce and all such activities passes at once into the hands of the Irish people; the development of all our national characteristics, language, literature, music, art, becomes at once possible in a matter not hitherto possible.[5]

However, Mary MacSwiney who had been elected in May 1921, spoke vehemently against the Treaty:

Half measures are no longer possible because on the twenty-first of January 1919 this Assembly, elected by the will of the sovereign people of Ireland, declared by the will of the people the Republican form of Government as the best for Ireland, and cast off for ever their allegiance to any foreigner.

Donal O'Callaghan opposed the Treaty on similar grounds and strongly opposed the oath of allegiance and the proposals for Dominion status.[6]

At local level, there were immediate reactions to the Treaty debate and the military leadership of Sinn Féin in Cork began to flex its muscles. The staff of the 1st Southern Division wrote to the four TDs instructing them to vote against the Treaty. The letter, dated 12 December 1921 and addressed from 'Headquarters: Cork No. 1 Brigade', is reproduced in de Róiste's diary. It contained the following message:

To all TDs in Cork 1 Area

(1) On December 10th the Staff of the 1st Southern Division and all Brigade Commandants met and sent forward to G.H.Q. unanimously a demand for the rejection of the Treaty proposals.

(2) You are reminded that it is your duty to support this demand.

(3) To act otherwise would be treason to the Republic to which we have all sworn allegiance.

De Róiste's interpretation of the note was that failure to vote against the Treaty would mean death. He informs us that Collins had heard of the note and had instructed headquarters staff to deal with it. De Róiste felt that the order illustrated that, at that moment, there was 'no liberty of conscience, or thought, no regard at the present time for the interests of the poor and lowly who crave peace not war'.[7]

During this period, de Róiste continually warned de Valera and Collins that the situation was 'getting out of hand' and that a split in the army was inevitable if discipline was not enforced from headquarters.[8] On 30 December, for instance, copies of a pamphlet that had been written by Alfred O'Rahilly were taken from Guy's printing works in Cork and the 'type' was broken. According to de Róiste, this action had been carried out by armed men who represented themselves as IRA men. The Sinn Féin Executive in Cork subsequently condemned the action. De Valera and Brugha assured de Róiste that army discipline would be maintained.[9] However, on 2 January 1922, a similar incident occurred. The Cork Chamber of Commerce had arranged for a petition to be signed in its offices by people who supported the

Treaty. That morning, armed men entered the rooms and took away the petition books. De Róiste assumed that these men were probably the same people who had destroyed O'Rahilly's pamphlet and that the Officer Commanding of the Cork No. 1 Brigade, Seán Hegarty, had authorised these actions, the same individual who had sent the 'notice' to the TDs informing them that it would be considered 'treason to the Republic' if they voted for the Treaty.[10]

The political leaders in Cork, however, tried to prevent a split. On 29 December 1921 the Standing Committee of Sinn Féin met to discuss the matter. Before them was a letter of provisional resignation from de Róiste. His reasoning was that as it had been the Standing Committee which had been responsible for his selection as a candidate in May 1921, he was ultimately responsible to them. If the Standing Committee endorsed his favourable stance on the Treaty, he would carry on. However, if a majority rejected the Treaty, he would resign so that the Executive would not be misrepresented on the issue in Dáil Éireann. When the Standing Committee met on 29 December, the meeting ended inconclusively. Nine people attended. Among these was Seán Nolan who was TD for the western division of the county. He insisted on presiding and on forcing the issue to a vote, he being opposed to the Treaty. Of the other eight, four were for approval: Alfred O'Rahilly, Barry Egan, Seán Jennings and C. Crowley (chairman of the committee). Against the Treaty were Seán French, T. Daly, Séamas Walsh and Diarmuid Hurley. De Róiste seemed amused at French's decision that his 'being against makes everyone laugh, and I wonder myself if he is not playing some joke'.[11]

On the following evening, the complete executive met to decide the issue and de Róiste and Walsh were

invited to attend. De Róiste attended but withdrew from
the meeting on the grounds that de Valera had asked
Dáil members not to become embroiled in public contro-
versies on the matter. O'Rahilly also refused to attend as
a protest against what had happened at Guy's printing
works that same day and argued that if the 'rule of the
revolver' was to prevail and debate stifled, there was no
liberty. The meeting came to no definite decision.
However, it reaffirmed its trust in the members of the
Dáil, thereby allowing the Cork city deputies to act as
they saw fit. According to de Róiste, it 'was fear of a
split that prevented any decision being come to even on
my resignation'. The Sinn Féin members of Cork
Corporation had also met on the previous night (29
December). It also did not force the issue and reaffirmed
the Corporation's allegiance to Dáil Éireann.[12]

During January 1922, meetings of Sinn Féin
cumainn were held throughout Cork city to select
delegates for the Ard-Fheis which was to be held on 7
February. Although de Róiste claimed that Volunteers
played an active role in ensuring that anti-Treaty
delegates were selected, this is difficult to corroborate.[13]
However, the political representatives continued to
project the appearance of unity. This was reflected in a
decision of the Sinn Féin members of the Corporation to
propose the outgoing Lord Mayor, Donal O'Callaghan,
for re-election to the position, even though he had
opposed the Treaty. This was achieved but not without
difficulty. De Róiste noted that there was a lack of
suitable candidates, owing to Sinn Féin's rule that the
Lord Mayor had to be able to speak Irish. However, the
real problem on this occasion was whether O'Callaghan's
election as Lord Mayor would be construed as a vote
against the Treaty and whether he would use his
position to oppose the Provisional Government.

Another important consideration was the realisation that a divided Sinn Féin would facilitate the emergence of a non-Sinn Féin candidate. Hence the meeting's eventual decision, as recorded by de Róiste, that it was:

> apparent to all that if we do not hold together, as at present, in the Corporation, we can at any time be outvoted by the other parties in that body. So an understanding was arrived at, to be reduced to writing by a small committee tomorrow night; that Donal be purely a 'Civic candidate' and that party politics be not introduced.[14]

De Róiste's diary entries also reveal that his 'Labour colleagues' were, by this stage showing a degree of independence of Sinn Féin. There was even a possibility that Labour would put forward Robert (Bob) Day as a candidate for the mayoralty. De Róiste calculated that if he received the support of all the opponents of Sinn Féin, in addition to five of his own supporters, then he would win. Day had been elected on the joint Sinn Féin and Transport Union ticket in the 1920 local elections and according to de Róiste, was supposed by many to be a 'Red Flag Republican' and more 'extreme' or 'advanced' than the Republicans themselves.[15] In the event, Day did not stand but he did, along with Councillor Kenneally, protest at O'Callaghan's re-election because of the way in which he had treated them the previous year. Day also protested against both 'Free State' and 'Republic' declaring that his ideal was a 'Workers' Republic' as opposed to the type of republic which existed in France or America.[16] As a result, Sinn Féin held a meeting on 31 January which spent an hour discussing relations with the 'republican labour members' of the party. This discussion was a consequence of the attack which Day and Kenneally had made on the Lord Mayor at the mayoral election. Some members felt that it was an attack against the party while others, including de Róiste, felt it was a reflection of purely personal hostility against O'Callaghan. It is not without interest that de Róiste informs us that these two members 'do not attend party meetings now'.[17]

Despite the appearance of unity, a number of private meetings also took place among pro-Treaty members of Sinn Féin with a view to breaking away from the anti-Treatyites. In an entry on 1 February, de Róiste describes what happened at one such meeting:

> I met a few pro-Treaty supporters last evening to discuss with them the position in Cork and relations with our friends on the anti-Treaty side . . . AJR [Alfred O'Rahilly] was strong for a break in the Corporate party, but in the end the understanding was that we would all go on in that party; agree where we can, disagree where we must; that no written agreement be drawn up, but let circumstances decide.[18]

At the subsequent full Sinn Féin party meeting, this course of action was agreed. Donal O'Callaghan also agreed with de Róiste's prognosis.[19] However, by this stage, it was becoming increasingly difficult to avoid a split. On Wednesday 8 February, a meeting was held of what de Róiste termed 'the pro-Treaty party' – '"party" in the sense of organisation leaders': Collins, Richard Mulcahy, Eoin O'Duffy, Gearóid O'Sullivan, Joe McGrath, Seán Milroy, Dan MacCarthy and J. J. Fawsitt. De Róiste's diary gives the following description of what took place:

Apparently several meetings have been held recently for the same purpose as on Wednesday night, but this meeting was the most important of those that had been held. My attendance was only accidental. I gathered from the discussions that the ideas that had been considered were the formation of a pro-Treaty political party, in preparation for a parliamentary election, the issuing of a weekly paper and of propagandist literature, and the raising of a party fund. Of course, if the Sinn Féin Ard-Fheis, by a majority, should declare pro-Treaty that organisation would be at hand. But it is evident there will be two organisations in any event as a result of the Ard-Fheis decisions.

De Róiste took the opportunity to brief the meeting on the situation in Cork and stressed the importance of securing order. He also undertook to secure funds for the party.[20]

Despite the fact that serious political differences were emerging within the leadership of Sinn Féin, an armed conflict in the South was not an inevitable consequence of the Treaty split.[21] However, violence was on the increase. All the senior members of Cork's brigades voiced their opposition to the Treaty. As Peter Hart has pointed out, 'Seán O'Hegarty and Cork 1 adopted the most belligerent course of action, breaking up public meetings, harassing local newspapers, and suppressing pro-Treaty publications. When a *Times* correspondent reported that many members of the IRA in Cork city actually supported the Treaty, in line with public opinion, O'Hegarty sent his gunmen to Dublin to kidnap him and force him to write a retraction'.[22] Although 'the pro-Treaty Publicity Department of the Dáil government documented an increasing drift towards chaos in both parts of Ireland in early 1922', several attempts were made to avoid strife.[23] These culminated in the 'pact election' of June 1922.[24] It would appear that de Valera and other anti-Treaty leaders wanted to avoid civil war as did those on the pro-Treaty side. The agreement between de Valera and Collins to put forward a national panel of Sinn Féin candidates appears to have reflected such a desire. However, at grass-roots level, it is also clear from de Róiste's diary that not all pro-Treaty Sinn Féin supporters were happy with the agreement and wanted instead to confront anti-Treaty candidates at the polls. Against this background, de Róiste perceived the essential fragility of the pact:

> One is forced to conclude that for real friendship the agreement between Dev and Collins came too late. Dev's 'blood speech' and the actions of the irregular Óglaigh have seared bitter thoughts into many minds.[25]

In Cork, the 'pact election' of May 1922 saw the emergence of the Labour Party into the electoral fray at a national level. Sinn Féin nominated the four outgoing members of the Second Dáil: J. J. Walsh, Liam de Róiste, Mary MacSwiney and Donal O'Callaghan. These fought the election, ostensibly on the same platform. Frank Daly, chairman of the Harbour Commissioners, stood as an Independent Commercial candidate, as did Richard Beamish. Robert Day was the candidate of the Labour party.

The major themes of Sinn Féin's platform were the necessity to maintain national unity and restore order to the country; an appeal to the electorate on the basis of the party's record; and an exhortation to the electorate not to be influenced by class or sectional interests. The party placed daily advertisements in the *Cork Examiner* during the week before polling day which repeated these themes. The advertisements had the names of the four 'National Panel candidates' printed on them, with the following message to the electorate:

> Those candidates stand for the supreme National interests. They represent the National ideals to which the Irish people gave adherence during the past four years. They represent the unity of the forces that worked and fought for freedom during those years. They stand for ordered Government and stabilised conditions and the utilisation of every advantage which had been secured to advance the nation in strength and freedom.[26]

Sinn Féin held two major rallies before polling day in Cork city. The first was held on 11 June 1922 with de Valera as the main speaker. Significantly, Walsh was not on the platform and de Róiste attended only after much argument:

> As there was no word from J. J., the Secretary impressed on me that, if any semblance of the Pact is to be preserved in Cork, I had better attend. After argument and cogitation, I decided that I would attend tonight, but not to 'orate' – and indeed I can say nothing, for I have nothing to say! I feel as a dumb man – and have no heart in the meeting.

De Róiste was annoyed by the hurried manner in which the meeting had been arranged by the anti-Treatyite Lord Mayor as well as by the lack of prior consultation. He felt that this meeting was a typical example of how the anti-Treatyites were 'utilising' the pact and endeavouring to 'climb back to power on the back of the pro-Treaty side of Sinn Féin'.[27]

De Valera made a particularly interesting speech at this meeting, the content of which appears to indicate that he did not foresee the possibility of armed conflict in the immediate future. He acknowledged that the two parties in the Dáil had differed fundamentally on one question but that they had agreed to differ and to concentrate on those points on which they were agreed. According to de Valera, these points included the establishment of a free and independent nation which he also identified as a 'Gaelic-speaking Irish-Ireland'. De Valera stressed that the restoration of order was fundamental.[28] Earlier, at a meeting in Mallow, he had also given a clear message to people who were taking the law into their own hands:

> They [Sinn Féin] wanted the restoration of a reign of public law. The conditions of the past four or five years were such that individuals and groups of individuals had to act with a large amount of immediate responsibility. They took powers upon themselves very often for the good of the nation. These powers must now be relinquished to the central authority established by the nation, and it is to bring back the restoration of those powers to a central authority and as a first step to restore conditions of law and order that both sides have come together and decided for the moment that we forget, in so far as we could, our differences and concentrate upon the things on which we agree.[29]

This was a clear message to the militarists that the civil authority was the supreme authority and that it alone should control all military activity. Implicit in this speech is a rebuke to those who were engaged in the type of activities described by de Róiste in January and February. At the Cork meeting, de Valera also reiterated his belief that the time was not yet ripe for the emergence of class interests and that it would be best for the nation's welfare if these interests were stood down. In de Róiste's words,

> And if for the last four or five years special class interests were subordinated to the general interest, they could afford to do so for the next eight or ten months. He knew that such an agreement could be abused, but he would not again ask special interests to stand down except the circumstances were precisely the same.

The Lord Mayor, Donal O'Callaghan, saw the electoral pact as evidence of the determination of both sides to avoid bloodshed. He asked the electorate to re-elect those 'who had worked up to now'. In her speech, Mary MacSwiney echoed these sentiments but was also quite clear in her mind on what the electorate was being asked to decide upon:

> They were not asked to vote on any matter concerning the one great difference that concerned Dáil Éireann. They were only asked to send back to the third Dáil the members they had sent to the second in order that the common enemy might see that he would not have the pleasure of disuniting the Irish people.

She praised the role of the Labour Party during the previous four years but like de Valera, asked them to 'have patience for a few months longer'. MacSwiney was of the opinion that all classes were already represented in the Dáil and that it was absurd to suggest otherwise. Finally, she had a particularly harsh and bitter message for Richard Beamish, stating that 'no one, who is or has been a Unionist in Ireland has any right to go before the people of Ireland and ask for their vote in this crisis'. She added that to elect a Southern Unionist, even if he had 'changed his coat', would allow England to say that Ireland always wanted to be in the Empire.[30]

De Róiste was the last of the Cork Sinn Féin candidates to speak. Like de Valera, he stressed the need for unity and the restoration of law and order. He also appealed for support for the Sinn Féin candidates on the basis of their record. Privately, however, de Róiste was unhappy with the tide of events. In particular, he was annoyed with the efforts that were being made by the anti-Treaty candidates to dissuade other interests from participating in the election:

> As he [de Valera] was tired, I spoke first, very briefly indeed and very carefully – and have felt a humbug since. For, both sides on the Panel are only playing a political game; and it seems to me exceptional audacity and assurance to ask the people so seriously to vote only for us and for no others.[31]

Earlier, on 6 June, de Róiste had recorded his views about non-Sinn Féin candidates going forward:

> It is the old assumption of autocracy, so prevalent in the days of the Irish Parliamentary Party, that none but the existing party, or representatives knew what was best for the country. It is an effort to torpedo the expression of the people's opinion upon their present representatives.[32]

The *Cork Examiner* also, in a number of editorials in the days leading up to the election, strongly upheld the right of sectional and independent interests to contest the election. In its editorial of 12 June, the paper commented disapprovingly that:

> Whatever way such things may be viewed there is no denying the fact that the intervention of independent candidates under Clause 4 of the Pact is regarded by many electors as a thing not undesirable, despite the efforts now being made to retain all the sitting deputies in Office.[33]

And on polling day, the paper's editorial concluded with the following message to the electorate: 'It may be repeated that the fullest freedom exists for electors to vote for whom they please and extend their preferences in any order they please'.[34]

In any event, irrespective of what the *Cork Examiner* or Sinn Féin felt, Labour was determined to stand as an independent political party and with its own programme. In a message to the electorate from the National Executive of the Irish Labour Party and Trade Union Congress, the party acknowledged that it would not win a majority but nonetheless stated its determination to win for the 'workers of Ireland' a small but direct and independent representation in the new parliament. Referring to the party's role in the past and its expectations for the future, the message declared that:

> Labour has played no mean part in the recent national struggle. Labour in the future, as in the past, will stand firm in defence of the Nation's rights against any outside aggression, but Labour is not willing any longer to forgo its own right to an effective voice in the National Legislature.[35]

Labour selected one candidate in Cork, Robert Day, and as a result, was able to organise a highly personalised campaign. They had daily advertisements in the *Cork Examiner* in the week before polling day. At public meetings, Labour speakers stressed the right and necessity of Labour to contest the election in order to secure the interests of the working class. Housing and education were the two issues on which Labour concentrated. The party ran an effective campaign with a clear and appealing programme. At a public meeting, held on 13 June, Labour speakers outlined the party's programme and rejected any calls for Labour to step down. Alderman Kenneally of the Transport Union who had stood on the Sinn Féin ticket in the 1920 local elections, put it bluntly: 'Labour is going forward and is not going to stand down for de Valera, the Lord Mayor or anyone else'.[36] At this meeting, Richard Anthony, another Labour leader, stressed Labour's commitment to better housing and a more egalitarian educational system which would enable working-class youngsters to attain the highest level of educational achievement. He condemned the fact that there were so few working men's sons enjoying the advantage of university education. Day also spoke at length on education:

> One of the first points in the programme of the Labour party is to establish a properly co-ordinated system of education, whereby the children of the workers, if they have the brains and ability, may be enabled to pass from the National Schools to the technical school or the secondary school and from there to the University. Up to now the children of the workers depended almost entirely for their education on the National School. This being so, we will see in the future at any rate that the National

Schools must be decent buildings, with ample space and every accommodation for the children. They must be properly heated and cleaned, and must have playgrounds where games suitable for the children can be played. The health of the children must be our first consideration, as we want sound minds in sound bodies. Towards this end we must have a system of school meals, whereby children who cannot afford a lunch will be provided with a substantial meal in the middle of the day . . . Means must be found to provide them with all school books and requisites free of charge.[37]

This speech illustrated the difference between the Sinn Féin and Labour programmes in this election. Sinn Féin speakers made very general statements which were essentially attempts to paper over the divisions which had emerged as a result of the Treaty. On the other hand, Labour seemed to have received a new lease of life and their speakers and candidates concentrated on social and economic issues throughout the election campaign, using language which the layman could easily under-stand. Their speeches were certainly not couched in abstract socialist terminology. A good example of Labour's direct and outspoken campaign style is provided in the daily advertisement which appeared in the *Cork Examiner* on Day's behalf. The advertisement listed eight points to which the candidate was committed. Included were a guarantee of work and a wage to those who were willing to work, a pledge to provide free education, the establishment of a housing authority to build houses for workers at a low rent, the granting of pensions to mothers who had been left without support, and a family allowance for all children up to sixteen years of age. It also declared that the state should accept responsibility for the support of all widows and orphans and for men who had been disabled during the Anglo-Irish War.[38]

The two independent candidates, Frank J. Daly and Richard Beamish, also had regular advertisements in the *Cork Examiner* before polling day. Both of these supported the Anglo-Irish Treaty. The former gave his priorities as the improvement of the circumstances of the working classes, the development of trade and commerce, and the promotion of agriculture as it was, in his view, the 'mainstay' of the prosperity of Ireland. Daly was also in favour of making Irish the national language of the country.[39]

In his advertisement in the *Cork Examiner*, Beamish declared that the economic development of Ireland was his priority. He saw agriculture and the city's harbour as two major planks upon which the future prosperity of Cork could be built.[40] Although Mary MacSwiney had some harsh words to say about Beamish's former Unionist beliefs, it is apparent from the de Róiste diaries that during the War of Independence, Beamish had been sympathetic to Sinn Féin. He certainly had the capacity to adapt to changing circumstances, as is evidenced by his eventual election to Dáil Éireann in 1923. Interestingly enough, it appears that before his decision to stand, he offered the pro-Treaty Sinn Féin group funds for the election. This offer was made on 3 June at a private meeting with de Róiste who described what took place:

> Then very cleverly, but 'not as a bribe old chap', so he put it, he asked if I considered £500 as an adequate contribution from his firm, Beamish and Crawford, brewers, to the pro-Treaty Sinn Féin funds for Cork City and County. I made no remark as to whether it was adequate or otherwise, but said

that collectors would probably call upon him in due course. My reason for this was that I at once decided, if he were to be a candidate himself we would not take money from his firm – if he were not a candidate it was a different matter – the rule of Sinn Féin has been to collect generally, without distinction of politics.[41]

The apparent unity which Sinn Féin exhibited throughout the campaign was shattered in Cork on the eve of polling day, when Collins and Walsh addressed a large rally. According to de Róiste, the only notice of the meeting was a small paragraph in that evening's newspaper. Fearing that there would only be a small crowd at the railway station to meet them, de Róiste was very surprised, on arrival at the station, to find a huge crowd was waiting to greet Collins. Collins and Walsh were led by a parade from the station to Turner's Hotel in Oliver Plunkett Street where they addressed the people. Neither Mary MacSwiney nor Donal O'Callaghan were on the platform. Collins' speech was short and very different from de Valera's a few days earlier. In effect, he told the electorate to vote for whom they wished:

> You here are facing an election on Friday, and I am not hampered now by being on a platform where there are Coalitionists. I can make a straight appeal to you citizens of Cork to vote for the candidates you think best of – to vote for the candidates whom the electors of Cork will think will carry on best in the future the work that the citizens of Cork want carried on . . . You understand fully what you have to do and I will depend on you to do it.[42]

These speeches were interpreted by the Republicans as breaking the electoral pact. Collins' message was certainly the antithesis of what de Valera, MacSwiney and O'Callaghan had said a few days earlier, particularly in relation to the participation of non-Sinn Féin candidates. Collins did not, in so many words, ask the electorate to vote for pro-Treaty candidates only although his speech did not endorse all the panel candidates. Indeed, implicit in it was a rejection of the pact.[43]

It is difficult to assess the electoral impact of Collins' speech. It certainly did no harm at all to either the Labour candidate or the Independents. If anything, it was an endorsement of their decision to stand and a rebuke to the anti-Treatyite members of the panel who had been exhorting sectional interests to stand down. Like all the other major newspapers, the *Cork Examiner* reprinted his speech in full. Its editorial the following day interpreted Collins' speech in this light, believing that it exploded the idea 'that independent candidates were acting in opposition to the spirit of the agreement reached by Messrs. Collins and de Valera'. It also gave a lengthy defence of the right of other candidates and interests to stand and suggested that some of the Sinn Féin deputies were not accurately reflecting the views of their constituents in the Dáil. Rather, it suggested, they were pursuing their own personal views to the exclusion of all others:

> Will it be seriously urged that such persons are to be retained in office, and the misrepresented con- stituencies be prevented from giving effective expression to their political views?[44]

According to the *Cork Examiner*'s political correspon- dent, the election campaign was disappointing – 'one of the tamest elections on record in a country notorious for election excitement'.[45] And in a report after polling day, the paper reported that the campaign was the most uneventful in the history of elections in Ireland:

> If there was an absence of the vigorous methods of older days there were many evidences of . . . less strenuous methods of electioneering. The poster, handbill, and advertisements in the newspapers, were availed of to make appeal to the voter and impress the claims of the candidate.[46]

But this calm had come only after the storm that had surrounded the nominations. Intimidation had been a prominent feature of the period before the nomination deadline. However, this faded, as it did in most other parts of the country, after the nominations had been made. Only in Sligo–East Mayo did violence and 'vigorous methods of older days' persist until polling day. The major significance of the results was the poll-topping performance of the Labour candidate, Robert Day, who received 6,836 first-preference votes (22.52 per cent) and the poor performance of the Lord Mayor, Donal O'Callaghan, who finished last on the first count.[47] The two pro-Treaty candidates were elected comfortably enough. Mary MacSwiney was the fourth candidate elected, just four votes short of the quota. The first count was as follows:

Robert Day (Lab.)	6,836
J. J. Walsh (Pro-T.)	5,731
Liam de Róiste (Pro-T.)	5,657
Mary MacSwiney (Anti-T.)	4,016
Richard Beamish (Ind. Com.)	3,485
Francis Daly (Ind. Com.)	2,826
Donal O'Callaghan (Anti-T.)	1,796

MacSwiney was elected on the fifth count after Daly was eliminated. Beamish did not receive sufficient transfers to oust MacSwiney and was nearly 1,300 votes behind her at the end.[48]

Commenting in its editorial of 19 June, the *Cork Examiner* saw the results as conclusive proof that the freedom to vote for the candidate of choice 'is the right which the people under no circumstances will forgo'. According to the paper, the election had also demonstrated the appeal of the Treaty to the citizens of Cork while Day's victory was hailed as a 'striking tribute to the completeness of the Labour organisation'. It also felt that an Independent Commercial candidate could have been elected if there had been only one such candidate and not two. It attributed O'Callaghan's poor performance to the possibility that since he was already serving as Lord Mayor, the electorate were insisting not only on 'one man, one job' but also to the simpler possibility that the Lord Mayor's 'anti-Treaty proclivities weighed against him with the electorate'.[49]

Undoubtedly the general election of June 1922 was a severe blow to the anti-Treatyite candidates and a major boost to the Labour Party. Cork had voted for the Treaty in overwhelming terms and it could even be argued that Mary MacSwiney, sister of the self-sacrificing Lord Mayor of Cork, Terence MacSwiney, had won a large number of personal votes on account of that fact rather than because of her rejection of the Treaty per se. Peter Hart's analysis is worth quoting at length:

> Whatever their claims of statehood, the republicans had become just one party among many, and not a very successful one at that. Cork's 'high political spirit', largely suppressed by the enforced unities of war and revolution, was revived by the Treaty

debate and the June election. Bands, tar barrels, and faction fights returned to the welcoming streets of Cork. The guerrillas tampered extensively with the vote but, like guns and sticks, the attempted theft of traditional seats was a traditional part of the game which had many expert players. Outside the county, die-hard republicanism may have seemed to speak with a 'Cork accent' but, in the city and in West Cork, the mantle of William O' [Brien] passed on to Mick Collins – whose electoral coat-tails, as it turned out, were almost as long. The Labour Party repeated the rewards of a decade, of unionization, while the antagonistic Farmers' Party fought to defend their own wartime gains.[50]

The success of the Labour campaign proved conclusively that it had the potential to become a major electoral force and that its decision not to contest the 1918 General Election had not inhibited its development. Robert Day had received more votes than the combined vote of the two anti-Treaty candidates.

The results in Cork were also typical of those in the nation at large. Those deputies who were in favour of the Treaty, including the Farmers' Party, the Labour Party and some Independents, won well. Of the 128 seats, the pro-Treaty group won 58, the anti-Treaty group 35, Labour 17, Farmers 7, Independents 7 and Dublin University 4. As Erhard Rumpf and A. C. Hepburn have put it, 'the proportion of explicitly anti-Treaty voters was therefore less than 22 per cent of the whole'.[51] All of the parties, with the exception of the anti-Treaty deputies, were prepared to take their seats in Dáil Éireann.

Perhaps of most significance in this election was the number of votes that had been given to parties whose primary concern was not the Treaty. These groups combined received a total of 247,000 votes out of 620,000 vote cast (or 39.84 percent of the vote). The pro-Treaty group received 134,000. Thus, as John A. Murphy has succinctly concluded, 'in the midst of the political crisis the electorate was expressing its interest in social and economic issues'. Moreover, as Michael Laffan has suggested, many voters wanted to put past troubles behind them. Indeed, many of the most symbolic figures of that period, including Pádraig Pearse's mother and Thomas Clarke's widow, had been defeated at the polls. As Michael Laffan has put it, 'the people wished to be saved from their saviours'.[52]

However, the vote received by the Labour Party was particularly significant and more or less equalled that of the anti-Treaty group. Although some writers feel that Labour's inability to take the centre stage of Irish political life was primarily due to its failure to participate in the 1918 general election, thereby leaving the field open to Sinn Féin, its relatively good performance in 1922 seemed to suggest that the potential existed for further electoral progress during the 1920s. This suggestion appears more plausible when one considers that the anti-Treaty group of deputies formed the basis upon which the third Sinn Féin party of 1923–26 and later Fianna Fáil built their support. In addition to this, by December 1922, the old Sinn Féin party was virtually in a state of collapse and the attempts made by de Valera and Austin Stack, the party secretary, to revive it, failed miserably. The Labour Party, although by no means a model political party in terms of organisation and policies, was at the very least considerably better organised than the anti-Treatyites at this stage. In Cork, it had fought a much better campaign and had a greater sense of direction and co-ordination. De Róiste was of the view that the anti-Treaty candidates would have fared even worse if they had stood on an explicitly anti-Treaty platform.[53] He even went so far as to suggest that 'so unpopular are the anti-Treaty candidates here in Cork that if the pro-Treaty Sinn Féin candidates appear on one platform with them, it will mean a loss of votes: a probable gain, however, for "independents". This, of course, is impossible to corroborate but their low poll and the success of pro-Treaty candidates would seem to confirm this.'[54]

The failure of the Labour Party to build on its vote of 1922 in subsequent years is significant in relation to the formation and growth of Fianna Fáil. The origins of Fianna Fáil are to be found in the disorganised, abstentionist and intransigent anti-Treaty group, a group whose political and electoral prospects seemed pretty grim in 1922. But from 1922 onwards, the electoral fortunes of anti-Treaty Republicans improved, unlike those of the Labour Party, which failed to increase significantly on its 1922 showing. In the drift to the Civil War, a battle-weary electorate had declared a plague on the two sides of the Treaty debate. Labour would never again benefit from such a mood.

By the end of June 1922, however, electoral politics seemed of little consequence as Ireland became embroiled in a bitter civil war. Many of the anti-Treaty IRA forces had taken matters into their own hands by taking over various barracks and buildings in the country, most notably the Four Courts in Dublin. The decision by the Provisional Government to retake the Four Courts on 28 June 1922 is generally regarded as the beginning of the Civil War. The anti-Treatyites were strong in Munster, particularly in Tipperary and Limerick. Many brutal atrocities were committed on both sides and many of the leading figures in the War of Independence died. On the pro-Treaty side, the President of Dáil Éireann, Arthur Griffith, died of a heart attack on 12 August, while on 22 August Michael Collins was shot dead in an ambush at Béal na mBláth in west Cork. On the anti-Treaty side, men like Rory O'Connor, Liam Mellows and Erskine Childers were executed by the Provisional Government. Harry Boland and Cathal Brugha were also victims of the strife.[55]

De Róiste himself became profoundly disillusioned with politics during the Civil War period and found it 'impossible to carry on a Constitutional opposition within the Dáil as long as revolver rule continued'. He himself was opposed to the oath and felt that certain clauses of the Free State constitution could be amended without violating the terms of the Treaty. He refused, however, to countenance violent activity in the pursuit of such amendments and was scathing in his comments on the anti-Treaty forces. He was also critical of the Provisional Government for acting without the authority of Dáil Éireann and for generally behaving in an intransigent manner. De Róiste believed that the Civil War could have been avoided or, alternatively, could have been brought to a quick conclusion if there had been 'a bit of give' on both sides. He felt, for instance, that many of the rank-and-file Republicans in Cork were looking for a way out and had no stomach for a confrontation. As Moss Twomey has observed, 'it's not war. We're losing because the fellows are not fighting. We're fighting at their legs'.[56] He found himself increasingly at odds with the Provisional Government and the subsequent Free State administration during the period. When the Dáil reassembled in September 1922, he attempted to pursue an independent line, voting against the government on a number of occasions. The government wanted complete backing from all pro-Treaty deputies and did not welcome de Róiste's behaviour. Indeed, de Róiste informs us that Patrick Hogan, Minister for Agriculture, charged him with being a 'Tadhg a Dá-Thaobh' (playing on both sides) while Kevin O'Higgins also bitterly attacked him.[57]

De Róiste was also angered by the government's response to peace moves that were being made in Cork about this time. His diary shows that people like T. P. Dowdall (a wealthy businessman and future Fianna Fáil TD), Frank A. Daly, (a Dáil candidate in 1922), Professor Alfred O'Rahilly (who was to stand for the government party in 1923) and de Róiste himself were continually trying to arrange a settlement between the two sides. However, the government apparently was not interested. In a telling remark, de Róiste confided to his diary on 26 September that 'both sets of ruling elites seem intent on defeating each other rather than harnessing public opinion'.[58] De Róiste's frosty relationship with the government at this juncture graphically illustrates the degree of polarisation which followed the Civil War. There was simply no place for the middle ground.

In Cork, the Civil War was characterised by much commandeering of goods by the Republicans, the seizure of police barracks and the takeover of customs duties. In addition, the *Cork Examiner* was taken over for a period by the anti-Treatyites and used for the dissemination of propaganda. Interestingly enough, the revenue that was being collected through customs and excise duties was lodged in the National Land Bank of which Robert Barton was a director. It seems that by October 1922 the government was putting the squeeze on these Republican funds. Liam Lynch, Chief of Staff of the Republican forces, wrote on 1 October 1922 to his colleague Ernie O'Malley, asking him to withdraw the money which the government had ordered the banks not to pay:

Regarding the money in banks which the enemy forces in Cork [led by Dalton] have instructed the banks not to pay over. They claim to have discovered the accounts in which the money collected by us by way of Customs and Excise at Cork, was lodged. I do not know at the moment the exact amount held up in this manner. I want you to arrange to meet Barton and ask him if it could be arranged by the bank to advance us the money privately, as it is doubtful if the Provisional Government can prove the money was that collected as Revenue. The money is all in the National Land Bank of which Bank Barton is a Director. I will be very anxious to hear what he has to say. We would badly require this money now, and if we cannot get it we must adopt other methods of it anon.[59]

During the earlier part of the Civil War, de Róiste had been involved in altercations with Dowdall over arrangements that had been made by the businessmen of the city and the Republicans in relation to the commandeering of goods and supplies. One notable incident which occurred during the hostilities and which the pro-Treaty party never allowed their opponents to forget during subsequent elections, was the destruction of Mallow Bridge. By May 1923, however, the Civil War was over, leaving a legacy of bitterness and discord throughout the country. Despite the fact that many people recognised the need for strong action on the part of the government, the executions of Republicans caused much bitterness and ill-feeling, something which was later to benefit the Republicans. Cork experienced its own particular tragedies. The deaths of Collins, Lynch and Seán Hales, the execution of Dick Barrett, and the events at Béal na mBláth and Bandon all record the toll of civil war.

The Civil War itself dealt the death blow to Sinn Féin and both sides went their separate ways. The bitterness created was to last for generations. Two political parties emerged from its ashes, the Cumann na nGaedhael party led by W. T. Cosgrave and the third Sinn Féin party led by Éamon de Valera. The latter was later to suffer a further split, leading to the formation of Fianna Fáil. But in the immediate aftermath of the Civil War, the predominant impulse throughout the country was for peace, stability and a return to normal life. This aspiration was reflected in the general election of August 1923, the first electoral contest in the new Irish Free State and the first to be held in normal electoral conditions since the Dáil's original declaration of independence.

3
1923–1926: A REALIGNMENT OF POLITICAL FORCES

B y January 1923 the Free State government had established a political party which drew on a broad spectrum of pro-Treaty support. However, it was a party which encompassed different views. While these would later come to the surface, for the moment differences were submerged by a desire to maintain unity on the Treaty. The Cumann na nGaedhael papers show that from as early as September 1922, measures were being taken to establish a national political party. On 7 September 1922, at a special meeting of the 'General Election Committee' which had organised the Pro-Treaty group's election campaign in 1922, a formal decision was taken to establish a political organisation. Desmond FitzGerald proposed and J. Dolan seconded that:

> A Political Organisation [should] be formed to safeguard the national position which would work through the Treaty towards a united and distinc- tively Gaelic Ireland, and that the executive of the Free State party be utilised to launch the party.[1]

Earlier in the meeting, the Minister for Finance, Ernest Blythe, TD, had highlighted the need for a party in parliament that would specifically seek to 'complete' the 'national cause' under the Free State. He believed that other elements in the assembly would be primarily concerned with sectional interests. He suggested the name 'National Party' after which it was agreed to appoint a subcommittee, with Deputy Séamas Ó hAodha as Secretary, to draft the objectives and structures for the new party. From an early stage in the committee's deliberations, the parish was identified as the basic unit of the new party. At subsequent meetings of the General Election Committee, a subcommittee was also appointed to make arrangements for a private convention of pro-Treaty supporters. This was to be held on 7 December 1923 and it was decided to invite all constituency directors of elections and other named supporters who were offered grants of free railway travel to enable them to attend.[2]

An account of that meeting, known as the 'Preliminary Conference' of Cumann na nGaedhael, is available in both the Cumann na nGaedhael and Mulcahy papers. The meeting was chaired by George Murnaghan, TD, and was attended by President Cosgrave, thirty-eight TDs and fifty-eight constituency representatives. A lengthy discussion took place on whether to form a completely new organisation or take over the machinery of Sinn Féin in order to achieve the suggested objectives. Blythe spoke against taking over Sinn Féin but argued that the government should implement its programme. It was not necessary to reiterate ideals when 'we had in our hands the legislative power to realise them'.[3]

A resolution to set up a new organisation was carried by a large majority. A Provisional Committee was appointed consisting of ten residential members, three others from each province, and three from Cumann na Saoirse (the Women's Section). Its task was to 'carry on' the organisation until a convention of branch representatives could be held to decide finally on a programme, constitution and name. A draft constitution was then discussed in detail and slightly amended. The suggested title in the draft, 'Cumann Náisiúnta', was replaced by 'Cumann na nGaedhael'.[4] President Cosgrave, addressing the meeting, stressed that the government was looking for nation-builders who would nurture the new Ireland in the light of the old ideals.[5]

The Provisional Committee subsequently set about building the organisation at constituency level. Each deputy undertook to attend a convention in his or her own constituency and to take immediate steps to have Cumann na nGaedhael established in every town and parish. At a meeting of the committee that was held in February, a decision was taken to include everybody who accepted the party's programme. This decision had been taken in response to a query as to whether those who had been Unionists before the Treaty were eligible for party membership or not. The answer was that they were.[6]

The objectives of the party, as outlined in the draft programme, were so broad that anybody who had supported the Treaty would have little difficulty in joining, with the exception of those who supported Labour.[7] These objectives included the reunification of Ireland, the fostering of the national language and culture, and the development of manufacturing industry and natural resources. In a fund-raising circular that was issued by party headquarters in June 1923 to all branches, the new party is described as not standing 'for any particular sectional interest, [and that] its policy objective is to harmonise the different sections and give justice and fair play to all'.[8]

The Provisional Committee appointed paid organisers to assist in forming new *cumainn*, although, as a secretary's report of later years observed, this system of organisation had many pitfalls.[9] Since it was the government party, Cumann na nGaedhael had a problem in that the party leaders, owing to their governmental responsibilities, could not make exhaustive trips throughout the country to rally support for the new organisation. This was to be of crucial importance in the development of the new party and helps to explain the gap that existed throughout the organisation's existence between the Cumann na nGaedhael executive and parliamentary party on the one hand, and the political organisation on the other. It could also be argued that the national objectives of the party were too vague and did not have sufficient power to sustain its membership and supporters. In the short term, the government's commitment to upholding the Anglo-Irish Treaty sufficed as a moral bind on its supporters and indeed, on the majority of the people of the country. However, by the end of the decade, the Treaty issue was wearing thin and was an inadequate and insufficient platform upon which to fight an election.

The first public annual convention of Cumann na nGaedhael was held on 27 April 1923, with a delegate from each *cumann* attending. The draft objectives and constitution were passed with a few minor alterations.[10] Given the considerable public acceptance of the Anglo-Irish Treaty as expressed in the 1922 general election, Cumann na nGaedhael could face the 1923 election with some degree of confidence.

The political climate immediately after the Civil War was one of seemingly unrelieved gloom for the Republicans. The old Sinn Féin party was shattered and its unity destroyed. Many Republicans were in hiding and a considerable number had emigrated. Moreover, W. T. Cosgrave and his government were firmly in control, buttressed by the formation of a national party to support its objectives. A general election was inevitable.

Consequently, during the month of May 1923, it was decided to reorganise Sinn Féin as a specifically Republican party. On 11 June 1923, at a public meeting that was held in the Mansion House in Dublin, a Reorganising Committee was appointed to establish the new party, which would draw on the anti-Treaty element of the second Sinn Féin party. Pro-Treatyites were discouraged from joining. The new organisation held on to the title of Sinn Féin despite protests from members of the old Sinn Féin party.[11]

The Reorganising Committee of the new party had two main objectives. The first was to direct and organise the Republicans for the forthcoming election; the second was to establish a national political organisation. The new party faced formidable challenges. There were tremendous forces operating against the Republicans in the 1923 general election. Most of their leaders were either dead, in jail or in hiding. Overall, up to 16,000 Republicans were interned at this time. Éamon de Valera, their leader, was arrested during the campaign and relatively little media coverage was given to the Republicans. In contrast, the Cumann na nGaedheal party received major headlines. All the national dailies and a sizeable majority of the provincial newspapers, were in favour of the government party as were most of the Catholic hierarchy.[12]

Sinn Féin's election policy rehashed the 1918 programme of its predecessor. The party committed itself to an abstentionist policy, a decision which was primarily responsible for its ultimate decline. Its economic policies were vague and generally followed Griffith's line of self-sufficiency. However, despite the many factors which operated against the Republicans, their electoral performance in 1923 was impressive, winning 27.4 per cent of the poll and 44 seats of the 153 seats in the Dáil.

Undoubtedly, the decision to use 'Sinn Féin' proved to be a master stroke. It was also clear that the appeal of de Valera had not yet waned. The election clearly demonstrated that republicanism was far from being a spent force. Nevertheless, Cumann na nGaedhael gained 38.9 per cent of the poll. It won 63 seats and took over the reins of office once again. The Labour Party's vote dropped from its 1922 level, an apparent victim of the increased polarisation resulting from the Civil War.[13]

The general election of 1923 in the Cork City Borough constituency is particularly interesting in that it throws some light on the realignment of political forces that took place after the Anglo-Irish Treaty was signed and the Civil War had taken place. Under the Electoral Act of 1923, the constituency's electorate of 66,700 returned five members.[14]

Although Cumann na nGaedhael had been launched in Cork in July 1923, it is clear from the account given in de Róiste's diary that it was not an organised body at this stage. T. P. Dowdall told de Róiste that the July meeting had been forced on them, Dowdall himself having to pay the expenses for it. De Róiste thought that at this early stage, it was an organisation solely for the benefit of J. J. Walsh, then the Minister for Posts and Telegraphs.[15] The public meeting was a major affair with President Cosgrave addressing a large crowd along with Walsh, Kevin O'Higgins, Minister for Home Affairs, Eoin MacNeill, Minister for Education, Professor Joseph Whelehan, Assistant Minister for Industry and Commerce, Ernest Blythe, Minister for Finance, and a number of TDs. Cosgrave's speech was reproduced in full in the following day's *Cork Examiner*. He outlined the Provisional Government's achievements since taking office: the establishment of a system of government, the formation of an army and a police force, the setting up of a fiscal commission and proposals to reorganise the judicial system. Concluding, the President asked for support 'for the national organisation Cumann na nGaedhael':

> They asked for that because the time was not yet ripe for sectional representation . . . but under the banner of Cumann na nGaedhael they asked that the national position should predominate in the country.

Once again, the call for national consensus, as opposed to the proliferation of sectional interests, was made. In his speech, O'Higgins attacked the Republicans, claiming that they were more tyrannical than the Black and Tans.[16] It was a taste of the vitriol of elections to come.

Bishop Cohalan was invited to the meeting but declined on the grounds that he had made it a rule not to attend political meetings. Nonetheless, he let it be known that he considered it an honour to have been invited. In a letter to the meeting, published in the *Cork Examiner* the following day, he made no secret of where his sympathies lay:

> But may I be permitted to express my admiration for the ability, the capacity, the resourcefulness, the determination, in the face of appalling difficulties, which President Cosgrave and his colleagues have shown in establishing government in the country, and in governing. I congratulate the President and his colleagues in the Government on their wonderful success.

The Bishop went on to suggest that irrespective of what parties would emerge from the forthcoming elections, President Cosgrave and his colleagues in government should be continued in office. The Bishop contended that all revolutions brought unrest and instability in their wake and that consequently the country required stable government. He concluded that 'it is important for the country to consider whether the present Ministers should not be continued in office, whatever parliamentary groupings may issue from the coming election'.[17] Clearly, the Cumann na nGaedhael party had an episcopal blessing as it approached the general election.

The 1923 election in Cork also witnessed the emergence of a 'Progressive Party' as a party of industrialists and business people. Although working independently of Cumann na nGaedhael, it was more or less allied to it and there was a considerable overlap in membership. T. P. Dowdall, for instance, who was prominent in the Cumann na nGaedhael organisation at this time, was also chairman of the Progressive Association and in this capacity, asked de Róiste to stand for that party in the election.[18] De Róiste declined because other candidates who shared the same platform were not of an 'Irish-Ireland' outlook. This was probably a reference to Richard Beamish who had stood for the Commercial Party in the 1920 local government elections and who, according to de Róiste, had Unionist sympathies. In addition, it seems that de Róiste himself had become tired of the idea of a career in politics and this may explain why he had decided not to stand. In an entry in his diary on 19 July, de Róiste recorded his growing disillusionment with public life: 'I am sick of it, of its insincerities and futilities, its hypocrisies and degradations. A cheek of brass and a glib tongue are the best equipments for public life'.[19]

De Róiste's independent stand on many issues had strained relationships with the government. Such was the extent of the friction that de Róiste was not invited to the public launching of Cumann na nGaedhael in Cork.[20] However, this did not stop his friends from making every effort to persuade him to stand on its behalf. On 30 July, a number of people led by Dowdall, urged de Róiste to declare himself as a candidate once again. They were even willing to allow him to go forward independently, assuring him that they would not ask him to support the government in all matters. They guaranteed him the support of both the Cumann na nGaedhael and the Progressive group. They also told de Róiste that the difficulty was in getting someone with 'Irish-Ireland' ideas to stand and that most of the party felt strongly that at least two candidates with those ideas should stand. De Róiste, however, declined the invitation.[21]

This concept of 'Irish Ireland' is of crucial importance in understanding the evolution of the major political parties in Cork at this time. Throughout the period under study, a considerable section of Cumann na nGaedhael remained committed to the ideal of an Irish Ireland. During the 1920s, however, this group became disillusioned with Cumann na nGaedael and began to distance itself from the core of the party. The prominent members of this group were J. J. Walsh, T. P. Dowdall, Senator J. C. Dowdall, Councillor Barry Egan, de Róiste and Mrs Collins-Powell (sister of Michael Collins).[22]

In any event, the Cumann na nGaedhael and the 'Progressive Party' executives met before the election to come to a working agreement. The latter party nominated Andy O'Shaughnessy and Richard Beamish as their candidates. Some members of Cumann na nGaedhael objected strongly to Beamish on the grounds that, as has already been mentioned, many thought him to be sympathetic to Unionism.[23] Walsh and Alfred O'Rahilly were nominated for Cumann na nGaedhael.

The nomination of O'Rahilly was a major surprise to de Róiste. He confided to his diary that he would 'never believe that man again! . . . After all our talks and arguments to find him a candidate and under Cumann na nGaedhael auspices with J. J. Walsh is indeed a surprise'.[24] It would appear that it was direct pressure from President Cosgrave that had led to O'Rahilly's candidature.[25] In a letter to O'Rahilly, dated 17 August 1923, Cosgrave asked the UCC professor to stand for the party in Cork, adding that 'we want men of your type in this Dáil'. Apologising for the lateness of the request, he told O'Rahilly that he was deliberately 'keeping himself' from exercising any influence in the selection of candidates and continued that 'apart from two other men who have not yet consented to stand I have not yet interfered'.[26]

In pursuing such objectives, it would appear that Cumann na nGaedhael was having difficulties selecting suitable candidates for Cork. At a meeting of the National Standing Committee of the party on 9 August 1923, the matter was raised. Letters were read from one C. Buckley and one D. Tobin indicating that the situation was difficult. The selection convention had selected J. J. Walsh, Con Crowley, William Murphy and Mrs Collins-Powell. Both Crowley and Murphy offered to step down if Mrs Collins-Powell would go forward and this was to be arranged.[27] Although there was no mention of O'Rahilly, Cosgrave was in touch with him in the meantime and, as a result, O'Rahilly's name was added to the ticket. At a subsequent meeting of the Standing Committee on 22 August, Senator Mrs Wyse Power asked 'for information as to why the decision of the Committee re the number of candidates sanctioned had not been adhered to'.[28] No answer to her question is recorded in the minutes but the episode illustrates clearly how, at an early stage of the development of the party system, the leadership could exert significant influence over local selection conventions whenever it was considered that such intervention was warranted. At a reconvened Cumann na nGaedhael Convention on 15 August over which Walsh presided, Crowley and Murphy formally withdrew in order to allow Mrs Collins-Powell to stand.[29]

The imminent anniversary of her brother's death may have been a factor in this decision. Nothing further appears in the *Cork Examiner* concerning O'Rahilly until 20 August, when in a report on the handing in of nominations, it was noted that:

> An interesting development took place in connection with the nomination for Cork City on Saturday. The candidates for Cumann na nGaedhael were nominated as Mrs Collins-Powell and Mr J. J. Walsh, Postmaster General, but at the last moment Mrs. Collins-Powell withdrew in favour of Professor Alfred O'Rahilly – of the University. The new candidate is very popular, not only in Cork but all over Ireland and is generally regarded as one of the greatest intellectuals in the country. The citizens may rely that at his hands the most important question of education and other vitally important matters will receive the attention which they deserve.

No doubt encouraged by its success in the Pact Election of 1922, Labour offered three candidates: the outgoing deputy, Robert Day, Alderman William Kenneally, a member of the Transport Union, and Richard Anthony, a linotype operator. Sinn Féin also nominated three candidates: Miss Mary MacSwiney (outgoing), Alderman Fred Murray and Dr Con Lucey. The Farmers' Union nominated one candidate (Timothy Corcoran) and there were two Independents, Sir John Harley Scott and Captain Jeremiah Collins, making a total of thirteen candidates in all.[30]

Cumann na nGaedhael and the Cork Progressive Association worked hand in hand during the campaign. For instance, T. P. Dowdall, the chairman of the Progressive Association, appears on the list of proposers for all four candidates, as do Barry Egan and Michael J. Nagle. Both parties also placed joint advertisements promoting the four candidates in the *Cork Examiner*. The advertisements of the Progressive Association had the names of Beamish and O'Shaughnessy in bold print, with those of Walsh and O'Rahilly in lesser print, with the following message:

Our Watchwords: Employment, Good Houses, Prosperity and Peace, A Contented People, A Happy Country.

Likewise, Cumann na nGaedhael advertisements promoted O'Rahilly and Walsh and urged further preferences for the Progressive candidates. Together they ran a high-powered and high-profile campaign and made considerable use of the media in doing so.[31]

The Cork Progressive Association held regular public meetings in support of their candidates. These meetings were attended by prominent businessmen in the city and the speakers generally praised the Cumann na nGaedhael government and the personal qualities and achievements of their candidates. On 15 August, a lengthy address from the Association's candidates appeared in the *Cork Examiner* which outlined their main objectives. They pledged support for the government of the Free State in its efforts to restore law, justice and order in the country and identified commerce, farming and labour as major issues of concern. On the question of industrial relations, they were equivocal stating that employers were entitled to a loyal, efficient and effective service from their employees. On the other hand, it was conceded that employers could not demand this unless their employees were fairly paid and reasonably housed. On agriculture, they committed themselves to developing sound agricultural education throughout the country. They felt that the only way to improve efficiency, raise standards and increased regularity of supply was through the education of the country's young farmers. They concluded by expressing the hope that workers and employers would join together in a spirit of co-operation to ensure the economic development of the country.[32]

At a meeting on 18 August, the chairman of the Association, outlined the credentials and qualities of their candidates:

> Mr O'Shaughnessy was not, perhaps, as well known to the citizens as Mr Beamish whose name was a household one in the city. Mr O'Shaughnessy was one of the largest employers in the South of Ireland. The Newmarket Dairy Co., of which he was chairman and managing director, had over 30 creameries employing over 200 men and women, while the woollen mills at Dripsey and Sallybrook, of which he was proprietor, were employing considerably over a hundred. Mr Beamish was, of course, the proprietor of a very large concern in the city, and the greatest friendliness existed between himself and the men under his control . . . Everyone recognised what he had done for the improvement of Cork while Chairman of the Public Works Committee.[33]

At this meeting, Beamish identified the promotion of employment as essential and that morale and confidence must be generated among the people to rid the country of depression and hopelessness. O'Shaughnessy revealed to the meeting that he had only decided to stand as a result of pressure from his friends and commented that:

> on this matter he was rather glad to find that old order in which a man sought the office was reversed by the new order in which the office seeks the man and he hoped that that would continue to be extended.[34]

At a subsequent meeting of the Progressive Association, O'Shaughnessy made no secret of his admiration for the government:

> Let us take an impartial bird's eye view of our country to-day. One year ago to the day Ireland received a staggering reeling blow in the loss of Michael Collins, the brave and fearless. But stunning as the man was the country stood bravely, and the Government, led splendidly by President Cosgrave, overcame the manifold difficulties it encountered, and to-day we have order firmly established and compelling respect.

He was of the opinion that the firmness of the government in restoring order to the country obliged the Association to support it unreservedly.[35]

Cumann na nGaedhael's campaign in Cork was led by J. J. Walsh who had been first appointed to office as Postmaster General by the then Provisional Government.[36] The party's strategy involved appealing to the various sections of the electorate. For example, it issued advertisements which were directed at workers and women while Walsh made special efforts to court the ex-servicemen, flour-mill workers and the licensed trade.

On 21 August, the party also appealed for the support of workers through an advertisement in the *Cork Examiner*. It claimed that the Free State had paid unemployment benefit to a weekly average of 30,000 since the previous October and that furthermore, 12,000 workers had been placed in employment and eighty industrial disputes settled by the government. The advertisement declared that 'the Free State is above Labour or Capital, but the Free State stands for the Square Deal between both. The Free State Government is the only Body in Ireland in a position to give employment to you on a big scale'.[37]

On the following day the party published a further advertisement which appealed to women for support. Reiterating that the government stood for order, stability and a fair deal between worker and employer, the advertisement also highlighted a matter of which it regarded as a particular concern of the housewife – the price of food:

> Women of Cork! You do the buying for your homes, and you know something about the high prices. The Government is out to bring down the cost of food and commodities. The Government will smash the Profiteer. Help, by your votes the Government, that will make living worthwhile in Ireland.[38]

The fact that Walsh addressed a large meeting of the Ex-Servicemen's Association which was chaired by the former Nationalist Lord Mayor of Cork, W. F. O'Connor, and subsequently received that body's support, indicates the degree to which political alignments were changing in Ireland's evolving political system. In the general election of 1918, and the local government elections of 1920, the Ex-Servicemen's Association were bitter opponents of Sinn Féin. Conversely, for most of his political life, Walsh had been a bitter opponent of the Ex-

Servicemen's Association. Indeed, while his memoirs expressed his sympathy for those who had died in the Great War, he still recalled with distaste when 'Cardinal Logue, John Redmond and William O'Brien called on their unsuspecting countrymen to go out and die with the Ghurkas and Sikhs for Christianity, Civilisation and Small Nations. It was enough to make every Irishman who had died for Freedom [to] turn in his grave'.[39] Nevertheless, the chairman of the Association, in welcoming Walsh to the meeting, expressed the hope that the ex-servicemen in Cork would support the Cumann na nGaedhael candidates and by doing so, to confirm that they were a body of some influence in the city.

In addressing the meeting, Walsh acknowledged the considerable number of ex-servicemen in the city. He recalled how during the Civil War, when Cork had been held by the Republicans, he had sent a special group of armed men to the city who had been given considerable sums of money for the relief of the Association's members whose pensions had been held up. He promised that he would take immediate action to ensure that the provisions of the newly passed Housing Act would be applied to Cork. At the end of the meeting, Walsh also signed an undertaking in which he agreed to use his influence to obtain from the British government a just and equitable fulfilment of the claims of Irish ex-servicemen. He also promised to ensure that past services in the British army or navy would not militate against such men in any way, especially in getting a job. Finally, he undertook to oppose any interference by the Irish government with pensions, allowances and the housing of ex-servicemen and their dependants, to make every effort to have ex-servicemen accepted for work in the public departments of the state and to ensure that they would not be treated any differently in this respect to any other citizen. It is difficult to ascertain how Walsh squared this last commitment with demands from Cumann na nGaedhael supporters for preferential treatment for pro-Treaty old-IRA men in public appointments but his reaching out to the Ex-Servicemen's Association for endorsement and support must be considered as a significant broadening of Cumann na nGaedhael's electoral base.

Walsh also addressed woollen-mill workers at Morrogh and O'Brien's at Douglas in which he highlighted the benefit of government contracts for the industry. He claimed that £323,000 had been spent in the Free State in contracts for clothing material which could have been secured much cheaper abroad. Walsh stated that he was a consistent and lifelong supporter of Irish industry and that when an opportunity 'like the present came his way', where large sums of public money were to be disposed of by him, he was in no need of reminders as to what he should do.[40]

Walsh addressed these meetings alone. Alfred O'Rahilly disliked pandering to sectional interests and was not prepared to engage in the hard slog of campaigning for votes. In a letter to the editor of the *Cork Examiner*, O'Rahilly made his position clear:

> I have been requested to give pledges and promises by various interests and organisations. As far as I am concerned all these sectional appeals are irrelevant to the vital issues before the country. Were the issue not so national and overwhelming, I should not, in spite of my strong personal distaste and at considerable inconvenience and sacrifice, have offered myself to represent Cork City. If the people of Cork prefer ordered government to moral and financial disorganisation they can avail of my

services: on subordinate issues they must trust to my own judgement and record. I had hoped that it was made quite clear that consistently with the assertion of majority rule I can be relied upon to do all that an individual can to secure amnesty and peace, and that I am entirely opposed to any vindictiveness, injustice or class-domination. Those who are not satisfied with the declaration may vote for some more suitable candidate. I have done my duty. I have not the remotest intention of pledging myself to any party or interest of indulging in clap-trap oratory or of adapting vote-catching expedients. The issue is too plain for that.[41]

This was to remain O'Rahilly's only public contribution to the campaign.

At national level, Cumann na nGaedhael concentrated on the government's success in restoring law and order. Speaking in Ennis, County Clare, Cosgrave made a scathing attack on de Valera and the anti-Treatyites. In particular, he criticised de Valera for not heading the delegation to London that had negotiated the Anglo-Irish Treaty and referred to the destruction that had been caused by Republicans during the Civil War:

Last year they had soldier politicians swaggering around the towns and the country, and no man knew whether or not he would own his own house in the morning. Today, after twelve months they saw many smoke-begrimed ruins and many graves in many a graveyard. There was many a home with a vacant chair and for what? For the three Graces he supposed, Miss McSwiney, Mrs Sheehy Skeffington and he forgot the name of the third lady. The three Graces and Mr De Valera, they had beaten them by two to one, notwithstanding the damnable destruction and desolation they had accomplished.[42]

Cosgrave's tour of the country opened a new chapter in electioneering by using the aeroplane for the first time. As a result, Cosgrave was able to address meetings at Ennis and Carlow on the same day.[43] The progress of his tour was followed in detail by the *Cork Examiner* which published his speeches every day and gave them a high profile on the main political page of the paper.

The anti-Treatyites did not receive anything like the same publicity. Their speeches concentrated on the conditions of Republican prisoners, the promotion of Irish-manufactured goods, and of course, the Anglo-Irish Treaty, the oath and the establishment of the Irish Republic. At a public meeting held in Blackpool on 13 August, Councillor Seán Nolan spoke about the difficulties that Sinn Féin had in organising an effective campaign:

> All the workers on the Sinn Féin side were in gaol or on the hills, and on a few of them devolved the work of organising the election and trying to put the facts before the people. Had they got a few months to prepare he had no doubt that a majority of Republican candidates would be returned. But the time was short and they could not organise properly or use propaganda. The Press was against them though they had reporters at their meetings.[44]

Constitutional issues dominated at this particular meeting. Professor William Stockley, addressing the meeting, reiterated Ireland's right to independence and said that although they had been offered some advantages by

England which the plenipotentiaries had said would mean independence, they were still in England's power and the king was the head of the government. Mary Comerford was also scathing in her attack on the Anglo-Irish Treaty and condemned the fact that Ireland was still part of the British Empire:

> NO. They wanted full independence for the whole country – North and South. They wanted to be recognised as an independent State and to have European countries recognising Ireland's neutrality . . . If they could put down the Free State murder gang; if they could put out of power the fifty odd men responsible for the executions and the detention of the prisoners, and the waging of war on the Republic – then they would have the Republic.[45]

This type of rhetoric was used consistently throughout the campaign by Sinn Féin. However, Mary MacSwiney linked the constitutional issues with economic matters. At a meeting held on 24 August, she suggested that those who were urging the Irish people to acquiesce in membership of the British Empire would very soon lose all pretence of keeping up the language or of purchasing Irish manufactures. She suggested that those who had sworn the oath of allegiance to the Republic were determined to make Ireland prosperous and that this could be done only by purchasing Irish goods and by protecting Irish industries and guarding them against profiteering. She also condemned the government's treatment of Republican prisoners who, she claimed, were not receiving any of the letters or parcels of food that were being sent to them by relatives. She also called for free speech, claiming that the reason why the Republicans had to get pamphlets printed in Manchester was because twenty printing presses had been destroyed by the Free State government.[46]

The election also took place against the background of a serious industrial dispute between the city's employers and employees, adding a local dimension to the 1923 campaign. The issues were whether the employers had the right to lay off members of staff when trade was slack and whether they could reduce wages. The *Cork Examiner* reported that only two or three unions were directly concerned, of which the drapers and grocers were the dominant groups. But the trade union movement as a whole adopted a united stand against the employers. On 20 August, a mediation attempt failed as a result of the employees' refusal to accept a decision by the employers to suspend their proposed revision of wages and terms of employment until 3 September, pending a conference at which Professor Whelehan, Assistant Minister for Industry and Commerce, would decide on the matter. The trade unions feared that this was nothing more than an election ploy and refused to accept the compromise. Instead, they called for an adjournment of the employers' demands for six months and the appointment of a commission of inquiry. These demands were refused by the employers. The result was a strike.[47]

Obviously this dispute influenced the campaign of the Labour Party, which used it to attack the Progressive Association and employers in general. At a public meeting which was held as part of the Labour Party's campaign on 18 August, the president of the Cork Workers' Council attacked the employers of Cork on their stance in the dispute:

> The Cork Employers' Federation had been sitting by day and night to make a scheme for the reduction of the wages of the workers of Cork, and secure increased prosperity for themselves, but they never

made any attempt to reduce the prices of the commodities that the workers had to purchase.

Richard Anthony, one of the Labour candidates, addressed the gathering and claimed that uniforms for the Irish army were being manufactured in England, in addition to 50,000 mattresses. It was 'bad economics', he claimed, for any government to send such work out of the country. He also referred to the lockout notices that had been sent out by the employers and suggested that trade unionism itself was under attack and that employers wanted to employ whom they liked. The outgoing Labour deputy, Robert Day, claimed that the Progressive Association was simply a new name for the Employers' Federation and had this to say regarding the industrial dispute:

> They were at present engaged in an industrial and political fight, but if they stood together they would succeed in resisting all the attacks that were made on them. It was all nonsense to say that low wages would mean more employment. The condition of affairs in England and Belfast and the six counties disproved that allegation.

Day then launched a blistering attack on Councillor Barry Egan who was a member of both the Progressive Association and Cumann na nGaedhael. He was a city jeweller with an establishment in Patrick Street. Commenting on a statement by Egan that if the Progressive Association had representatives in the Dáil during the past twelve months, Mallow Bridge would have been rebuilt, Day made the following personal attack:

> If the man himself had been there it might have been built [laughter]. That man had a shop in Patrick

101

Street and last month he got his compensation for its destruction but since that time he had not put a stone on it. That was what they would get from the Progressive Association.[48]

At a subsequent meeting in Bishopstown to support the Labour Party, Day returned to the issues of government contracts as well as to the matter of compensation for business people whose premises had incurred damages during the War of Independence. On the former, he claimed that Labour had done its best to keep contracts in Ireland and had exposed 'the game of exporting the contracts'. On the question of compensation he pointed out that:

> A large number of the Progressive Association were owners of the burned-out premises and yet they had done nothing to put a stone on a stone towards rebuilding in Cork, and it was through his [Day's] exertions that one gentleman of the party got the interest stopped on his money, if he didn't start building at once. A big fight was being waged in Cork to bring down the wages of employees, and that fight was backed up by the Progressive Association, the Cumann na nGaedhael and the other Associations that had employers' representatives on it.[49]

Clearly, therefore, while Cumann na nGaedhael and Sinn Féin clashed on constitutional issues, another battle was going on at another level between Labour and the Progressive Association. The Progressive Association did not respond directly to the attacks that were made on them by Labour candidates but constantly spoke of the necessity of maintaining good relations between capital and labour.

The issue of government contracts for clothing became a subject of further public controversy, with J. J. Walsh of Cumann na nGaedhael and Richard Anthony of the Labour Party making conflicting claims and allegations. At a meeting in Blarney, Walsh contradicted Anthony's allegation that army contracts had been sent to England. He stated that one-third of those who were working in woollen mills were working because of government contracts and that the clothing of the army came under his department. He added that, since taking office in March 1923, he had ensured that not one pennyworth of clothing material had been secured from anywhere other than Ireland. Even at the risk of contradiction, he further said that of every £5 that the Free State spent on contracts, £4.17 was spent in Ireland although he added that at least two of the three remaining shillings were spent abroad because the materials that were needed were not always manufactured in Ireland. However, Anthony dismissed Walsh's argument and pointed out that his views on the matter were supported by the secretary of the Wholesale Clothing Factories' Association who had made a similar comment regarding the 50,000 uniforms that were made for the army in England. According to Anthony, Smith's remarks had been made in a reply to a statement in the Dáil by General Mulcahy in which the minister had defended sending clothing contracts to England on the grounds that £224,000 had been saved as a result of placing them there.[50]

That a controversy like this should have become a major part of the election battle suggests that constitutional issues such as the Treaty and the oath were not dominant. Economic concerns were of equal importance, including the desire to return to an orderly economic climate. Those who were going to vote for Cumann na nGaedhael were not necessarily indicating their whole-hearted approval of the Treaty, or indeed of the oath, but rather felt that they were voting for a party that, at the very least, held out the prospect of an early return to 'normal' living. The Republicans' programme was too abstract for the ordinary voter, to whom the 'Republic' was an indefinable and intangible political objective.

The *Cork Examiner* called for the return of Cumann na nGaedhael to government and condemned Sinn Féin for its 'irresponsibility' during the previous twelve months. On polling day, the paper gave a clear message to the electorate:

> President Cosgrave and his Ministers, brushing aside all platitudes and speaking in plain language for the plain people, in spite of irresponsible opposition, have put forward an irresistible case for a renewal of the confidence of the electors. Rarely have men had to handle a task as onerous as theirs since the standard of revolt against the people of Ireland was raised.

The editorial then went on to attack the behaviour of the Republicans during the Civil War, citing the destruction of railways and food supplies as examples of what it termed 'an extraordinary form of warfare'. It compared the Republicans' activities to the edicts of the Roman dictator Sulla:

> When Sulla ruled the destinies of the Eternal City the individual names of victims were posted up, giving his enemies an opportunity of seeking security in exile. History is supposed to have no greater instance of injustice than these pernicious enactments, but the Irish Republican Executive

secretly condemned to death all the Irish Ministers, all the Senators, all the members of the Dáil, and several other classes too numerous to mention.

The editorial also questioned whether members of Sinn Féin understood the full implications of their slogan 'Up the Republic'. Was the Republic to be fashioned on the lines of America or France or of Russia? The editorial suggested that de Valera and 'his most important lieutenants' held divergent views on what constituted a republic.[51]

In addition, the paper endorsed comments made by T. P. Dowdall, chairman of the Cork Progressive Association, when he said that 'the running of a country is nowadays largely a business concern'. In this connection, the editorial emphasised that:

> the necessity of selecting persons to carry on the business of the nation who are prepared to look facts in the face and to do their best to make the country a fit place for every section to live. This cannot be done by reviving old hatreds or by tail-twisting 'our late predominant partner', but by administrative capacity.

The two Independent candidates, Jeremiah Collins and Sir John Harley Scott (a former Unionist who had been elected to Cork Corporation in 1920 on the Commercial ticket), both listed as their priorities better housing, creating employment, better relations between capital and labour, and the restoration of peace and order. Collins was also at pains to stress his nationalist credentials by reminding the electorate that during the War of Independence, he had been responsible for the escape of Liam Mellows and many more, and that at the commencement of the Volunteer movement, he had 'brought the arms from Belgium'. The Farmers' Party candidate, Tim Corcoran, supported the restoration of peace and order and sought the reduction of rates and taxes. He stressed the overriding importance of agriculture to the economy.[52]

The election took place on 27 August and passed off peacefully. As the *Cork Examiner* noted, 'as far as Cork was concerned, it proved one of the most orderly and unexciting elections within memory of the older inhabitants.[53]

The result gave the combined forces of the Progressive Association and Cumann na nGaedheal a sweeping victory, winning four out of the five seats. The election was a complete turnaround for Labour. Having headed the poll in the 1922 election, the party now lost its only seat. Mary MacSwiney increased her first preference vote and won a seat for Sinn Féin. Richard Beamish for the Progressive Association polled very well, improving significantly on his 1922 performance and winning a seat. The election was a major personal triumph for J. J. Walsh ,who polled a staggering 17,151 first preference votes. His huge surplus helped to bring in his party colleague, Professor Alfred O'Rahilly and Andrew O'Shaughnessy of the Progressive Association who only polled 766 votes on the first count. The result of the first count was as follows:

J. J. Walsh (CG)	17,151
Mary MacSwiney (SF)	6,109
R. H. Beamish (Prog)	5,822
Prof. Alfred O'Rahilly (CG)	2,506
R. S. Anthony (Lab)	2,492
Dr Con Lucy (SF)	1,870
Timothy Corcoran (Farm)	1,618

Robert Day (Labour)	1,431
William Kenneally (Lab)	1,358
Sen. J. Harly Scott (Ind)	786
Andrew O'Shaughnessy (Prog)	766
Frederick Murray (SF)	461
Capt. Jeremiah Collins (Ind)	243[54]

The Labour debacle was the major surprise of the election. In the general election of 1922, Robert Day had headed the poll with 6,836 votes and Labour had received 22.5 per cent of the total valid poll. However, in the 1923 election, Day received only 1,431 first-preferences, and Labour only 12.39 per cent of the vote. The total first preferences of the three Labour candidates combined was still 1,821 short of one quota.

A number of reasons can be advanced for Labour's poor performance. The party ran too many candidates and its campaign strategy and performance suffered as a result. It is much easier to promote one candidate than three. The advertising campaign for the Labour party in 1922 had been simple, clear, effective and highly personalised. In the 1923 election, there was no such advertising campaign, possibly owing to a shortage of funds. The content of the Labour party's speeches and propaganda was also different on this occasion. Labour speakers did not concentrate on issues such as education and housing, as they had done in 1922. Instead they concentrated on attacking the employers of the city and in particular, the Progressive Association, over the industrial dispute that was occurring at the time. In retrospect, it is possible to argue that this dispute harmed the electoral chances of the Labour party more than those of anybody else. The fact that a large number of workers were on strike on behalf of other workers also contributed to the Labour defeat.

It must also be acknowledged that the Progressive Association and Cumann na nGaedhael ran a high-powered campaign with prominent daily advertisements in the *Cork Examiner*. Furthermore, their meetings, in particular those of Cumann na nGaedhael, received better coverage from the *Cork Examiner*, with bigger headlines and subtitles as well as better placings.[55] Walsh's courting of various interest groups obviously worked to his benefit. That the campaign coincided with Collins' anniversary also did Cumann na nGaedhael no harm. Labour's campaign was nowhere near as dynamic. Furthermore, Cumann na nGaedhael was the party in power. Given that it had been in government for less than a year and had managed to emerge victorious from a civil war, it must have appeared as the only party which was capable of forming a government. Sinn Féin certainly was not. Most of its leaders were in jail. In any case, it was committed to overthrowing the Anglo-Irish Treaty and was not prepared to 'operate' the Free State apparatus of government. The MacSwiney name was undoubtedly an influential factor in helping the party to gain a seat in Cork. However, in general terms, the election must be viewed as an overwhelming endorsement of the Cumann na nGaedhael government by the people of Cork city, especially as the Progressive candidates clearly stated that they would support the government.

The *Cork Examiner* certainly saw the result in this light. In an editorial on 31 August, the paper interpreted the results as expressing a desire on behalf of the electorate for stabilised conditions of law and order. For the Republicans the paper had this advice:

> Having tested the feeling of the country and got their answer in no uncertain terms, Mr de Valera and his followers ought decently to retire from public life or

else cease to disfranchise their constituents and take their seats in the Dáil to get the most out of the Treaty and the Constitution. That is all the country wants from them.

The same issue also noted the failure of other groups, namely the Farmers and Labour, 'to secure any striking numerical victories'. In relation to the former, the paper suggested that the fact that several of the government's candidates were farmers was a contributing factor to their poor performance. In addition, it stated that the desire for stable government was a major reason for the farming vote to swing behind the government candidates, as opposed to the Farmers' Union.

With respect to Labour's performance, the paper expressed the view that the Labour movement had been prone to 'extremism of late' and that the results of the election reflected this. It called on the party to develop a more moderate approach which would be attuned to the needs and desires of the worker:

> He [the worker] is no revolutionary and does not expect to find the millennium in this world. If those who direct the Labour Party will formulate a policy more suitable to the outlook of the Irish worker they will find him prepared to trust them with his vote. We can not believe the Irish Labour Leaders are at heart extremists or unprepared to make a sensible compromise on many points that seem at issue. But there has been some loose 'speechifying' recently, and this together with the holding up of the port and other incidents of the present wage dispute contributed to the 'landslide'.

Finally, the *Cork Examiner* offered the view that Richard Anthony's securing of the highest share of the first-preference votes of the Labour candidates was evidence of a trend of opinion among rank-and-file workers, and identified Anthony as representing the right wing of the party.[56] Nationally, Cumann na nGaedhael polled 38.9 per cent of the vote, winning 63 seats, and took over the reins of office once more. Sinn Féin, despite the many factors operating against it, won a respectable 27.4 per cent of the vote, capturing 44 seats of the 153-seat Dáil, a relatively good performance given the circumstances.

With Cumann na nGaedhael now firmly in control, Sinn Féin began a new organisational drive after the election. It enjoyed rapid growth. Inspired by its electoral success and aided by funds from America, paid organisers were employed to accelerate the establishment of a strong countrywide organisational network. At its Ard-Fheis in October 1923, 680 branches were represented, a strong indication of the party's growth. This growth continued during the first half of 1924 although it was still a far cry from the party's initial fortunes. As Michael Laffan has pointed out, only sixteen branches were represented, and 'less than 150 attended', at a meeting that was held on 11 June to re-establish the party.[57]

As Peter Pyne notes, this revived 'third' Sinn Féin party belonged 'to a comparatively rare species of political party in that it not only refused to recognize the political legitimacy of the new order, but attempted to duplicate many of the powers and functions of the state'.[58] During its short life, the party attempted to set up what virtually amounted to a state within a state. It had established its own government and Dáil and had conferred upon them a *de jure* right to govern. It attempted to erect a separate judicial system, an educational alternative, and an employment exchange for its own members. It also ran an economics department. Foreshadowing Fianna Fáil's establishment of the *Irish Press*, the party also attempted to launch a national newspaper but failed because of a lack of capital. However, most of these ventures did not succeed. Between 1924 and 1926, the party declined in strength and influence. Its financial position deteriorated rapidly from 1924 onwards. The number of branches also diminished, so much so that by July 1925, the number stood at just over half the total of the year before. Electorally, its fortunes declined also. Between October 1923 and February 1926, the party contested twenty by-elections and had relatively little success. The local government elections of 1925 resulted in a further setback for the party. This unimpressive performance led to much frustration and disappointment. Not surprisingly, therefore, many leading figures in the party began to question its abstentionist role and by the end of 1925, rumblings of discontent were increasingly apparent within the organisation.[59]

In Cork, however, the party made some headway with the election of Seán French as Lord Mayor in January 1924. French was later to break from the MacSwiney group in Cork and follow de Valera. He stood for Fianna Fáil in the June and September elections in 1927 and was elected on both occasions. He was a Cork city chemist who had first been elected to Cork Corporation in the 1920 local elections. He retained the position of Lord Mayor until the end of the decade owing to the fact that Cork Corporation was dissolved by the Free State government in November 1924. De Róiste was very angry at French's victory, particularly since it was the vote of Sir John Harley Scott that secured French's election. Scott was a former Unionist and in return for his support, the Republicans placed his name first of the nominees for sheriff. De Róiste commented caustically on his election:

In the former Republican Party it was considered an act against our principles to nominate a Sheriff at all: but neo-Republicanism is founded on such a bed-rock of the Republic that anything may be done 'in principle'.[60]

French also secured support from some of the Labour councillors who felt that he had stood by Labour in the past. The nine Labour councillors were split on the issue, another illustration of how national political issues were reducing the effectiveness of the Labour party as an independent and cohesive political party. According to a report in the *Cork Examiner*, a meeting of the Labour party in Cork a few days earlier had decided to vote for French by a majority of four votes. Labour's Councillor Allen complained that Labour members were being coerced into voting against their political opinions: 'There is no alternative for me, he concluded, when there is no Labour man put forward, but to vote for the Treaty man, and for that reason I will support Barry Egan'. Likewise, Councillor John Good, who had been elected on the joint Sinn Féin and Transport Union in 1920, declared that initially he was not going to vote unless a Labour candidate was proposed. However, on hearing the debate, he felt that he had no alternative but to change sides. In his opinion, if anything 'was to be done for Cork, it was by voting for Councillor Barry Egan of Cumann na nGaedhael' and that he 'would vote in order to challenge the Labour movement to say who was right and who was wrong in asking them to come forward and vote for a political party'.[61]

In reply, Councillor Kelleher stated that he always 'took his stand by Labour ' and would continue to do so. He declared his support for French on the grounds that he had 'sprung from the working class'. French was proposed by Councillor Dan Gamble who had contested the local elections of 1920 as a Nationalist and who declared himself to be a Labour man while Councillor Kenneally of the Labour Party seconded.[62]

Of considerable interest also was the position of Councillor Michael Egan who had stood for official Labour against Sinn Féin and the Transport Union in 1920. He was also to stand for Cumann na nGaedhael in the by-election of November 1924 which had been brought about by O'Rahilly's resignation from the Dáil. At this meeting, he obviously still regarded himself as a Labour man, when he declared that had 'Labour put forward a candidate. I firmly believe we would have elected him today. But the people who are talking about Labour are the very men who prevented us from putting forward a candidate'.[63] Yet by the end of the year, Michael Egan was elected to the Dáil as a member of Cumann na nGaedhael. Meanwhile, the *Cork Examiner* attacked the election of Seán French, declaring that the people of Cork felt that a particular section of the Corporation was paying little attention to the wishes of their constituents and that this had been graphically illustrated when, by a narrow majority, a 'coalition' succeeded in electing as Lord Mayor a gentleman who, whatever may be his personal attributes, had openly associated with a party which the electors of Cork had repudiated by a nine to two majority. The paper concluded that the decision effectively meant that the Corporation did not represent the feelings of the citizens. It was, of course, referring to the anti-Treaty Sinn Féin party, of which Seán French was a member.[64]

The 1924 by-election was also of considerable importance to both the membership and development of Cumann na nGaedhael in the city and provides an insight into the role and behaviour that was expected of a backbench TD and of a party organisation in action. It had been caused by the resignation of Alfred O'Rahilly who was dissatisfied with both his role as a TD and, as he saw it, his ineffectiveness in relation to the formulation of government policy. In a long letter to Richard Mulcahy, Minister for Defence, O'Rahilly criticised the government's failure to give a general amnesty to Republican prisoners, particularly after the end of the 1923 hunger strike, believing that 'there is too much unnecessary militarism and that the armed forces and the demobilised men are really more dangerous now than the irregulars [Republicans]' had been. During the Republican hunger strike, O'Rahilly had intervened on a number of occasions with the prisoners urging them to give up the strike and indeed, he is credited by the *Cork Examiner* with having played an influential role in bringing it to an end. On a personal level, O'Rahilly's letter to Mulcahy contains a stinging critique of the government's treatment of individuals:

> I do think from my short experience that the government does not treat individual members like myself fairly. I can fairly claim to have a national outlook, to have my fair share of brains and commonsense and also to represent opinion down here better than any other. But I find when I go to Dublin that the powers that be treat me as an outsider and as a negligible automaton useful only in divisions of the Dáil.

In addition, O'Rahilly asserted that he had never been given an opportunity to discuss matters of policy. He concluded that:

> it was grossly unfair and deceitful to ask me to stand for the Dáil at all. Even my views on education, on

which subject I can surely claim some competence – are turned down by the Government without even according me the courtesy of a reasoned refusal.[65]

One could perhaps speculate that a person of O'Rahilly's stature would have expected more than a backbench role, perhaps a ministry. In any event, O'Rahilly made it clear in his letter to Mulcahy that he would be resigning in the near future. Cosgrave also discussed O'Rahilly's criticism in a memorandum which he sent to Mulcahy on 3 January 1924. In this, he strongly rejected O'Rahilly's criticisms and gave it as his opinion that the professor had never intended to remain in the Dáil and that he simply wanted to get out at the earliest opportunity. That O'Rahilly had also taken his views on these matters to the press did not enhance his reputation. In any event, it was easier to consider that the professor was contrary rather than concede that the party had problems.[66] On 27 December 1923, Mulcahy replied to O'Rahilly and urged him not to take any action until he had a discussion with him. O'Rahilly responded that the matter was beyond reconsideration and explained that he had waited patiently for several months for an answer to a request for the establishment of an education commission, but to no avail. He also reminded Mulcahy that he had stood for the Dáil at the personal request of President Cosgrave,

at great personal sacrifice (as he fully knows). What on earth am I there for? Any fool can vote the ticket. Why waste the time of 'men of my type' when important literary work is waiting for me – work for which I have been twenty years preparing, work which will bring credit to the country.

He concluded by saying that if Mulcahy had any information as to the 'carrying out of this educational matter' he might possibly reconsider his decision.[67]

But his disillusionment extended beyond his own personal position. He criticised the insularity of the Executive Council and despaired that 'everyday brings home to me how out of touch the Government is with helpful brains in almost every department'.[68] To O'Rahilly, the party had no policy of its own. Cosgrave had even asserted that O'Rahilly and himself had never discussed education. The memorandum concluded with a general comment on the state of the party that 'the new party is getting and has got a bigger show than the last and if it goes on demanding the same show it will want an executive of its own'.[69]

This concluding remark by Cosgrave seemed to indicate a general impatience with demands and deputations from his party. The government's reluctance to listen to rank-and-file criticism is a constant theme in the record of events kept by de Róiste and indeed, he attributes much of his own unpopularity to this problem.[70] The pattern examined above was not unique to Cork. At national level, there is also evidence in the minutes of the Ard Chomhairle (National Executive) of Cumann na nGaedhael of a lack of communication between the government and the organisation. At a special meeting of the Ard Chomhairle held on 13 May 1924, to which all TDs were invited, the relationship between the organisation, the parliamentary party and the government was discussed. The following resolutions were discussed and unanimously passed:

> That this meeting demands that in future when legislation is intended on matters that stir popular feeling a real effort be made to sound the public

through the organisation as to what views are held on controversial points, and if the Government have to adopt unpopular measures under pressure of necessity that an adequate explanation be furnished through the TDs to their constituency committees of the reasons for such measures. That all members of the Cumann na nGaedhael party be paid up members of the organisation and promote and attend meetings of the organisation so as to keep in personal touch with the people who have elected them.

The proposer of both motions, one P. McIntyre, from the constituency of Dublin North, felt it was necessary that the organisation should be in a position to advise the government as to the political effect of its own measures and that, in return, it should receive from its parliamentary party members a clearer grasp of legislative measures, especially those that were unpopular. The President and several ministers, including Kevin O'Higgins and Patrick Hogan, agreed that there was a need for 'closer relations' all round.[71]

At a subsequent meeting of the Coiste Gnótha, the activities subcommittee of the Ard Chomhairle, held on 30 May 1924, the matter was again raised, with Pádraic O Máille, TD, complaining that the party contributed very little to 'current' legislation which was usually presented ready-made by the Executive Council to be accepted or rejected. In his opinion, the permanent officials in the civil service had too much influence on policy formulation, for which, according to O Máille, they were not qualified. He concluded that a constructive policy common to the organisation and the party was urgently needed. After considerable discussion, the meeting decided to form a consultative committee or committees to draw up a national and economic policy for adoption by the organisation.[72] Clearly, therefore, more than a year after its establishment, Cumann na nGaedhael members (of both the parliamentary party and the organisation) had no clear perception of what constituted its party's national policy and felt the need for the development of such a policy. Of course, the point should be made that this debate took place in the immediate aftermath of the Army Mutiny crisis of 1924 which severely rocked the government and its organisation.[73]

However, in September 1924, there is further evidence of the continued strained relations between members of Cumann na nGaedhael and the Executive. A row occurred between the Minister for Finance, Ernest Blythe, and Cumann na nGaedhael's Coiste Gnótha over the government's decision to reduce the old-age pension and a subsequent revision of means which resulted in even further reductions. In a communication from the Coiste Gnótha to the minister dated 17 September 1924, Blythe was left in no doubt about the considerable anger which had been aroused by the government's measures. The Coiste Gnótha felt that the necessary economies would have been effected with far less friction had the formal decision of the one-shilling reduction been shelved and the revision that was now taking place been tabled in the first place. The letter, which was signed by the party secretary, Séamus Dolan, made it clear to Blythe that party members regarded the revision of payments as most inopportune, having regard to the prevailing poverty, the bad harvest and the coming by-elections. In a comment, the secretary added that 'I am to add that the Coiste Gnótha are at a loss to know whether in arriving at such administrative decisions, the ministers responsible take any account of the political effect produced and of the possible consequences on the stability of the state of continuous public displeasure.'[74]

In his reply, the minister was totally unapologetic and expressed considerable annoyance with the party's attitude. Indeed, his opening sentence represented a slight on the party secretary:

I have your letter of the 17th instant purporting to communicate the views of the Coiste Gnótha of Cumann na nGaedhael in regard to the recent revision of the means of Old Age Pensioners and in regard to the administration of Old Age Pensions generally.

The minister stressed that the revision of means had been carried out in strict accordance with the Act which left no discretion to the Revenue Commissioners or to himself and which had fixed 5 September as the date on which the revision of means was to come into effect. He then outlined the reasons behind the government's decision and stated that as the Old Age Pensions Act was now law, there was no option but to enforce it. However, he was quite critical of rank-and-file Cumann na nGaedhael members, writing that 'I think the state of mind which your letter indicates reflects the state of mind which is responsible for a good deal of harm in the country'. Blythe felt that it was the duty of the political organisation once the government had decided on certain measures, and a majority of the Oireachtas had supported them, to explain and to convince the people of the necessity for such measures. Instead of this, he wrote that 'I find that Cumann na nGaedhael and its branches, so far from trying to realise the position and appreciating the needs of the case, has joined in the ignorant and irresponsible chorus of criticism.' In a handwritten addition to the document, Blythe made his final comment that:

In view of all the circumstances, it appears to me some what deplorable that responsible people are so unwilling to defend the reduction and make clear the causes which rendered it necessary. I think that when the government faces the facts of a difficult situation and decides on measures which receive the approval of the elected representatives of the people in the Dáil, it is entitled to look to well informed and responsible citizens for support and encouragement.[75]

The Coiste Gnótha replied on 22 September, having met on 19 September, and pointed out to the minister that 'terrible hardship' was being caused by the drastic reductions being implemented by the local pension officers. It further added that the local pensions committees were being continually overruled and that in every instance, the pensions officers' decision was upheld on appeal. The letter concluded by stating that the committee was compelled to take notice of the volume of opinion centring around this question and suggested to the minister that where possible, more generous consideration should be given to the views of the local pensions committees in cases of appeal. Finally, it requested that the minister reconsider the whole question of pensions in the light of the committee's representations.[76]

The minister's reply to this communication, dated 26 September 1924, was a carbon copy of his previous letter to the Coiste Gnótha and envisaged no change in government policy. Once more, the Coiste Gnótha reiterated its request that the minister should direct his attention to the way in which the revision was being carried out by the pensions officers and the failure in many cases to give any weight to the views of local pensions committees. The secretary also informed Blythe that endless protests were continuing to arrive at the party's head office from every part of the country and that one government supporter, returning from Connemara, said that 99 per cent of the population there would vote against the government at the next election. The secretary added that the responsible people in the organisation had continually defended the government and its measures against attack but that in relation to the passing of the Old Age Pensions Act, the vast majority of members, including TDs, were opposed to it, and that there was an overwhelming volume of anti-government feeling abroad in relation to the issue. In conclusion, the secretary protested indignantly:

> Re the use of the word 'purporting' in the beginning of your letter, I would like to point out that my letter in question was sent to you on the strength of a written order of the Coiste Gnótha signed by the Chairman of the meeting, who was a TD, and not only purports to, but actually does give the views expressed by the members present, who included three TDs.[77]

The above correspondence illustrates the testy relationship that existed between the organisation of Cumann na nGaedhael and certain of its ministers. Blythe's assertion that the organisation should blindly support the government on every issue, irrespective of merit, was bound to annoy party members who felt that democracy was a two-way process and that party members should have the right to articulate their views to the cabinet. The authoritarian tone, tenor and apparent indifference of Blythe's letter would hardly inspire good relations between the government and party organisation. Blythe's approach, no matter how admirable in some respects, was not one attuned to electoral realities. Certainly O'Rahilly was unhappy with the lack of influence which backbench TDs had over government policy. To this extent, O'Rahilly's decision to resign reflected a real mood within certain sections of the parliamentary party of Cumann na nGaedhael.

The by-election was held in November 1924. The nomination of Councillor Michael Egan to stand on behalf of Cumann na nGaedhael caused uproar with the Irish-Ireland section of the party in the city. As John Regan has noted, 'de Róiste and the old guard in Cork, believed that Egan had been foisted upon them. The convention for the selection of a candidate was openly "packed" by Doctor Magner, uncle-in-law of Kevin O'Higgins, for support of Michael Egan [and] this was known to Batt O'Connor TD, who presided on behalf of the Dublin Executive'.[78] The selection was divisive but instructive. De Róiste confided to his diary that Egan 'is now supported by his one-time antagonists of the same school, the Hibernians and the United Irish League who followed Redmond and Devlin. Cumann na nGaedhael, the pro-Treaty organisation in Cork, is now ruled by such men'.[79]

Another dissident was Mrs Collins-Powell, who wrote to the *Cork Examiner* alleging that the convention was not a proper one.[80] A number of caucus meetings were held by the Irish Irelanders within Cumann na nGaedhael, as a result of which it resolved to regain control of the party organisation in Cork. The old Sinn Féin element had become either discontented or remained away from party meetings altogether.[81] Egan's nomination was also raised at the Coiste Gnótha meeting of Cumann na Gaedhael on 24 October 1924 when, after a lengthy discussion, it was decided to ratify the convention's selection of him.[82] At a further meeting of the Coiste Gnótha on 31 October 1924, a signed protest against the nomination from a number of constituents (presumably the 'Irish Irelanders' referred to by de Róiste) was read. A decision was taken to reply 'as in previous cases of protest'.[83]

De Róiste, commenting on the composition of the Cumann na nGaedhael party at this stage, noted in his diary:

> The 'pro-Treaty' party is not a cemented political party. It is a combination of diverse elements held together for the time being, by the opposition of the anti-Treaty section. Pro-Treaty consists of Sinn Féin, Old Unionist, old Parliamentarian, Labour, Industrialists, Farmers sections with diverse outlook. The binding force is acceptance of the Treaty. Otherwise there is great divergence of opinion.[84]

In any event, Egan won the by-election with a majority of 12,000 votes. Councillor Seán French, Lord Mayor and nominee of the Sinn Féin party, had polled 14,000 votes, an increase of 5,000 on the anti-Treatyite vote in the 1923 general election.

By March 1925, the reorganisation of Cumann na nGaedhael in Cork was complete, with the 'Irish-Ireland' section back in control. Because of this development, de Róiste decided to rejoin the party's executive in Cork at the invitation of Mrs Collins-Powell.[85] Throughout 1925 and 1926, there seemed to be a resurgence of the Irish-Ireland movement in Cork. According to de Róiste, men like T. P. Dowdall and Frank J. Daly were anxious to make peace with the Republicans in an endeavour to persuade them to enter Dáil Éireann.[86]

In November 1925, de Róiste presided at a meeting of a new Irish-Ireland society in Cork. Unifying Republican and Treatyite Irish Irelanders was the declared aim. But

as de Róiste was to complain, no plan of work was
expounded for the accomplishment of such an aim.[87]
The movement did have one positive achievement,
however, in the establishment of a weekly journal in
Cork named *The Irish Tribune*, a nationalist alternative
to *The Irish Statesman*.[88] Its financial backing was
guaranteed for a period by a consortium which included
T. P. Dowdall, Hugo Flinn, and O'Rahilly.[89] The first
edition of *The Irish Tribune* was published on 12 March
1926, and it ceased publication the following December.
In its first editorial, the paper declared: 'No apology is
necessary for starting a new Irish weekly' and went on
to allege that 'The Irish Press is notoriously without
influence on public opinion. The Anglo-Irish struggle
was carried on in spite of the practically unanimous
opposition of the more important newspapers'. In
outlining its standpoint and fundamental principles, the
paper dedicated itself to the ideal of an Irish Ireland:

> While allowing opportunity for divergences in detail,
> we intend clearly and unambiguously to uphold the
> cultural, political and economic ideal of Irish Ireland.
> We are opposed to anglicisation and alienation alike
> in morals, culture, language and industry.

Moving on to the more specifically political level, the
editorial concluded that:

> accepting the Treaty position as a fact, our aim will
> be so to utilise and develop it as to rally together all
> Nationalists and to heal our present deplorable
> divisions while never losing sight of the estrange-
> ment of the North East.[90]

One could suggest that the individuals who were behind
this newspaper in policy terms differed little from those

on the pragmatic wing of Sinn Féin which, during this period, was trying to extricate itself from the abstentionist straitjacket into which it had tied itself. It would appear that the major objection of people like Dowdall and Flinn to Sinn Féin was its refusal to recognise the legitimacy of the new state. Thus, when Fianna Fáil was founded and eventually entered the Dáil in 1927, it was not uncommon to find people like the Dowdall brothers and Flinn appearing on its platform. *The Irish Tribune*, throughout its period of operation, published articles on protectionism, tillage farming, land annuities, the oath of allegiance and partition, all of which were issues which became central planks of Fianna Fáil's policy platform in later years. Professors O'Rahilly, Stockley and Busteed were regular contributors.[91] The emergence of this somewhat independent Irish-Ireland group also indicates a certain unhappiness on the part of the people who were involved with the government's realisation of the ideal of an Irish Ireland.

The emergence of this Irish-Ireland group and its desire to heal Civil War wounds seems to have coincided with a movement within the Sinn Féin party at national level to change its abstentionist policy towards the institution of the Irish Free State. Throughout 1925, there was considerable speculation that Sinn Féin was reconsidering its policy in this regard. It was perhaps significant that this was a time of reassessment and change within the IRA. By November 1925, at the organisation's first post-Civil War convention, it was decided that the army should withdraw allegiance from the 'republican government' and that the Army Council would have complete control over the military wing.[92]

De Valera was also considering a change of policy during 1925. Indeed, as early as August and September 1924, confidential police reports that were submitted to the government indicate emerging splits among the anti-Treatyites, between what the Garda Chief Commissioner, Eoin O'Duffy, described as 'ultra-militarists' and the 'politicians'. In one such report, he wrote that:

> the former element is inclined to hold to the original 'death or glory' attitude; the latter seem to consist of a large party which is anxious to pin its faith on the chance of an irregular working majority at the next election and a smaller group which would be prepared to enter the Dáil if certain difficulties such as the Oath could be overcome.

However, the report stressed that a general decision by the 'Irregular' political party to enter the Dáil was most unlikely, as such a step would inevitably lead to an absolute break with the militarists and the consequent break-up of the whole political organisation.[93]

The failure of Sinn Féin to make any appreciable electoral gains after the 1923 general election as well as the decision of the IRA to break from its political wing and a reassessment of the party had been crucial to its effectiveness. Throughout 1925, the Republican press published many criticisms of the party from members and sympathisers. The most significant and perhaps enlightening criticism came from Seán Lemass. In a series of six articles that were written in *An Phoblacht* between September 1925 and January 1926, Lemass questioned the wisdom of the party's continuing abstentionist policy. He warned that unless radical changes were made, the party would continue to decline and would eventually cease to have any realistic chance of becoming the government party. Perhaps the most significant idea in Lemass' articles was his insistence that the party should concentrate on an immediately realisable political objective, such as the abolition of the oath of allegiance.[94] Such a viewpoint foreshadowed the policies of Fianna Fáil when, shortly after its foundation, it launched a nationwide petition to abolish the oath.

Despite increasing discontent within the organisation, the 1925 Ard-Fheis produced a compromise resolution which aimed to keep the party unified. Within two months, however, the party had split irrevocably on abstentionism from Dáil Éireann. The major reason for such a change so soon after the 1925 Ard-Fheis was the decision by the governments of the Irish Free State, Northern Ireland and Britain to sign the Boundary Agreement on 3 December 1925.[95] In the words of Peter Pyne, this event was crucial in convincing a section of the party's leadership to abandon abstentionism under certain conditions.[96] The event demonstrated to many members of the party its powerlessness to influence the destiny of their country as long as they remained outside Leinster House. Despite a number of meetings and much soul-searching, the Sinn Féin deputies did not enter the Dáil. However, the Boundary Agreement introduced a significantly new element, in that it generated a sense of urgency among the political pragmatists in Sinn Féin who were now convinced of the need to change policy. It also set in train a series of events which culminated in the formation of Fianna Fáil.

On 6 January 1926, de Valera publicly announced that he was prepared to enter the Dáil if the oath was abolished. A special Ard-Fheis of the party was convened on 9 March 1926 to decide the issue once and for all. Before the meeting was a resolution, circulated by de Valera to all the branches, proposing:

That once the admission oaths of the 26 and 6 county assemblies are removed it becomes a question not of principle but of policy whether or not Republican representatives should attend these assemblies.

This motion was opposed in an amendment from Fr O'Flanagan, a member of the Ard Chomhairle, which stated that 'it is incompatible with the fundamental principles of Sinn Féin as it is injurious to the honour of Ireland to send representatives into any usurping legislature set up by English law in Ireland.'[97]

Over 500 delegates attended the Ard-Fheis. After two days of repetitive and often emotional speeches, the Ard-Fheis narrowly decided in favour of O'Flanagan's amendment. Throughout the two days, there had been intense canvassing, the moderates being led by Gerry Boland and Seán Lemass while Mary MacSwiney, Fr O'Flanagan and Michael Price campaigned vigorously to uphold abstention. The latter group were hampered by the lack of support for abstention at local level although the eventual outcome would throw some doubt on such a contention.[98] Although the Ard-Fheis received scant attention in the press, a subcommittee was appointed by the Ard-Fheis to restore unity but it failed to achieve its objective. Within days the leading members of the moderate wing of Sinn Féin were holding meetings to establish and organise a new political party. During the following weeks, many leading members of Sinn Féin defected from the party. Of the forty-seven Republican deputies who had been elected in 1923, twenty-one followed de Valera into the new party. By April 1926, the third Sinn Féin party had disintegrated into two nearly equal factions. In the words of Peter Pyne, 'the schism of March 1926 marks the dividing line between the Third and Fourth Sinn Féin parties'.[99]

The Boundary Agreement also had significant repercussions for Cumann na nGaedhael. At an Ard
Chomhairle meeting held in December 1925, the issue
was raised. Nineteen TDs attended, together with three
delegates from Cork, T. P. Dowdall, Councillor Barry
Egan and A. O'Shaughnessy who had been elected as a
TD in 1923 on the Progressive Party platform. The
following resolution was proposed by Jeremiah
O'Connell of Sligo and seconded by T. P. Dowdall and
was put to the meeting:

> That this meeting of the Ard Chomhairle records its
> conviction that under no circumstances can the Free
> State consent to the alienation of any part of the 26
> counties and that all future negotiations about the
> Boundary question should be conducted directly
> with the British Cabinet only.[100]

Dowdall urged that a decision of two Boundary
Commissioners would not be valid unless it was endorsed
by a plebiscite. He argued that the Executive Council
should cease from bargaining and stand on its rights under
the Treaty. The proposer, Jeremiah O'Connell, suggested
that if attacked, the Irish Free State should put the English
'to the trouble of a reconquest'. Ernest Blythe, Minister
for Finance, replying, maintained that the Executive
Council had nothing to reproach itself with. He stated
that the weakness of their position was inherent in Article
12 of the Anglo-Irish Treaty, which practically left the
decision in the hands of the chairman of the commission.
Article 12 had proved a failure, he said, but that fact did
not break the Treaty. He went on to say that 'to talk of
fighting the issue militarily was codology. We would be
walked on, and it was very doubtful if a mandate to fight
could be got from a people weary of strife'.[101]

Another delegate, Fr Malachy Brennan from Castle-maine, who later joined Fianna Fáil, reacted strongly and said that Blythe's 'jeremiad of despair had increased tenfold the prevailing depression'. In his opinion, the Free State government had been too reasonable, in comparison with the inflexible attitude of the Northern Ireland premier, Sir James Craig. Brennan added that many who had accepted the Treaty would have been on the other side if they had foreseen that the chairman of the Boundary Commission, Mr Justice Feetham, would be allowed to ignore the wishes of the inhabitants of Northern Ireland. He concluded that 'as the Treaty was now violated, we should let it be known that if the abstaining TDs entered the Dáil the Oath would not be bound to them, and so we might end the more important partition in the South and let England do her worst'.[102]

However, other speakers who were not identified, came to the rescue of the government and urged that any declaration from the meeting showing lack of faith in the government would be disastrous. The resolution was eventually withdrawn.[103] Fr Brennan's proposal to allow abstentionist TDs to take their seats without having to take the oath of allegiance is significant, since at this very time, efforts were being made in Dublin by a group of politicians, including Frank J. Daly, Hugo Flinn and T. P. Dowdall, to have the oath of allegiance abolished, modified, or to have a 'conscience clause' inserted, in order to allow de Valera and his followers to enter the Dáil.[104] These individuals were later to join Fianna Fáil and represent the party in Dáil Éireann and it is clear that at this time, they were far from happy with government policy, particularly in relation to the Boundary Agreement.

In Cork the Cumann na nGaedhael Executive also had problems in relation to this issue. De Róiste's diary reveals that Dowdall managed to organise a small meeting of Cork party members on 3 December 1925. Six Executive members were present, together with two 'not of the Executive'. According to de Róiste, Dowdall's idea was tantamount to telling the government that they had bungled the issue and should resign. De Róiste himself urged caution and expressed the opinion that the inhabitants of Northern Ireland should have been consulted on the boundary question, as laid down by Article 12 of the Anglo-Irish Treaty.[105]

Similar meetings were held throughout the crisis, the principal speakers being de Róiste, Dowdall, Daly, Flinn, John Punch, Seán Jennings and Mrs Collins-Powell. It is difficult to assess Flinn's party allegiance at his stage. He later became a member of Fianna Fáil and as such, was elected to the Dáil in September 1927. De Róiste describes him as a very wealthy man, owning the Palace Theatre of Varieties and having considerable investments abroad, and gives the following assessment of him:

Hugo Flinn is the professor or schoolmaster mentality; well read and well spoken, but impresses one as too sure of his own opinions. I would regard him as a doctrinaire politician and economist.[106]

Thus, the significance of the Boundary Agreement in relation to the evolution of the Cumann na nGaedheal party in Cork was that it created further disillusionment among the Irish-Ireland element of the party who as time went on, would become even more aggrieved over other aspects of the government's policy, in particular, over its reluctance to pursue a wholly protectionist economic policy. The continued alienation of this group from the leadership of the party led eventually to several members resigning from Cumann na nGaedheal and joining

Fianna Fáil, thereby bestowing increased credibility on the latter party as well as helping to broaden significantly its electoral support base in Cork.

Before dealing with the formation of the Fianna Fáil party in 1926 and the consequent decline of the third Sinn Féin party as a major political force, it is necessary to discuss the reasons which caused the latter's demise. In doing so, one begins to find some clues as to why Fianna Fáil had managed to become the most successful political organisation in the country by the end of the decade. In analysing the remarkable growth of Fianna Fáil, it is helpful to explore the relationship between it and Sinn Féin. For instance, it could be argued that while the years spent in Sinn Féin constituted an important learning process for the future leaders of Fianna Fáil, that party also learned from the mistakes of the third Sinn Féin party and thus avoided many of the pitfalls into which it had fallen.

Electorally there was a very definite relationship between Fianna Fáil and Sinn Féin. Electoral patterns between 1923 and 1927 show that, to a very large degree, Fianna Fáil was supported by former followers of the Sinn Féin party.[107] In a socio-economic and geographical analysis of the Sinn Féin party's support base in the period 1923–26, Peter Pyne has also concluded that 'Sinn Féin in 1923 was largely the party of the lower middle class, the party of the owner occupiers and small shopkeepers and traders . . . the party of the people who were perhaps the most valuable in economic recession.' The party was largely supported by small farmers and landless labourers. There also seems to have been a tendency for the Sinn Féin vote to increase as the urban vote decreased. Thus, at this stage it appears to have been a predominantly rural-based party.[108]

It would appear that the two major factors responsible

for the decline of Sinn Féin were its abstentionist policy and its inability to devise a coherent social and economic programme which was relevant to the needs of its supporters.[109] It was simply not feasible to sustain a political party with considerable mass support on an abstentionist platform in the post-independence Irish Free State. The majority of the people had decided in 1923 to accept the new order and were clearly not in favour of abstentionism. Popular support, a capacity to establish an alternative administrative machine which would be capable of supplanting the existing state administration, and most important of all, tangible and realisable goals, were the ingredients which ensured the success of Sinn Féin from 1918 to 1922. These ingredients were simply not present during the period of the third Sinn Féin party.

The abstentionist policy also prevented Sinn Féin TDs from carrying out effective constituency work which was central to the Irish party political system and later perfected by many a backbench Fianna Fáil TD.[110] As a result, the Sinn Féin parliamentary party was an unlikely pressure group playing a largely irrelevant and isolationist role in the political scheme of things.[111] However, perhaps the major weakness of the third Sinn Féin party was its preoccupation with constitutional issues, resulting in a failure to deal adequately with the social and economic issues of the day. As Peter Pyne has put it, 'its social and economic policies had little to offer the class that formed the backbone of the party, with the result that their support was gradually alienated'.[112] The supporters and members of Sinn Féin suffered considerably from the economic crisis of the early 1920s. During 1924 and 1925, agricultural prices declined rapidly, with a consequent decline in exports. Furthermore, by 1925, the cost of living reached its highest level of the 1922–32 decade. It was also one of the worst years for unemployment. Emigration, particularly in the west, continued with monotonous regularity. Many of those emigrating were members of the Sinn Féin party who were unable to find employment as a result of economic recession and government discrimination. Despite the economic misery of the period 1924–26, Sinn Féin neglected to produce an alternative set of social and economic policies to those being enacted by the government. It failed to articulate effectively the bread-and-butter concerns of its own followers. Such a policy, or rather lack of policy, was bound to have electoral repercussions.

A number of efforts were made during 1925 to develop social and economic programmes. However, these efforts were vague and general in character. For instance, no mention was ever made of the land annuities, an issue which was to be a major plank on the social and economic platform of Fianna Fáil. In any event, the party realised that there were many opportunities to exploit the economic policies of the then Cumann na nGaedhael government. For example, there was considerable unemployment over the 1920s. It also underlined the fact that voters were more concerned about such issues rather than the abstractions of abstentionism. While constitutional issues remained important, the ideal electoral formula was a synthesis of the socio-economic and constitutional issues. Fianna Fáil tried to achieve just such a synthesis and produced, in combination with its constitutional policy, economic and social policies that were objective and realisable and were calculated as a realistic alternative to the laissez-faire policies of the government.[113]

The results of the 1922 and 1923 general elections show that during the period when the constitutional issue was most hotly debated, a considerable section of the electorate voted for parties who were not prominent in the Treaty debate and whose electoral platforms were not based on the Treaty divide. The proportion in 1922 was 40 per cent of the electorate. In 1923 the non-Treaty parties received up to 33 per cent of the vote. In the general election of June 1927, they received up to 46 per cent of the vote.[114] It was not until September 1927 that the parties which had been born out of the Treaty gained a hold over the electorate with 74 per cent of the vote. And it could be argued that the factors governing the September 1927 result were not entirely related to constitutional issues since in this election, Fianna Fáil took particular care to concentrate on socio-economic issues in order to downplay its reversal of policy in relation to the taking of the oath.

Tom Garvin's suggestion that the the political elite of the early 1920s was somewhat out of touch with the everyday concerns of the electorate seems plausible in the light of these figures.[115] Certainly Peter Pyne's analysis of Sinn Féin shows that its failure to develop social and economic policies was a major factor in its decline. The Labour Party, on the other hand, tended to neglect unduly the constitutional issues. But more significantly, its economic and social policies were not attuned to the electoral realities of the day. Its policies, as Peter Mair has pointed out, were aimed at the 'urban and rural proletariat', a group which in relative terms, was 'electorally peripheral'. In 1926, for instance, only 8 per cent of the employed population were engaged in industry. Mair argues that it was Labour's irrelevance to both the constitutional relationship between Britain and Ireland and the economic and social issues that led to its decline.[116] Fianna Fáil's economic policy seems to have been the most realistic alternative to that of the government.

4
1926–1927: TOWARDS STABILITY & CONSOLIDATION

After that fateful Sinn Féin Ard-Fheis on 9 March 1926, a group of de Valera's followers met in the Wicklow Hotel in Dublin to discuss future strategy. With or without de Valera, there was a determination among certain moderates to follow the course that he had outlined and to establish a new political organisation.[1] De Valera did not attend many of the preliminary organisational meetings. However, he did attend the two meetings where definite plans were made to launch a new party. On 12 April 1926, an organising committee announced that a new party was to be founded. Three days later, it issued its manifesto. The choice of 'Fianna Fáil' as the party's name together with 'The Republican Party' as a subtitle, was a compromise between de Valera and Seán Lemass. Lemass had been anxious to maintain a link with the Old IRA, Sinn Féin and the neutrals. The first full-scale meeting of the party was held on 16 May 1926 at the La Scala Theatre in Dublin.[2] Robert Briscoe recalled that 'that day formulated the philosophy and creed by which Fianna Fáil has lived and governed Ireland'.[3]

The initial organisational drive was spearheaded by the party's TDs, local representatives and the organising committee, with de Valera making key speeches in populous areas or at multi-constituency meetings. From the beginning, the organisation was given an explicit electoral orientation with the local *cumainn* or branches founded to coincide with electoral districts. The constituency organisation was therefore the cornerstone of the election machinery and provided the main link between the branches and national headquarters. The party leadership stressed the importance of organisation and at each Ard-Fheis between 1927 and 1932, the honorary general secretary's report discussed in detail the strength of Fianna Fáil's organisation throughout the country. In that report, certain constituencies were singled out for special mention, some for their increased activity, some for their lack of initiative.[4] One of the major differences in organisational terms between the third Sinn Féin party and Fianna Fáil was the latter's capacity to generate finance at home. The 1927 Ard-Fheis decided to hold an annual collection. In the 1928 National Collection, the party collected £3,702 6s 1d.[5] Hitherto, the party had depended almost entirely on funds from abroad, a precarious and unpredictable position. Such an annual operation also helped to keep the organisation at local level in an effective condition.

To establish local branches, party leaders travelled the length and breadth of the country seeking the assistance of known Republicans or former members of Sinn Féin. Public meetings were held throughout the country. Many years later, Seán MacEntee vividly recalled this period of intense activity by the party's itinerant organisers:

> For more than five years hardly any of us were at home for a single night or any week-end. Lemass bought up four or five second hand Ford cars, 'old bangers', and with them we toured every parish in the country founding Fianna Fáil branches on the solid basis of Old IRA and Sinn Féin members.[6]

So successful was the organisational campaign that in 1927, the number of *cumainn* registered was 1,307. Although this figure decreased to 1,033 in 1928, the party secretary's report indicates that this was due mainly to the amalgamation of small *cumainn* which had been initially formed for election purposes, with more permanent units of the organisation.[7]

There was a significant difference between the formation of Fianna Fáil and Cumann na nGaedhael. Unlike their Cumann na nGaedhael counterparts who had to establish a party while governing a war-torn state, the Fianna Fáil leaders had the time to tour the country at their leisure. Fianna Fáil's organisational drive was also greatly aided by the presence of its 'star performers' at the various constituency meetings. Unlike the third Sinn Féin party, Fianna Fáil also did not restrict its appeal to those of a purely anti-Treaty persuasion. From the outset, the party sought to attract the uncommitted sections of the electorate, either those who had not taken an active political role in the past, or groups such as the neutral and post-Treaty IRA that had not expressed support for any political party. Throughout this period, Fianna Fáil constantly appealed to nationalists of all types to join. The party manifestos called for a healing of past conflicts and there was a clear emphasis on playing down past dissensions. So successful was this policy that by 1932, candidates who had been members of Labour, the National League, Cumann na nGaedhael, Clann Éireann, Sinn Féin and the National Group stood in the election of that year under the banner of Fianna Fáil.[8]

The aims of the party, as published in 1926, included the abolition of the oath, the restoration of the Irish language, securing the political independence of a united Irish republic, the redistribution of land, nationalisation of insurance, the establishment of a state bank, and an economic programme designed to make Ireland 'as self-contained and self-sufficient as possible with a proper balance between agriculture and other essential industries'.[9] The last of these objectives became a crucial element in future Fianna Fáil election campaigns. During the 1920s, the Free State economy was in crisis, plagued by rising unemployment, emigration and appalling housing conditions. The government's strict fiscal policy ruled out the possibility that these conditions might be alleviated by the injection of large amounts of state capital. The government was firmly opposed to large-scale borrowing. While the depressed agricultural sector was primarily responsible for the economic decline of the period, all of these factors, when taken together, had electoral implications for the Cumann na nGaedhael government. As Brian Reynolds concludes, 'it is safe to assume that this problem of depressed agricultural conditions was a prime reason for dissatisfaction with government policy'.[10] However, this is not to say that Cumann na nGaedhael's period in office was not marked by considerable achievements, particularly in the area of state building. These included the establishment of a state civil service, an efficient police force and a system of local government. Of revolutionary significance was the successful Shannon hydroelectric scheme of 1927 which brought electricity to rural Ireland for the first time. But, as F. S. L. Lyons has written, these changes 'far-reaching though they were, were essentially changes of practice and procedure rather than of principle'.[11] The government's fundamental approach to the management of the economy was, despite some exceptions, largely governed by free trade principles.

A final point concerning the formation of Fianna Fáil and one which is of particular significance in relation to the development of the Irish party political system, is the fact that many of those who left the IRA and Sinn Féin to join the new party were themselves social radicals. The Sinn Féin party after 1916 contained many left-leaning members and this helped to retard the growth of the Labour Party. Peadar O'Donnell, reflecting on the Sinn Féin split in 1925, noted that many of the most radical and militant IRA men who had voted at the IRA Convention in 1925 to break with Sinn Féin and de Valera, voted with de Valera on this occasion, surprisingly in his view, so great was that leader's influence. O'Donnell added that the left wing of both Sinn Féin and the IRA and some 'fine Republicans' went with de Valera. Both organisations lost men like Seán Moylan, for whom O'Donnell had a great admiration, Patrick Routledge, 'a real radical', Tom Derrig, Michael Kilroy, Dan Breen, Seán Lemass, Tom Mullins, Oscar Traynor 'and hundreds of others, many of whom were social radicals'.[12]

The point here is that many members of Fianna Fáil, both leaders and rank-and-file, had a left-of-centre approach to economics, a factor which had an influence on the party's subsequent policies. A perusal of the *clár* (agenda) for the first five of the party's ard-fheiseanna confirms this, with motions calling for an incoming Fianna Fáil government to guarantee employment, or adequate maintenance for those who were willing to work, to increase old-age pensions, and to provide generous measures 're Workmen's Compensation, Widows and Orphans, Endowments etc.'[13] Another motion on the clár of the 1926 Ard-Fheis demanded that 'profiteering' be made an offence punishable by imprisonment. At the same Ard-Fheis, motions condemning the low wages which were being paid on the Shannon hydro-electric scheme and the 'awful' exploitation of the poorer classes by 'money-lenders' were passed.[14]

At the 1927 Ard-Fheis, a motion calling on Fianna Fáil to include in its foreign policy the recognition of Soviet Russia and the opening up of trade and diplomatic relations with that power was debated, as was another calling for an adequate 'Workers Housing Scheme at a rate of rent to meet the needs of the ordinary Labourer'.[15] Significantly, a motion tabled at the 1928 Ard-Fheis instructing its elected representatives to 'support the principle of the eight-hour day and the forty-four hour week, in all industries to which it can appropriately be applied', was adopted by the National Executive of the party, as was a motion adding a new section to the Constitution of Fianna Fáil: 'Section 7. To carry out the Democratic Programme of the First Dáil'.[16] While these motions do not, collectively or individually, constitute a coherent economic philosophy, they indicate a certain political outlook or approach which had a strong social democratic dimension. This dimension also dampened the appeal of the Labour Party. The differences between the two parties on social and economic issues were less than clear. Moreover, there was a marked absence in the late 1920s of any definite left/right cleavage between Fianna Fáil and Labour of the type that existed between parties of the right and left in continental Europe during the same era.

From its inception, Fianna Fáil geared its organisational drive towards the general election that was expected in 1927. As early as August 1926, the party's head office had approved circulars to be sent out explaining various aspects of election work, the preparation of a register and the electoral laws themselves. Furthermore, the party promoted its policies continuously throughout 1926 and 1927 through speeches made by its leading spokesmen and the activities of the local *cumainn*. In one such speech on 27 June 1926 in Clare, de Valera appealed to those with a pro-Treaty background to forget past differences and support Fianna Fáil.[17] In relation to the development of its agricultural policies, Fianna Fáil organised an 'All-Ireland Agricultural Conference' in early 1927. It was held on 3 February in Jury's Hotel in Dublin. It was ostensibly non-political and farmers from all over the country were invited to attend and give their views. The exercise proved useful from the point of view of recruitment. Above all, it signified a desire on Fianna Fáil's part to court the rural electorate. The conference also marks the beginning of Fianna Fáil's attempt to promote the advantages of protectionism among the farming community.[18]

Protectionism was a major issue during this period. It was a central feature of Fianna Fáil's economic policy and proved to be something of a thorn in the government's side. The cabinet was badly split on the issue, with J. J. Walsh, Minister for Posts and Telegraphs, favouring a degree of protective tariffs while Kevin O'Higgins, Minister for Justice and External Affairs, and P. J. Hogan, Minister for Agriculture, were resolutely opposed to such measures. Walsh was later to concede that 'credit must be given to the fact that Fianna Fáil went all out to implement the self-sufficiency programme of Arthur Griffith.' Cumann na nGaedhael had, he said, 'scrapped these ideals without mercy'.[19] It was an issue that received considerable media coverage and, in addition to helping Fianna Fáil maintain its rural support, it won for the party considerable business support, particularly in Cork.

The election campaign of June 1927 provided Fianna Fáil with its first electoral test. In the period leading up to the election, a number of attempts were made to forge an alliance between Fianna Fáil, Sinn Féin and the IRA. The moves were initiated by Eamon Donnelly, a Northern TD. In a letter to Mary MacSwiney who had remained committed to Sinn Féin, Donnelly outlined headings under which an agreement could be reached with Fianna Fáil with a view to forming a common Republican platform on which to contest the election. Donnelly felt that the present situation was hopeless and that there was an overwhelming desire on the part of the rank-and-file for unity between Republicans.[20] His 'headings' for discussion were as follows:

(1) Abolition of Oath before entry of any Republican TD to any elected assembly.

(2) Repudiation of all imperial commitments, financial and otherwise.

(3) Repudiation of Partition and the immediate utilisation of every available weapon to bring it to an end.

(4) Ulster constituencies to be dealt with on the principle of the Collins–de Valera pact of 1922.

(5) All Republican TDs returned must in case a majority is secured be pledged to enter 'Merrion Street' so as to secure at the first meeting, the removal of the present Free State Ministry.

(6) Minister of Defence to be acceptable to the Volunteers.

(7) After debts are paid balance of deposit fees to be used at the forthcoming election.

(8) This is the immediate republican objective and prejudices in no way ultimate objectives.

(9) If agreement can be secured Dev and A.O'C. [Sinn Féin leader, Art O'Connor] to be cabled the terms and appear afterwards on common platform in USA.[21]

MacSwiney's initial reaction on receiving these proposals was to inform Donnelly that they were too vague and that, in her view, Fianna Fáil's policy was unacceptable.[22] However, on reconsidering the matter, she stated in a further reply to Donnelly on 10 April that there could be a chance of effecting unity and that another electoral landslide similar to 1918 could be achieved.[23]

MacSwiney outlined her own proposals on 9 April in a letter to the Standing Committee of Sinn Féin. Before doing so, she expressed the view that Donnelly was correct in stating that the rank-and-file everywhere desired unity before the next election. Her position was that if Fianna Fáil gave certain guarantees, then unity could be effected. The guarantees, as expressed in her letter to the Standing Committee, were as follows:

(1) The Minority Position: The first of those guarantees would have prevented the minority party from entering the Free State Parliament, under a conscience clause or some other such device, while claiming to be Republican, and helping to stabilise it by their presence.

(2) The Majority Position: This second guarantee would have obliged a majority, which claimed to be Republican, to summon an All-Ireland parliament immediately and repudiate the Free State Constitution at once and set about framing an Irish one.

(3) The third made it quite clear that the only de jure government in the country was the government of the Republic.[24]

MacSwiney concluded her letter by stressing that if Fianna Fáil could be brought to accept these guarantees, Sinn Féin should do everything possible to prevent the 'present junta' being returned: 'If they come back as the biggest party again it will be harder than ever to convince the world that the Free State does not really satisfy the Irish people'.[25]

It appears that Mary MacSwiney and others in Sinn Féin were being motivated by the realisation that Sinn Féin on its own was not in a position to put up enough candidates to win a majority. Furthermore, there appears to have been considerable pressure from the rank-and-file of both organisations for unity. For example, MacSwiney herself received a communication from a Michael O'Donnell of County Kerry, dated 21 April 1927, informing her that a joint conference of Sinn Féin and Fianna Fáil delegates had been held in Tralee, attended by Tom McEllistrim, TD, and a number of county councillors, at which it was unanimously agreed:

> That the meeting, representative of all Republican organisations in Kerry call on our leaders to make a final effort to settle all differences whereby one could face the electorate with a united front.[26]

It is difficult to gauge Fianna Fáil's response to these overtures but in an undated letter to MacSwiney from Donnelly, the latter revealed that Fianna Fáil was prepared to accept her proposals as a basis for discussion and that a deal was expected.[27] Furthermore, it is known that a meeting of Fianna Fáil, Sinn Féin and IRA representatives was held on 26 April 1927 and that those who were present agreed on a set of proposals to submit to the executives of Sinn Féin and Fianna Fáil. It was agreed beforehand that the chairmen and vice chairmen of the respective organisations would meet on the understanding that any proposals for unity or co-operation in the coming elections, unanimously agreed to by these representatives, would be adopted as national policy. It was further agreed that if they failed to secure a policy for the elections, an effort would be made to arrive at an agreement as to the line to be followed by a Republican majority comprised of both parties if they took over the machinery of government, and that such an agreement would be published.[28]

De Valera himself was absent in America during these developments. On his return, he received a letter from MacSwiney informing him what had been happening and urging Fianna Fáil to drop its 'minority' position. She could not see why they could not join together. Foreshadowing a future dilemma for Fianna Fáil, she concluded that:

> There will be no going into the Parliament unless the Oath will be removed. There is not one chance in a thousand that the Oath will be removed if you only get a minority. Would it not be worth while telling that to the people, and promising not to use the minority position this time in order that we might join together and rouse the enthusiasm of the people which seems from all I hear possible to do at this juncture.[29]

De Valera replied in a short and negative manner, writing that the 'minority position' of Fianna Fáil was an essential part of the whole programme, and that to give it up would be 'to cripple the policy as a whole'. He accepted that MacSwiney could not agree with him, and so he felt that they should agree to differ. On the matter of preference votes, de Valera wrote that on their side they were determined that no Republican votes would be lost. Concluding, he stated that 'it is a pity that Sinn Féin cannot see eye to eye with us on our policy as a whole, for I believe that together on that programme we would be almost certain of success'.[30] De Valera's reply is interesting in that it indicates that Fianna Fáil did not want to tie itself down regarding possible entry into the Free State parliament after the election, even if the oath was not abolished. As subsequent events show, Fianna Fáil did enter the Dáil in July 1927 having taken the oath but in doing so, declared it to be an 'empty formula'. De Valera's reply marked a certain finality in relationships between Sinn Féin and Fianna Fáil. There was now no turning back for Fianna Fáil.

While the leadership of both organisations failed to come to an agreement, it is difficult to assess the situation at grass-roots level. However, the results indicate that the vast majority of former Sinn Féin supporters voted for Fianna Fáil.[31] Cumann na nGaedhael's platform was based on its record in office. In the words of its leader, W. T. Cosgrave, 'we believe that performance, not promise, should be the touchstone'.[32] It warned the electorate that the only alternative to the status quo was 'another round with Britain'. The party received considerable support from the media. During the election campaign, it revived memories of the Civil War, firmly laying the blame on the shoulders of Éamon de Valera. Fianna Fáil based its campaign on the abolition of the oath and the withholding of the land annuities. It also promised to promote the growth of tillage farming, to better the lot of the small farmer and to protect native manufacturing industry by imposing tariffs on imports.[33]

In Cork city, it is difficult to trace the individuals who split from Sinn Féin to join Fianna Fáil. Undoubtedly, the most important figure was the Lord Mayor, Seán French, who had performed very creditably in the 1924 by-election. Of course, Mary MacSwiney remained committed to abstentionism and became Vice-President of Sinn Féin. Fianna Fáil's organisation was weak in Cork city. It had as few as eight *cumainn* in

1926 and 1927 and this was reflected in its electoral performance in June 1927.[34] Mary MacSwiney and the MacSwiney name still held a certain influence over Republican Cork.

The June 1927 election in Cork marked the return of de Róiste to the electoral fray. Before the election, he recorded in his diary that there was a general expectation on all sides that Cumann na nGaedhael would be reduced in strength and that the party would be lucky to have two candidates elected in the city. The party's selection convention was held in May. According to de Róiste, the basis of representation was laid down by the Executive as 'all members of the present Executive, six additional from each *cumann* in the constituency and not more than ten others – selected by the Executive'. The latter proviso was adopted as a response to an idea expressed by some that 'we should have "important people"(people of money) at the Convention'.[35] Thus, the Executive of Cumann na nGaedhael in Cork had considerable influence over the composition of the party's candidates. According to de Róiste, the Executive wanted four candidates nominated: J. J. Walsh, TD, Barry Egan, Michael Egan, TD, and de Róiste himself. As events turned out, the four who were favoured by the Executive came through the Convention on the first round of voting.[36]

Fianna Fáil nominated three candidates: the Lord Mayor, Seán French; Dr Con Lucey, who had contested the 1923 election on behalf of Sinn Féin; and Seán O'Leary, the party's constituency delegate. Outgoing TD Mary MacSwiney was the Sinn Féin standard bearer while Frank Daly and Timothy Corcoran stood for the Farmers' Party. Richard Anthony and Edward Fitzgerald contested the election on behalf of Labour. The National League which had been founded by Captain William

Archer Redmond in 1926 from the remnants of the old Irish Parliamentary Party, nominated Councillor John J. Horgan to contest the election on its behalf.[37]

Both constitutional and economic issues received considerable attention during the election campaign. Cumann na nGaedhael defended its record in office and reminded people of the dislocation that had resulted from the Civil War, claiming that it had impeded the economic progress of the country. Fianna Fáil called for the abolition of the oath, the adoption of a more aggressive protectionist economic policy and endeavoured to present itself as a 'catch-all' party. Labour identified unemployment, housing, education and partition as issues on which the government was vulnerable. The National League also attacked the government for allowing partition to occur and in addition, campaigned for a reduction in taxation and public expenditure. The Farmers' Party argued for increased representation for farmers, in view of the fact that agriculture was the mainstay of the Irish economy.

At the Cumann na nGaedhael Convention in Cork, Peter Hughes, Minister for Defence, set the tone of the campaign when he launched a highly personal attack on de Valera:

> The head of Fianna Fáil was vain enough to do anything so long as his own vanity was secured. That self-same vanity in 1921 was having the country laid waste and buildings destroyed, with innumerable lives lost and money wasted that would never be returned to the country in their time. Because of the vanity of one individual they were unable to do three or four years ago what they were doing only now. He had split the national ranks and even then he could not keep his head, but

had to cause a split in his own party and he would not be surprised, if the present Fianna Fáil lasted any little time longer, to see him split that again.[38]

The annual convention had provided the government with an excellent opportunity for launching its campaign. Walsh presided and in his opening address, refuted arguments made by political opponents which held the government responsible for partition:

> The basis of partition was laid before any of them was born – laid elsewhere and not by Irishmen. All the materials for partition were in readiness at the time of the Treaty . . . he was satisfied that no opportunity had arisen during the lifetime of the present government whereby the unification of the country could have been secured.[39]

Significantly, T. P. Dowdall, who was to join Fianna Fáil within a matter of months, addressed the convention on the issue of protectionism, an issue which caused considerable friction within the party. Dowdall said he was pleased to hear that the government:

> were definitely in favour of the protectionist policy and did not intend to put on indiscriminate tariffs. They wanted tariffs to increase trade at a not unreasonable cost which would prevent unemployment and emigration. They wanted to be very certain of that matter for up to now they had had it in homeopathic doses. He hoped their policy would be a courageous one while avoiding anything in the nature of indiscriminate tariffs on articles that could not be produced economically in this country.[40]

President Cosgrave, however, addressing the convention on the issue, was more equivocal, stating that the government had set up a commission of top civil servants to obtain all the required information for a thorough consideration of each new tariff proposal. This was essentially a compromise between the advocates and the opponents of protectionism within the party. Cosgrave declared that the government was 'frankly protectionist' and that it believed that the list of commodities which could usefully and economically be subject to a tariff was not yet exhausted.[41]

Cumann na nGaedhael's major election rally in Cork took place on 7 June with a crowd of over 20,000 attending, according to the *Cork Examiner*. The main speaker was Kevin O'Higgins, Minister for Justice, and he was accompanied by the four Cumann na nGaedhael candidates. Senator J. C. Dowdall chaired the meeting. In his opening address, Dowdall declared that in the settlement that had been made 'by two great Irishmen, Arthur Griffith and Michael Collins, an agreement was reached that contained all the essentials of liberty'. He argued that the government had control over every essential service and he submitted that its 'splendid' record of achievement, together with the restoration of law, order and security, was in itself, a justification for the re-election of the government.[42] Although this type of rhetoric did not betray any latent dissatisfaction with the government, within months, Dowdall was to appear on Fianna Fáil platforms in the city.

Both Walsh and de Róiste spoke on the Treaty and constitutional issues, the latter claiming that it had been forced on them during the campaign. De Róiste stated that Cumann na nGaedhael stood for peace, security and progress. Walsh briefly alluded to protectionism and then spoke of the government's record, claiming that, but for the Civil War, much more would have been achieved:

> The depressing aftermath of the world war, the civil war, with its Mallow Bridge episode, and no less important the general political strike of 1923, were each and all contributory factors in the prevailing conditions.[43]

Likewise, Kevin O'Higgins concentrated on the Civil War and the government's record in office, stressing in particular, the improvements that had been effected in the agricultural sector.[44]

Fianna Fáil held its major election rally in Cork early in the campaign, on 9 May, with de Valera addressing a crowd of approximately 7,000.[45] In contrast to the extensive coverage given to the Cumann na nGaedhael campaign, the paper's report of the meeting was carried on a centre page under a small heading and in a narrow column.[46] In the course of a wide-ranging speech, de Valera condemned the oath and partition and declared that 'when they elected representatives who would refuse to take such an oath they would lay the foundation stone for real national progress.' He then dealt with the economic programme of Fianna Fáil, affirming that their guiding principle was the 'making of their island as self-contained and self-sufficient as possible'. He advocated support for native industries, in order to protect them 'from unfair outside competition by putting up barriers sufficiently subservient to the needs of the people'.[47]

Seán T. O'Kelly also made an interesting contribution stressing Fianna Fáil's opposition to the political dominance of sectional interests and that the party represented all classes:

Some might think that by electing farmers they could restore Ireland's economic prosperity – some that by electing Labour members that they would benefit themselves and their class and some were suggesting that the publicans' trade should put in members to represent their business. The people should remember that no one or two or three of these sections could ever bring back to Ireland the possibilities of prosperity that had been lost since the Free State was established. Any chance they had of restoring economic prosperity to Ireland could only be given to them by electing a majority of men and women, representing truly every class in the community who had the interests of the nation at heart. Fianna Fáil was such an organisation ready to take power – ready to direct the country on the road to economic reconstruction.[48]

The meeting was chaired by Lord Mayor Seán French, who claimed that Ireland was economically bankrupt and that only a restoration of the unity of 1921 would restore economic prosperity.[49]

On 11 May, the *Cork Examiner*, through its editorial, hit back at Fianna Fáil, reminding them of the destruction of bridges and railways carried out by the Republicans in 1923 which had destroyed trade in Cork. In relation to the oath, the editorial noted sarcastically:

Judging by what speakers said at the Grand Parade, Cork, on Monday night, the bad trade, unemployment, etc. is not due to the depression of the world markets for agricultural produce, or even to the iniquities of the Free State Government, but to the oath which members of the Dáil take do not wish [to take] to disenfranchise their constituencies. Until this Oath is 'repudiated' farmers cannot till land, feed pigs, sell clean eggs, creameries cannot manufacture good butter, boot factories cannot make good boots and shoes, mills cannot manufacture good tweed or sell it; nor can workers bend their backs to the task and produce just a little more to increase the well-being of the country.

Commenting on de Valera's trip to America, the editorial questioned the commitment of Irish-Americans to the Irish economy, claiming that only £300,000 worth of commodities were bought by Americans annually from the Irish Free State. The paper felt that if Irish-Americans concentrated more on buying Irish goods than on oaths and constitutions, they would make a greater contribution to the country:

At present the practical interest shown by Americans in buying Irish products does not quite balance the value of the Irish biscuits bought by the hereditary enemy and is not one sixteenth of her purchases of Irish stout, not to mention cattle, butter, eggs, etc.[50]

Fianna Fáil's Seán French concentrated on the economy in his election speeches, stating that the economic salvation of the country was at stake.[51] However, his colleagues on the panel concentrated on the constitutional issues, with Seán O'Leary declaring that Fianna Fáil appealed for 'one Ireland and that Ireland free'. He attacked the treatment of workers on the Shannon scheme and condemned the underdevelopment of the fishing industry.[52] At a meeting in Blackrock on 7 June Dr Con Lucey appealed to the hurling fraternity of the area for support. He declared that 'he was depending on the spirit of the GAA which he knew was at its highest level in Blackrock to rally the people of that area under that banner, that of the Republican Party and of a free, happy and prosperous country'. He concluded by complimenting the chairman of the Cork County Board of the GAA for keeping the Association out of politics.[53]

The National League identified partition, the Boundary Agreement and the economy as the major issues in the campaign. At a meeting held on 1 May, the party's candidate, John J. Horgan, declared that the government had completely surrendered all of its interests in the North. He invited 'the attention of the Nationalists of the South to the fate of their brethren in the North and to the humiliation to all Irish nationalists of having their country partitioned.' The party leader, Captain William Redmond, attacked the government for its 'failure' in economic terms, citing unemployment, poverty, high taxation and excessive public expenditure as the major manifestations of this failure.[54] At a meeting held on 6 June, Horgan again reiterated the National League's concern with unemployment and high public expenditure.[55]

The Farmers' Party had two candidates in the field, County Councillor Tim Corcoran and Frank J. Daly, chairman of the Cork Harbour Commissioners. Both candidates concentrated on economic issues. Corcoran appealed for support on the grounds that agricultural industry was the basis of the country's economic and cultural life and called for a reduction in both taxation and public expenditure. Daly also spoke about high public expenditure and excessive taxation and appealed to all parties:

> to put aside futile and dangerous discussions about oaths, treaties, etc. which only tended to divide Irish men and to concentrate instead on the

practical policy on which all could agree, and that was to assist and develop our industries in order to provide a means of livelihood for the people.[56]

These demands for lower taxation and reductions in public expenditure were rejected by Labour. At a meeting held on 6 June, Richard Anthony argued that a more 'equitable levying of taxation and the more useful expenditure of the proceeds were of more concern to the Labour Party than its reduction'. He felt that public expenditure cuts would affect the working class severely and that education and housing would inevitably come under the axe. He saw the reform of the taxation system in terms of a redistribution of wealth from the wealthier to the poorer classes:

> In so far as the money is taken from the rich and spent by salary and wage earners and pensioners, what happened is that a demand for fur coats, motor cars and other imported luxuries is converted into a demand for Irish bacon, mutton, beef, butter, potatoes, oatmeal, stout, pork, etc. What they needed was more of this kind of expenditure met by taxation of superfluities and distributed without extravagance.[57]

The Labour Party launched its campaign in Cork on 1 May with a major rally. Its speakers identified unemployment, housing and education as the party's priorities. But at that meeting, Edward Fitzgerald spoke at length on the Northern issue and argued that Labour was the only party that could unite the people of Ireland. He cited the 'gatherings' at the party's annual congress as evidence of the party's capacity to attract members and supporters from all parts of the country. He declared that Labour would establish one government for the whole of Ireland, a government which would abolish:

> double customs, double police forces, double civil services, and many other duplicate administrations, and the big savings in such directions could then be devoted in the promotion and development of the industries that would secure employment and prosperity.

On public expenditure, he argued that only the poor and the working classes would suffer in the event of further cutbacks. He also attacked the disparity between the minimum wage paid to German and Irish workers on the Shannon scheme, the latter receiving much less.[58] Anthony, at the same meeting, attacked the manner in which, under the railway unification and amalgamation scheme, 'highly placed officials and managements got decent pensions and gratuities but the shopmen and workingmen on the railways were put on the scrap heap, or else on the three quarter time'.[59] Thus, it can be seen that, once again, Labour's candidates in Cork articulated their policies in clear, simple language and avoided political abstractions. The issues they raised were directly concerned with the realities of the day, i.e. wages on the Shannon scheme, housing and reductions in the old-age pensions. Labour was battling to win back a seat it had lost in 1923.

Bishop Cohalan also commented on the approaching election in the form of a letter to the *Cork Examiner*. Stating that he did not want to influence a single voter, he felt that the vast majority of the electorate wanted peace and public order. However, he did question whether or not it:

would contribute to public order if a number of
elected members were to continue the policy of
abstention from the Dáil? It surely would be a very
serious thing for the country. I do not suggest the
likelihood of it – if it were contemplated to set up a
rival assembly to the Dáil.[60]

Clearly, Dr Cohalan was indicating his opposition to
continued abstention from Dáil Éireann, a policy to which
Fianna Fáil was still committed, pending resolution of the
question of the oath. The Bishop observed that education,
agriculture, the Shannon scheme, protectionism and
reducing public expenditure were the main issues of the
campaign and that there was:

considerable agreement amongst most of the parties
on principles and on policies. The question for the
elector is: Which of the rival parties is most likely to
give effect to these principles and policies to promote
the general interest of the country, to maintain peace
and public order?[61]

The *Cork Examiner* had no doubt whatsoever as to
which party was not suitable for government. In an
editorial on 7 June, the paper blamed the country's
economic ills on the Civil War and the opposition to the
Anglo-Irish Treaty which had brought it about. The
people responsible for that opposition, declared the
paper, had cost the country millions of pounds and were
responsible for the prevailing misery:

Directly or indirectly the opposition to the Treaty
must have cost the country close on 100 millions.
And the people who are primarily responsible for
that ask the country to hand over the country to

them. Whatever fault the country may find with the present government or with the Farmers' Party or the Labour Party they will think more than twice before they install the visionaries of Fianna Fáil in power. The people have had enough of trouble already.[62]

Therefore, the *Cork Examiner*, unlike the Bishop, gave a clear and unequivocal direction to the electorate.

On the day after polling, the paper also noted that there had been considerable activity in and around the polling booths with 'all kinds of vehicles, especially motors' being used to bring voters to the polls, with three parties, Cumann na nGaedhael, Fianna Fáil and the Farmers' party, 'strongly supplied with such facilities'. On the behaviour of the participants the paper commented:

> One of the outstanding features of the polling throughout the entire constituency was the complete absence of any untoward incidents. It was uneventful in this respect and was probably the most orderly and efficiently conducted election in the South of Ireland for many years.[63]

This view is corroborated by de Róiste who noted in his diary that the election reflected toleration and goodwill.[64]

The results in Cork however were a severe disappointment for de Róiste and Cumann na nGaedhael. Although Walsh topped the poll, his first-preference vote of 1923 was halved. His later recollection of the result was slightly more rose-tinted.

> Starting with the Sinn Féin Election of 1918, I was elected on four successive occasions for Cork City. My vote, on all occasions except the last, was in the

neighbourhood of twenty-two thousands, which is the highest average vote ever recorded for a candidate in this country. In the 1924 election, so sweeping was the verdict that three of the four remaining candidates were swept in on my surplus. Certainly no man has ever had less reason to quarrel with the electorate.[65]

Labour recovered well from its 1923 debacle, with Richard Anthony comfortably taking a seat despite the fact that Independent Labour candidate, P. J. Bradley, polled an impressive 2,246 first preference votes. The overall Republican vote actually declined from the 1923 level of 18 per cent to 15 per cent. Nevertheless, Seán French was elected for Fianna Fáil. It was a particularly important victory for the party, since the seat had been taken from Mary MacSwiney. As one of Sinn Féin's best-known and influential figures, her defeat in Cork clearly signalled the disillusionment of rank-and-file Republicans with the policy of abstention from Dáil Éireann. John J. Horgan, a former member of Cumann na nGaedhael, was elected for the National League and that party's success seems to have been at Cumann na nGaedhael's expense. Barry Egan won the fifth seat for Cumann na nGaedhael without reaching the quota.[66]

In its review of the election results, the *Cork Examiner* noted that although no party had received an overall majority, the results represented a clear ratification of the Anglo-Irish Treaty and the Free State constitution.[67] The paper reflected on the reasons for Cumann na nGaedhael's poor performance. The party's disregard for public opinion was judged to be the major factor, followed closely by the over-officiousness of income tax officials, over-zealous customs officers and a costly and inefficient postal system. The *Cork Examiner* also suggested that thousands of parents had objected to compulsory Irish in the schools. However, the paper took heart from the fact that electorally, Sinn Féin 'has been wiped out of existence to all intents and purposes. Fianna Fáil has gained little in spite of its Utopian "economic programme". On a clear-cut issue for or against the Treaty the Government would have won hands down'. And in relation to the government, it declared: 'Nor can the country have forgotten the incalculable services which the Government whatever its minor faults rendered the country in the hour of need'.[68]

Nationally Cumann na nGaedhael dropped up to 12 per cent on its 1923 performance and polled a disappointing 27.38 per cent of the vote. Fianna Fáil polled 26.22 per cent, slightly lower than Sinn Féin in 1923. The Labour Party received 12.5 per cent of the poll, while Independents received a significant 13.51 per cent share. The National League picked up 7.36 per cent while the Farmers' Party won 8.85 per cent. The two minor Republican parties, Sinn Féin and Clann Éireann, mustered a little less than 4 per cent of the vote.[69] Clearly, at this juncture, a multi-party system had emerged with the two Treaty parties gaining just over 50 per cent of the total vote between them. Sectional interests polled well, demonstrating again that the Irish electorate in the post-Civil War period was concerned with economic and social issues as well as constitutional questions. The content of the various party campaigns in Cork reflected this, with economic and social matters receiving considerable attention.

The post-election situation brought its challenges for Fianna Fáil. The most immediate of these related to the oath and admission to Dáil Éireann. At the first meeting of the Fianna Fáil parliamentary party after the election, de Valera read from opinions submitted by counsel (A.

Wood, KC, James Creed Meredith, KC, and George Gavan Duffy, BL) to the effect 'that there was no legal authority in any person to exclude from the Dáil, before the Election of the Ceann Comhairle, any member who had not subscribed to the Oath'. After discussion, it was then decided that in the event of the Fianna Fáil TDs being present in the Dáil, Seán T. O'Kelly would be proposed for the position of Ceann Comhairle. Finally it was decided that if admission was refused a public meeting of protest would be held at College Green immediately afterwards.[70] On 23 June, the opening day of the Dáil, the Clerk of the Dáil, when presented with the legal opinion obtained by Fianna Fáil, simply rejected it and ruled that the TDs of that party could not enter the Dáil unless they were prepared to take the oath. At a parliamentary party meeting held later that day, the Fianna Fáil TDs signed a declaration which repeated their election pledge that 'under no circumstances whatsoever will they subscribe to any such oath'.[71] And on 18 July, de Valera, at another meeting of the Fianna Fáil party, referring to moves which had been made, and would be made, to try to force Fianna Fáil to take the oath, asked if 'there [was] any member of our Party who would be willing to take the oath of allegiance in the Free State constitution under any circumstances whatsoever?' There was no reply, though Deputy Belton did say that he had no moral qualms about taking the oath and that if the party did not succeed, he might have to review his position.[72]

The situation was dramatically changed by the murder of Kevin O'Higgins, Minister for Justice and Vice-President of the Executive Council, on 10 July 1927. He had been one of the most able and controversial ministers of the Cumann na nGaedhael governments since the foundation of the state.[73] The government reacted strongly, drafting a new and stronger Public Safety Bill which became law on 11 August. Secondly, legislation was introduced, in the form of an Electoral Amendment Bill, which provided that every candidate for election to the Dáil had to affirm on nomination that he or she was prepared to take the oath. Finally, the government proposed to amend the constitution in order to restrict the call for a referendum to members of the Dáil who had taken the oath. This last measure was designed to thwart the campaign which had been initiated by Fianna Fáil for a referendum to abolish the oath. Under Article 47 of the Free State constitution, a referendum could be held if a demand for it was backed by 75,000 signatures. Since July, Fianna Fáil had been busy collecting those signatures and had succeeded in amassing a considerable number. However, it was the second measure which required a statement of intent to take the oath which was of the greatest significance because it effectively closed the door on abstention and created an uncertain political situation. All opposition parties in the Dáil were opposed to such measures and public opinion in general was hostile. Many felt abstentionism was a safety valve. In addition, there was a good deal of disquiet over the government's intention to tamper with the constitution merely because it suited its own political needs.[74]

On 26 July, de Valera read to the Fianna Fáil parliamentary party the draft of a guarantee which he had drawn up with representatives of the Labour Party. He was prepared to give the guarantee and urged his colleagues to do likewise. The draft read as follows:

In the event of a Coalition Government being formed and succeeding in securing that all representatives of the people be free to enter the Twenty-Six

County Assembly without subscribing to any political test, the Fianna Fáil party will not press any issues involving the Treaty to the point of overthrowing such Government during the normal lifetime of the present Assembly.

The meeting gave full consent to de Valera's action, and clearly the way had been opened for negotiations to begin with Labour. The meeting decided also to continue collecting signatures in favour of holding a referendum to abolish the oath.[75]

However, at the parliamentary party meeting of 5 August, the winds of change were evident. For the first time, the secretary used the word 'formula' to describe the oath. A discussion was held as to whether or not commitments which had already been given precluded the deputies, even 'in the present emergency from deviating from our former line of action and the strict letter of our pledges with respect to non-subscription to the Free State formula for entry into the Free State Parliament'. The general view of the meeting was that if the issue were put to constituency conventions, they would release the party members from their pledges. It was accepted that whatever decision was arrived at would be accepted by the party as a whole. A sub-committee was then appointed to examine whether the party could defeat the government's measures by taking their seats in the Dáil.[76] A special meeting of the full National Executive was then arranged for 9 August to consider what action the Fianna Fáil TDs should take in relation to the present political situation. When it met, the National Executive decided by 47 votes to 7 to give the party deputies a free hand in deciding the issue.[77]

Meanwhile, negotiations between Fianna Fáil and Labour leaders were taking place with a view to deciding upon a strategy to defeat the Cumann na nGaedhael government in the Dáil.[78] On 6 August, de Valera, Seán T. O'Kelly and Gerry Boland met Thomas Johnson, William O'Brien and Luke Duffy of the Labour Party. At this meeting Johnson, the Labour leader, stated that his party would 'surely as a natural outcome of their policy be in favour of the abolition of the Oath by negotiation and of political tests for employment and the coercion, electoral amendment and constitutional amendment acts'.[79] On 8 August, O'Kelly, Boland and Frank Aiken put certain queries to Johnson and O'Brien. In effect, these queries were a set of demands calling on any government elected to immediately withdraw the Constitutional Amendment Bill, the Electoral Amendment Bill and the Public Safety Bill. It was also demanded that all political tests for employment in the public service be abolished and that steps be taken to allow elected representatives who had conscientious objections to the oath to take their seats without having to subscribe to it.[80] Johnson answered the queries in the form of a memo which he gave to Boland. In this memo, he committed the Labour Party to either withdraw or repeal the three contentious bills. On the oath, Labour would negotiate for its abolition with the British government. If a referendum resulted in a vote in favour of abolition, Labour would introduce legislation to give effect to such a mandate.[81] On 12 August, de Valera and O'Kelly met Johnson at 1.30 p.m. and again four hours later. At these meetings, Johnson said that in his view, it was unlikely that Labour would form part of a coalition with de Valera at its head but that he could come to an agreement with the National League with a view to forming a coalition.[82]

In any event, at the sixth meeting of the Fianna Fáil parliamentary party, Seán T. O'Kelly reported on behalf of the special committee that had been appointed on 6 August. He read documents which had been signed by Johnson and Captain Redmond in which they declared that their parties were in favour of abolishing the oath by negotiation, the repeal of the Public Safety Acts, and the establishment of the machinery for the initiation of constitutional amendments by the people. After a general discussion, it was decided that the party's elected deputies would take their seats in the Dáil, having made it clear beforehand that in taking this action, they had no intention of giving allegiance to the king.[83] In accordance with this decision, on 12 August the Fianna Fáil deputies entered the Dáil chamber and occupied their seats. In the public statement issued by the party on their behalf, it was claimed that the oath was nothing more than an 'empty formula' and that given the 'national emergency' that had been created by the government's legislation and the possibility that, as they saw it, such legislation might endanger the general peace, they were not going to allow themselves be debarred from exercising their functions as public representatives by an 'empty formula'.[84]

An attempt was made to defeat the government on 16 August when a motion of 'no confidence' was moved by the Labour leader, Thomas Johnson. Should the government be defeated, it had been agreed that Labour and the National League would form a coalition government supported by Fianna Fáil. A government defeat seemed inevitable because Fianna Fáil, the National League and the Labour Party together had one vote more than the government. However, John Jinks of Sligo, a member of the National League, failed to turn up to vote, having been persuaded that his constituents would not approve of him voting with de Valera.[85] The vote on the motion of no confidence ended in a tie and the Ceann Comhairle voted in favour of the government. President Cosgrave, however, realising the precarious nature of the government's position in the Dáil dissolved the Dáil and another general election was called.

Fianna Fáil had been encouraged to enter the Dáil by the prospect of defeating the Cumann na nGaedheal government. Although its initial attempt to achieve this objective had failed, it was now totally committed to the parliamentary process. At the parliamentary party meeting held immediately after the vote of no confidence, all members 'were instructed to familiarise themselves with the local needs of their constituencies, so that they could press them on the reopening of the Free State Assembly'.[86] Cumann na nGaedheal did not do the same. The entry of Fianna Fáil into the Dáil had been crucial to the development of the Irish party political system in that a major group which had hitherto stayed outside parliament, and indeed, had refused to recognise it, was now firmly part of the process and was no longer a potentially destabilising force in the state. One could argue that since the break-up of the old Sinn Féin party, de Valera had been heading in this direction and correspondence with Mary MacSwiney in the period leading up to the election seems to confirm this. De Valera had determined to work the system as it was. Certainly, he would have preferred to enter the Dáil without having to take the oath but he was not prepared to allow the oath to stop him from doing so. This is illustrated by his remarks to the parliamentary party meeting held on 5 August 1927:

The Chief then asked if members believed that the Free State formula must, in the condition of the future, be subscribed to by those who are going to remove it, did they think we should do it now rather than leave it to others? All who were present answered yes, except Frank Carney.[87]

It is clear that de Valera was committed to constitutional politics and had no intention of engaging in extra-parliamentary activities or indeed, of renewing hostilities with the Free State government. It is true that the government's legislation had placed him in a dilemma. Equally so, he believed (incorrectly, as it turned out) that his party's entry into the Dáil would result in the immediate defeat of the government. Nonetheless, his decision to enter the Dáil, oath and all, must rank as a courageous political decision which in the long term brought stability to Irish politics. The Electoral Amendment Act had presented him with a dilemma with, as Joseph Lee has noted, 'his stature possibly damaged by the capitulation . . . Seeing no oath, hearing no oath, speaking no oath, signing no oath, the Soldiers of Destiny shuffled into Dáil Éireann'.[88] Much to Cumann na nGaedhael's displeasure, they came as a united band.

The idea of Labour in government with the National League belongs to the realm of speculation. However, it can be argued that if Jinks had attended and voted against the government on 16 August 1927, then the Irish party political system would have evolved in a very different way. Finally, as will be demonstrated later, Fianna Fáil's entry into the Dáil helped to broaden its support base considerably and people who, up to this juncture, had been supporters of the institutions of the Irish Free State, were now prepared to support Fianna Fáil on the basis that it was now firmly on the constitutional path.

The calling of a second election so soon after the June election was calculated to freeze out the smaller parties. On the Republican side, Sinn Féin and Clann Éireann were unable to nominate candidates. Clann Éireann's national executive urged party members to support Fianna Fáil. On the other side, Cumann na nGaedheal came to an arrangement with the Farmers' Party. In addition, a number of Independents joined Cumann na nGaedhael to contest the election.[89] It was a whirlwind campaign with newspaper advertisements playing a dominant role. Cumann na nGaedheal hired a public relations firm, O'Kennedy Brindley Ltd, to handle its publicity.[90] Undoubtedly the fact that the election took place only three months after the June contest militated against the smaller parties which did not have the resources to mount an effective campaign. Furthermore, Cumann na nGaedhael benefitted from the sympathy aroused by the murder of Kevin O'Higgins. However, for the first time since the Treaty, the entry of Fianna Fáil into the Dáil placed the mantle of 'alternative President' on de Valera. From now on, the choice was not only between Cumann na nGaedheal and Fianna Fáil but also between Cosgrave and de Valera. The decision by Fianna Fáil to take the oath did not harm the party in electoral terms. The personality of de Valera was also crucial and played no small part in Fianna Fáil's advance. He had already acquired an aura of leadership and by the force of his personality alone appeared at the time as the only credible alternative to Cosgrave. Nevertheless, the outcome of the election was that Cosgrave, with the help of the Farmers and some Independents, formed another administration.

The September 1927 general election campaign in Cork was remarkable for its many surprises, most notably the departure of J. J. Walsh, Minister for Posts and Telegraphs, to the continent, ostensibly for health reasons. In a telegram sent to Barry Egan, chairman of the Cumann na nGaedhael Executive in Cork and published in the *Cork Examiner* on 3 September, Walsh wrote: 'Please withdraw my name from nomination, cannot in national interest support Free Trade Coalition. Please publish this fully'.[91] It had been an open secret for many years that Walsh was on a collision course with the cabinet over the question of protectionism versus free trade. As far back as May 1927, de Róiste had outlined in his diary how a deep cleavage was developing on the issue within Cumann na nGaedhael. He recorded that Walsh was making a bid for the leadership of those who supported protectionism and that he was prepared to split the government party on the question before the next general election if the Executive Council did not accept 'whole-hog' protectionism.[92] In the June general election campaign, Walsh allegedly urged Seán Milroy to stand against the party in Dublin North. *The Irish Times'* political correspondent even claimed 'that Walsh had suggested a merger with elements of Fianna Fáil at a Cabinet meeting before his departure from Ireland'. Although John Regan admits that this story was never substantiated, rumours of 'a new Cumann na nGaedhael–Fianna Fáil reorientation' were current in Cork in late August and 'de Róiste suspected that Walsh was behind the move'.[93]

In another entry, dated 22 February 1927, de Róiste described a meeting of the Cumann na nGaedhael Ard homhairle at which he was present:

> Chief contentious matter on the Agenda of the meeting was that of a protective tariff policy for agricultural products. It occupied about four hours discussion. The majority seemed strongly in favour of such a policy. Hogan opposed. Blythe opposed. Practically admitted – at least assumed that if put to a vote, the Ard Chomhairle would endorse the policy by a majority.

However, Walsh did not force a vote on the issue and as a result, the motion was simply sent as 'a recommendation to the government'.[94] Responding to the reference in Walsh's telegram to the 'Free Trade Coalition', Cosgrave said he could not understand it. He told the *Cork Examiner* that 50 per cent of imports (inclusive of agricultural produce) were being tariffed.[95] On 6 September, as news of Walsh's resignation appeared in the press, Cosgrave traveled to Cork city to 'steady the party'. Nevertheless, by 13 September, the Dowdall brothers had defected to Fianna Fáil.[96]

For its own economic reasons, Cork city had a strong lobby in favour of protectionism. Nearly all the major political personalities in the city favoured such a policy. The Dowdall brothers, Flinn, de Róiste, O'Rahilly and Barry Egan were all committed protectionists. They were also part of the Irish-Ireland group in the city which had founded an Industrial Development Association and a successful newspaper and which, since the beginning of the century, had been active in fostering the ideals of Irish Ireland in the cultural, economic and political spheres.[97] De Róiste noted a waning in the group's influence within Cumann na nGaedhael and commented on a new orientation within the party involving the elimination of those who, in his words, 'bore the brunt of the battle since 1918, and the bringing in of 'business men' and possibly "farmers", men who were not active politicians in the revolutionary years'.[98]

De Róiste himself was not considered by the Cumann na nGaedhael Executive for nomination and his diary entries provide a very detailed account of the behind-the-scenes manoeuvrings within the party. At the actual meeting of the Executive to select candidates in Cork, Walsh and Egan, the two outgoing deputies, were nominated. Then Mrs Collins-Powell nominated Alexander

Healy, nephew of the Governor General, to be followed by Michael J. Nagle. At this stage, before a fifth candidate was nominated, Egan took a letter from his pocket, signed by President Cosgrave on behalf of the Standing Committee in Dublin, containing names suggested for the Cork constituency. The names were those of James Dwyer of Dwyer & Co., Willie Dinan of Eustace & Co., and M. J. Nagle with, of course, those of the sitting representatives. Egan and Healy then left the room to contact Dwyer and Dinan. However, Dwyer refused to stand and Dinan could not be located. De Róiste was then proposed but replied: 'I said "no" I have no money. You have run after the men of money. Continue to do so'.[99] De Róiste felt bitter that he and Michael Egan had not been among those originally considered, or at least given the opportunity of refusing to become candidates. They had faced defeat in June when the government was unpopular and moreover, de Róiste had been only pipped in the June election by Barry Egan. But Cosgrave's intervention had antagonised others apart from de Róiste. 'Mary Collins-Powell 'flared-up': '1916 is of course forgotten . . . so are all those who ever did anything in the fighting days'. De Róiste summed up the alienation: 'The new "orientation" is accomplished in Cork at least'. As Hart has concluded, 'the O'Higginisation of Cumann na nGaedheal outlived its mentor'.[100]

Already troubled by the issues of partition and protection, Walsh had also become disillusioned with the party. As he later recalled in his autobiography, despite his efforts as chairman of the party, 'to many of us it was clear that it only needed time to kill Cumann na nGaedheal. Under Mr Cosgrave's leadership, it had no policy for the development of the resources of the nation . . . Its complete eclipse would long since have been a national gain'.[101] Like de Róiste, he was frustrated by politics and even public service:

> That the people had grown tired of abuse as a substitute for what had been expected from a native Government became clearer day by day, and everywhere a Minster went he was confronted with the cry 'What about your seventeen hundred?' This was the Ministers' salary. The salt on this salary issue was further rubbed in by the frequent assertion that not one of the Ministers could earn his own livelihood. Without a hope of doing further service to the country through politics, and smarting under the taunt that I could not earn my own living, though I had managed the biggest enterprise in the country and saved the taxpayer the annual deficit of over a million a year, I decided that never again would I take a cent of the public's money. When the autumn elections of 1927 were announced, I determined to get out and stay out. It was a long and trying road from that stormy November night, in 1913, when we started the Volunteers in the City Hall, to the same month in 1927, when I shook the dust of politics from my feet. It was worth it all, but I wouldn't care to go through it again. Once in a lifetime is enough.[102]

Cosgrave was in Cork when news of Walsh's definite refusal was published. De Róiste met the president and offered to stand as a candidate if he would approve. Such a candidature would show that despite Walsh's behaviour and the defection of the Dowdalls to Fianna Fáil, there was not going to be a general stampede from Cumann na nGaedhael. De Róiste recalled that before Cosgrave could reply, a four-man deputation, including two priests, arrived proposing that Cosgrave himself should stand in Cork. At a public meeting that night, Barry Egan announced that President Cosgrave had agreed to be a candidate for Cork. Thus, it might be argued that Moss' conclusion is not complete:

> There is a general dislike for the 'carpet-bagger', the candidate from some other part of the country who is presented to the constituency by the central office. But if they be a party leader of renown, the county may feel honoured that he should be its representative. Thus Cosgrave successfully stood for both Cork Borough and Carlow–Kilkenny in September 1927.[103]

Both de Róiste and Michael Egan refused to speak at public meetings during the election. De Róiste commented that 'it was my farewell. I now knew I was not wanted by the coterie that controls Cumann na nGaedhael.'[104] In relation to the evolution of the Cumann na nGaedhael party, de Róiste's assessment was that:

> To a large extent Cumann na nGaedael has gone over to the older elements in Irish politics – ex-Unionists, ex-Redmondites, ex-O'Brienites. The leaven of younger elements, those who were of the original Sinn Féin, Volunteers, Gaelic League movements, is small.[105]

De Róiste's account of events also indicates the loose manner in which Cumann na nGaedheal candidates were selected in Cork to contest the September general election. There did not appear to be a formal structure through which candidates could be selected. The evolution of the party, as outlined by de Róiste, is also interesting. One cannot help drawing the conclusion that since its foundation, the Cumann na nGaedhael party had a fluctuating membership, with people coming and going and that it failed to establish solid foundations upon which to build. During its early years, loyalty to the Treaty was the binding force, but over time this bond weakened considerably.

Fianna Fáil nominated Seán French, Hugo Flinn and Dr Con Lucey to stand while Richard Anthony and Luke Duffy stood for Labour. Outgoing Deputy John J. Horgan, stood once again for the National League.[106] Flinn's nomination reflects a significant broadening of Fianna Fáil's electoral base. He was a wealthy man, associated with the business community of the city and had participated in a 'no income tax' movement in 1925. He was the perfect answer to any allegations that Fianna Fáil was a party destined for 'another round with Britain'. In addition, the Dowdall brothers, Senator J. C. and T. P. (the latter of whom was to be elected as a Fianna Fáil TD), left Cumann na nGaedheal and appeared at Fianna Fáil election meetings, denouncing the government and assuring the business community that there was no need to fear the Fianna Fáil party. In particular, they spoke out against the new Public Safety Act. In one such election address, T. P. Dowdall condemned the Act and declared that those who had conceived it had no right to be in charge of the government of any country. He went on to assure the business community that it would be in their interests not to be misled into thinking that the country was in danger because a party which had hitherto refrained from going into the Dáil had now entered it. He had only been on the Fianna Fáil platform for a few days, he said, and even though he was not an official exponent of that party's viewpoint, he knew 'sufficient about it to know that they were going to work this country on constitutional lines and for the benefit of all the people'.[107] The Dowdall defection was not exceptional, nor was the like peculiar to Cork city or Cumann na nGaedhael. By 1932, Fianna Fáil counted ex-members of Cumann na nGaedhael, Sinn Féin, Labour, the National League, Clann Éireann and the National Group among its candidates. More tellingly, the converts included leading Cumann na nGaedhael figures. Along with Walsh, Robert Barton, one of the signatories of the 1921 Treaty, campaigned for Fianna Fáil on the grounds that 'Collins and Griffith had been betrayed by the Cosgrave administration.'[108]

Cumann na nGaedhael concentrated on its record in office and highlighted the inexperience and 'dangerous' nature of Fianna Fáil. In a clever advertisement in the *Cork Examiner*, the party argued that:

> If Mr de Valera has really seen the error of his ways as he now confesses, he owes it to the country to do full and ample penance by working loyally and submissively as the leader of a Minority party in the Parliament of the people until there can no longer be any doubt about his sincerity. Only after such a Probation can you be sure that he has really reformed.[109]

The *Cork Examiner* itself took up the same theme, declaring that those who wanted peace and stability should vote for the government candidates and that by the end of the next five years de Valera and his followers would have learned a lot.[110]

Fianna Fáil countered this line by concentrating on social and economic issues and by emphasising that it was not about to cause a revolution if elected. In a remarkable message addressed 'To the People of Ireland', de Valera declared:

The sinister design of aiming at bringing about a sudden revolutionary upheaval with which our opponents choose to credit us is altogether foreign to our purpose and programme. Our first and most strenuous effort must accordingly be devoted to repairing the present economic ruin.

There was no mention of the oath in this message and constitutional issues were, in general, played down.[111] Throughout the campaign, Fianna Fáil candidates across the country concentrated on economic issues, and Cork's candidates were no different. Despite the shadows and the gunmen on Cumann na nGaedhael's posters, social and economic differences were as important as any other issue.[112]

Speaking in Passage West on 9 September, Deputy Seán French declared that Fianna Fáil was an economic party which 'would attempt to improve the economic condition of the country according to the will of the people'.[113] At a meeting in Douglas, Hugo Flinn attacked the Public Safety Act before he committed Fianna Fáil to reversing the emigration of both labour and capital:

They would bring back the 250 millions of capital across the water by discrimination in taxation and induce the people to put that money into their own mills and guard them against unjust foreign competition.

At the same meeting T. P. Dowdall, stressed that there would be no chaos if Fianna Fáil was returned to power, and said that the party was in favour of a 'well-balanced' policy of protection for agriculture and for industry.[114] Fianna Fáil's election advertisements also contained a heavy emphasis on economic issues. For example, one juxtaposed de Valera's assertion that the primary duty of a modern state was to provide employment with Patrick McGilligan's infamous speech as Minister for Industry and Commerce in the Dáil in 1924, when he had stated that it was not the function of the Dáil to provide work.[115]

Observing the emphasis being placed on economic issues by Fianna Fáil speakers, the *Cork Examiner* reacted strongly. An editorial on 12 September declared that the main issue in the election was whether Treaty would be honoured. Commenting on Fianna Fáil's economic policy, the editorial continued:

> Some new converts to the Fianna faith are particularly strong on the economic position. Nothing is said from Fianna platforms – least of all by the new converts [possibly a reference to the Dowdalls and Hugo Flinn] – about what could have been done to develop the country with the huge amount – certainly not less than forty to fifty millions – which Mr de Valera's opposition to the Treaty cost the country. Folk in Cork are told about the high salaries paid to judges and heads of departments, but they are not reminded of how much more the destruction of Mallow Bridge cost.[116]

Cumann na nGaedhael concentrated on its record in office and in particular, on its success in restoring peace and stability after the Civil War. Speaking in Cork on 12 September, the party leader, W. T. Cosgrave, declared that the party was standing in this election for a 'single army, the balancing of the budget, helping industry, improving the public services, and keeping their word in the Parliament of the people'.[117]

At the launch of the party's campaign, speakers attacked Fianna Fáil on the issue of the oath and constantly warned of the possibility of a return to the Civil War days. Barry Egan justified the recent Public Safety Act on the grounds that there was a large criminal element across in the country who had to be dealt with. Egan concluded his speech by reminding his listeners of the local horrors of the Civil War:

> While those people were peace-making, and appealing for reconciliation they however, never uttered one word of regret for the misery and poverty and trouble caused by the destruction of Mallow Bridge. Was that for the good of Ireland, or for an ideal that would mean the building of houses and factories that were badly needed.

M. J. Nagle saw the election issue in even blunter terms:

> It was whether they were to go back to the condition of affairs which prevailed in '21 or '22 or whether they were going to have peace and order, security and happiness maintained in the country.

And Eoin Mac Néill commented that 'it took them five years to find out about the "empty formula" and what I'd now ask you to do is to give them five years more to find out other things'.[118]

Clearly, Cumann na nGaedhael felt that the Civil War was still a relevant electoral issue, and of course Kevin O'Higgins' murder gave them the opportunity to revive issues such as the need for public order and stability. The *Catholic Bulletin* made its feelings particularly clear on this tactic:

> The Free State Party survived up to the last Election, by virtue of the calamities of the Civil War! These it recited to the electors ad nauseam.

The whole case of Cumann na nGaedhael consisted in a recapitulation of the burnings, shootings, and depredations of Republicans in 1922–1923.[119]

Cumann na nGaedhael was supported unequivocally by the Cork Progressive Association – a body which had two candidates elected to Dáil Éireann in 1923. This organisation represented a broad spectrum of business and commercial interests in the city. Significantly, a meeting of the Association held on 9 September was dominated by speakers praising the government for its efforts in establishing peace and stability after the Civil War.[120]

The Labour deputy, Richard Anthony, attacked the Progressive Association's endorsement of the Cumann na Gaedhael government which, in his view, was the 'most reactionary' that ever existed in any country. Of the members of the Association, he had this to say:

They need only read the names of those attending the meeting of that association, to know they were men pledged to a long term of coercion for this country. Buckshot Foster or Oliver Cromwell would turn in their graves at the idea of the Public Safety Act.

Anthony concluded by saying that Fianna Fáil members were brother Irishmen and that the hand of friendship should be extended to them or any party that was prepared to work constitutionally for the country's benefit.[121]

Labour concentrated on social and economic issues, as it had done in June. On 14 September, the party outlined the policy programme that would have emerged if Labour had manage to form government with the National League in July:

Preference would be given in all public employment to men with families instead of the present preference which is given to ex-National Army men. If ex-National army men had dependents they would be given the fullest consideration, but the preference would be given because of the number of dependants. They would have already cancelled the ordinance which limits the wages paid to men on public road works to 26/-, 27/-, 28/- and 30/- per week in 25 counties out of 26. They would have increased the wages being paid on the Shannon scheme. They would have altered and improved the administrative arrangements in respect of payment of unemployment insurance. They would have reversed the instructions that had been given in the Old Age Pensions Department which have so unfairly deprived many pensioners of what they are entitled to. They would have taken steps to restore the 1/- cut to the old age pensioners. They would have put in hand a scheme for widows and orphans pensions.[122]

The programme illustrates how Labour remained very much attuned to the electoral realities of the day. It made straightforward, concrete proposals which would have considerably benefited the poor and the working class, in simple, understandable language and without socialist rhetoric.

On the issue of revising the Treaty, the Labour Party's view was summed up by Anthony when speaking at a meeting on 1 September:

To him it was of greater concern to put a hundred men at work who would be able to feed a hundred hungry families than all their shibboleths, oaths and clauses. Much could be achieved by friendly negotiation with Great Britain, but they could not put a pistol up to John Bull and demand that such-and-such a clause be taken from the Treaty.[123]

The National League candidate, Deputy John J. Horgan, echoed his remarks during the June campaign and condemned the 'extravagant' administration of the government. He also attacked the failure to give assistance to the working class. He described the licensing legislation as the most drastic that had ever been applied to the country. He felt the working man was entitled 'to a reasonable refreshment at the close of a heavy day's work'. Horgan also argued that a change of government was necessary if the country was to make any progress and that the country did not have to rely 'all the time on Mr Cosgrave and his party'.[124] There was one Independent candidate, Sir John Harley Scott, the well-known former Unionist politician in Cork city and a regular participant in elections of the period. A member of the Corporation before it was dissolved in 1924, Scott presented himself to the electorate as a representative of the commercial classes.

The *Cork Examiner* continued to support Cumann na nGaedhael in its leading articles and was unequivocally opposed to Fianna Fáil. In a hard-hitting editorial on 14 September, the paper declared that more than '40% of the people on the register of the Irish Free State last June did nothing to prove that they deserve to have the right of voting.' The editorial continued by recommending the electorate to give their support to the government party in the first instance, and after that, to give consideration to all other parties except Fianna Fáil:

But until Fianna Fáil gives proof that it is willing to accept the verdict of the people and to cease talking about breaking contracts, it deserves no consideration from electors with the least sense of responsibility.[125]

In spite of the criticisms that had been levelled against the party from all sides, the election results proved to be a major boost for Fianna Fáil. In Cork, the party gained a seat at the expense of the National League and increased its share of the vote by 15 per cent. Seán French was elected on the first count with 11,608 votes. Significantly enough, Hugo Flinn won a second seat for Fianna Fáil on the last count on the strength of National League transfers. By the final count, only 1,105 votes separated Flinn (who was leading) and Alexander Healy of Cumann na nGaedhael. The victor would be determined by the distribution of the votes of the outgoing National League deputy, John J. Horgan who had been eliminated with 3,440 votes in the penultimate round. Only 1,251 of Horgan's votes were transferable: Flinn received 730, and Healy 521.[126]

That a Fianna Fáil candidate should receive a greater number of transfers from a National League candidate was a clear indication how much the party's support had broadened. Its appeal was obviously extending rapidly to a much wider constituency. Cumann na nGaedhael also did very well, securing nearly 50 per cent of the first-preference vote in Cork, but just failing to take a third seat. W. T. Cosgrave topped the poll and his huge surplus brought in Barry Egan on the second count. Richard Anthony won the fourth seat for Labour although he had to wait until the seventh count to get elected.

Nationally, Fianna Fáil managed to increase its first-preference votes by just under 10 per cent to 35.2 per cent while Cumann na nGaedhael increased its first preference vote by 10 per cent to 38.7 per cent.[127] Labour's vote fell by 3 per cent but lost a disproportionate nine seats. A decline of over 2 per cent in the Farmers' Party vote resulted in that party losing five seats. The National League lost five seats also, largely as a result of the Jinks affair. This election marks the emergence of the two Treaty parties into a dominant position within the party system, capturing nearly 74 per cent of the vote between them. Party fragmentation within the system was checked, a trend confirmed in the 1932 election.

5
1927–1932: GROWING MATURITY

The Irish party political system was further consolidated between 1927 and 1932. For Fianna Fáil, it was a time of particular importance. Without its rivals' experience of parliamentary politics, it was the party's time to learn. Practicalities constantly arose for which abstentionism had left Fianna Fáil ill-prepared. However, both inside and outside the Dáil, the party quickly rose to the challenge. Appointing spokesmen to cover particular policy areas,[1] Fianna Fáil opposed the government on a range of national questions between 1927 and 1932. Considerable debate occurred on issues relating to the constitutional status of the state and its position within the Commonwealth. However, the party increasingly adopted Collins' incremental strategy towards the Treaty as part of its own national policy.

In addition to its determination to get rid of the oath, Fianna Fáil also opposed other institutions that had been established as a result of the Anglo-Irish Treaty, particularly the office of Governor General. Even Cumann na nGaedhael had no particular affection for the role of Governor General but felt obliged to maintain it, in accordance with the obligations that had been imposed on the Free State government by the Anglo-Irish Treaty. The Senate, with its strong Unionist representation, was another Fianna Fáil target and some newspapers supported the campaign for its abolition. Even outside the party there was a widespread view that there was no good reason for spending money to keep the Governor General and the Senate in operation. On all these issues, Fianna Fáil managed to portray the government as pro-Commonwealth and pro-British and itself as the custodian of the nation's ideals.[2]

Fianna Fáil's social and economic policies were also in direct conflict with those of the Cumann na nGaedhael government. The burning economic issue of the day was protectionism. Throughout the period, provincial newspapers as well as various groups and interests called for the introduction of a far-reaching protectionist policy. Fianna Fáil made the issue the key feature of its economic platform. Three major benefits accrued to the party as a result of this. By keeping the issue of protectionism at the forefront of Irish political debate, Fianna Fáil was able to bridge the urban–rural divide and in doing so, widened its electoral base. From 1927 onwards, the party concentrated on farmers, promoting its protectionist plans. The second major benefit to the party was that many provincial newspapers swung towards the Fianna Fáil view on protectionism, largely at the expense of Cumann na nGaedhael. Thirdly, as a result of Fianna Fáil's stance on the issue, many business interests began to support the party.[3]

Nowhere was this illustrated more clearly than in Cork where, as we have seen, the Dowdall brothers switched to Fianna Fáil in September 1927. Both were strong advocates of protectionism and their high status in the business circles of Cork helped to give the Fianna Fáil party a less revolutionary image. In addition, Hugo Flinn, another wealthy businessman, stood for the party in the general election of September 1927. In 1932, Professor Alfred O'Rahilly, former Cumann na nGaedhael TD, and J. J. Walsh, former Minister for Posts and Telegraphs, actually supported the Fianna Fáil candidates. Both Walsh and O'Rahilly were staunch advocates of protectionism and as already discussed, it was over this particular issue that Walsh refused to stand for re-election in September 1927.

In its agricultural policy, Fianna Fáil advocated switching emphasis from livestock farming to tillage. The party wanted smaller farms that would produce cereal crops and provide more employment. On the other hand, Cumann na nGaedhael favoured larger farms producing beef, butter, eggs and bacon for export to Britain. Fianna Fáil also believed in a Griffithite rural industrialisation programme to halt migration to the cities. Speaking in the Dáil in 1929, Seán Lemass said he wanted 'industry in this country decentralized: in other words, not grouped into towns with attendant slums and other evils'.[4] There was a general fear within Fianna Fáil that Ireland would end up with hopelessly overcrowded cities and a consequently barren and depopulated countryside.

On a general ideological level, there was a marked difference between Cumann na nGaedhael and Fianna Fáil. With the two exceptions of the Shannon hydroelectric scheme and the Carlow sugar plant, Cumann na nGaedhael was not in favour of the state playing an active role in the economy. As Brian Reynolds has pointed out, 'from 1927 onwards there is not one example of an attempt by the Cumann na nGaedhael government to create a new state or semi-state body, nor is there any example of the development of a long-term project by the administration'. Fianna Fáil, on the other hand, was totally in favour of state intervention in the economy. Between 1927 and 1932, the party urged the establishment of a whole range of state-sponsored bodies, including a Housing Board, a Wheat Control Board and a state agency to encourage the development of industry.[5]

Fianna Fáil's major organisational achievement during this period was the establishment of the *Irish Press* in 1931. The existing national dailies had never been favourably disposed towards Fianna Fáil and it was clear to de Valera that the party required a supportive national newspaper. A twofold scheme to raise money was organised. Shares to the value of £200,000 were issued, of which £100,000 worth were available in the Free State and £100,000 worth in the United States. The scheme was devised so that ordinary people could subscribe and by 1930, de Valera was able to announce that the stock was oversubscribed in the Free State. The entire organisation was involved in the development of the newspaper. The first issue of the *Irish Press* appeared on 5 September 1931. Its declared ideal was an 'Irish Ireland'. Its appearance was a tribute to the energy and commitment of the Fianna Fáil members and was a remarkable achievement to have been 'able to plan, fund and institute a national newspaper in less than five years'.[6] J. C. Dowdall was among the members of the first board of directors, another example of the importance of the party's broadening support base in Cork and the extent of the Dowdall conversion to Fianna Fáil.

It can be argued that growing support for Fianna Fáil from June 1927 onwards in Cork city also reflects the emergence of the business element on the party platform. Between 1927 and 1932, there was no appreciable growth in the party's organisation in the city. The party had eight *cumainn* in 1927 and seven in 1928. However, this had dropped to four in 1929. In 1930 and 1931, it had five *cumainn* while in 1932, this more than doubled to thirteen. Thereafter, the party made rapid progress, with twenty *cumainn* in 1933 and twenty six in 1934. During the same period the party's percentage share of the first-preference vote increased dramatically from 15 per cent (June 1927) to 31 per cent (September 1927) to 35.9 per cent (1932) and to 39.1 per cent (1933).[7]

Electorally, the local government elections of March 1929 were of particular importance in Cork city. The elections were held as a result of the passage into law, on 23 February 1929, of the Cork City Management Bill which provided for the election of a City Council. Together with an appointed manager, the Council was to administer the affairs of the city. Under the Act, the manager had considerable autonomy, unlike the members of the new Council whose powers were considerably less than those of their predecessors.[8] Cork had been without a City Council since November 1924 when the Cumann na nGaedhael government had abolished it, partly as a result of its alleged corruption, and partly because its anti-Treatyite majority was being used to promote a particular political point of view. Commenting on the new Act, the *Cork Examiner* was in no doubt as to why the old Council had been abolished:

> After the Treaty things rapidly worsened and reached their lowest level towards the autumn of 1922. From then until its dissolution the Council was used as a machine for propaganda against the Free State Government. It would perhaps be too much to expect a body which had in effect become a political organisation against the Government of the country to revert to its normal duties of managing the city's business in the best interests of the citizens. The sorely tried ratepayers and the residents generally were relieved when they learned of the appointment of a Commissioner to take control of the administration.[9]

The elections themselves were remarkable in that party-political considerations were given short shrift by the voters. In contrast to the local elections of 1920, national political considerations were relegated to the lowest level of popular concern. The recurring theme throughout the campaign was the welfare and improvement of the city. The elections were also marked by the emergence of a Businessmen's Party. T. P. Dowdall who had joined Fianna Fáil in 1927, was a major figure behind this group. In all, there were 68 candidates for 21 vacancies. The entire city was one constituency. In 1920, the city had been divided into eight wards and the former City Council had consisted of 56 members. The 68 candidates represented the following interests: Labour (21), Independents (16), Cumann na nGaedhael (11), Businessmen's Party (10), Fianna Fáil (9) and Town Tenants (1).

Nominations closed on 8 March and polling day was set for 20 March.[10] The campaign was of short duration and judging by the newspaper coverage it received, the election was a low-key affair. The *Cork Examiner*, in its editorial of 6 March, strongly advanced the view that the electors should consider only those candidates who were prepared to put the affairs of the city first:

> If the citizens pick out from the extensive list of candidates which will be submitted to them 21 who will sink all party and personal considerations and apply themselves to the work of attracting more trade to Cork; and what is as important, fostering the spirit of civic pride and civic responsibility, all will be well. The only politics which should find a place in the future Corporation are Cork politics.

This theme was taken up by the Businessmen's Party whose candidates were all high-profile businessmen in the city. T. P. Dowdall is listed as a proposer of most of the party's candidates and he also spoke at the party's election meetings. By any standards, their candidates were impressive. T. C. Butterfield was a former Lord Mayor of Cork and Patrick Crowley was a former president of the Cork Chamber of Commerce and had large business interests in the city. Francis J. Daly was a butter merchant and large exporter of agricultural products. William Desmond was a former member of the Corporation and a future TD for Cumann na nGaedhael; T. J. Fitzgibbon was the manager of one of the largest mills in Cork. William Griffin was managing director of a large warehouse in Cork; Graham Sutton was 'principal' of one of the largest shipping and distributing firms in Ireland. He was also a former president of the Incorporated Chamber of Commerce.[11]

The party based its campaign on a number of planks. First of all, spokesmen emphasised the business acumen and experience of their candidates. Secondly, they suggested that the city should be organised along business lines. Thirdly, they stressed their non-party political affiliations and echoed the *Cork Examiner*'s view that party politics should be kept out of the affairs of the new Council. The party's position was eloquently expressed by T. P. Dowdall at a meeting held on the eve of polling day:

> The Business Party were contesting this election so that if returned they would give all the assistance in their power to the officials to run the business of the city on business lines to secure the most efficient and economical administration of the city's affairs consistent with the welfare of the people.

At an earlier meeting, Sir Stanley Harrington stressed the party's non-party political nature:

He wanted the electors to understand very clearly that the Business Party were not out for politics, and would have nothing to say to them. Their members would leave politics outside the door of the Council chamber. They had no connection whatever with any of the political parties, though they had no antagonism to any of them. They were purely a party of business men.[12]

The Labour Party, with twenty-one candidates, constituted the main opposition to the Businessmen's Party. Its candidates were mainly tradesmen and workers, with one national schoolteacher and three insurance agents. At their election meetings, held under the auspices of the Cork Workers' Council, speakers questioned the sincerity and motivation of the Businessmen's Party. George Nason, president of the Workers' Council, attacked the Businessmen's Party candidates for making so many promises:

> The business men in their programme also advocated close cohesion between Labour and capital, the same as in England, but we all know . . . If we offered him a £1 reduction in our wages he would like us, but if we offered him a subscription of £2 a week he would love us. That is his cohesion.

Other Labour speakers outlined the party's programme for more and better housing and for better educational opportunities. One Labour candidate, Jeremiah Hurley, received the backing of the Cork branch of the Irish National Teachers' Organisation, of which he was secretary. Members of the branch urged teachers to vote for Hurley and the other Labour candidates. One member, C. P. Murphy, put the issue bluntly:

If everything were right it should not be necessary for them to appeal to the teachers for support for Mr Hurley and the Labour Party because their members should be quite clear and distinct as to who had been their friends whenever they required assistance. There was not a shadow of a doubt that the only party who had loyally supported the teachers in any matters appertaining to the betterment of their organisation was the Labour Party.[13]

Cumann na nGaedhael's campaign was low key, and received very little media coverage. The meeting held to launch the party's campaign on 10 March did, however, receive considerable coverage from the *Cork Examiner*. The chairman of that meeting, Michael Egan, a former TD, defended the party's right to contest the elections:

Did these people think that because a man had political convictions that he was not possessed of a mind or soul for anything else but politics? He would say that on the ticket selected by the Cumann na nGaedhael organisation they had selected eleven men whom they claimed for the administrative and the business point of view were second to none.

It would appear that both Egan and de Róiste managed to patch up their difference with the party organisation in Cork. Entering the electoral field once again, de Róiste also endeavoured to play down the party-political dimension. He argued that Cumann na nGaedheal was not merely a political organisation but was also interested in local civic affairs. He stressed that the Cumann na nGaedhael candidates were:

going forward, not in any political party spirit – as had already been stated, they were pledged not to introduce political matters, and to prevent such matters being introduced, so far as they have power – but they were going forward to do their utmost for the civic advancement of Cork.[14]

Of the eleven Cumann na nGaedhael candidates, eight were businessmen, owning their own premises; one, de Róiste, was a company secretary; another, Michael Egan, was a coach-maker and one an estate agent. Fianna Fáil's campaign took on an even lower profile and received no coverage at all. The party had nine candidates. Seán French, the outgoing Lord Mayor of Cork, was the party's big vote-catcher while Seán O'Leary, a former Dáil candidate, also stood. Of the nine candidates, two were accountants, three were insurance agents, two were self-employed, one was a warehouseman and one a commercial traveller. Of the sixteen Independents, six were businessmen, four were low-paid workers of various types and the other six were divided as follows: two ex-servicemen, one widow, one solicitor, one decorator and finally, Sir John Harley Scott, a veteran of many elections and a former member of the Corporation. The Town Tenants' Organisation had one candidate, Thomas O'Regan, who was the organisation's secretary.[15]

The results confirmed the theme of the election campaign, in that the established political parties fared very badly. The distribution of seats was: Independents (7), Businessmen's Party (6), Cumann na nGaedhael (3), Fianna Fáil (3), and Labour (2).[16] The election was undoubtedly a major success for the Businessmen's Party and for Independents. Labour fielded far too many candidates and failed to do itself justice. In terms of first-preference votes, the party was on a par with Fianna Fáil and Cumann na nGaedhael. However, the fact remains that in a straight electoral battle with the businessmen of the city, Labour was the ultimate loser. One reason for this must have been the high profile of the those who had stood for the Businessmen's Party. The Labour candidates would not have been as well known or as prominent in city life. Significantly enough, the party's Dáil deputy for Cork, Richard Anthony, did not contest the election. Neither did Fianna Fáil's Hugo Flinn or Cumann na nGaedhael's Barry Egan. Seán French was the only Dáil deputy in Cork to enter the contest and he topped the poll with a massive 1,568 votes, well over two quotas.

The results also clearly indicated that 'national issues' were no longer dominating politics. The electorate was clearly able to differentiate between electing a national government and a city council. They voted for personalities rather than parties. Issues such as the oath, the country's constitutional status or the role of the Senate did not generate sufficient interest or influence over the voters to determine their preferences in electing the city council. The number of candidates contesting the election, representing a broad spectrum of the city's electorate, was also a clear manifestation of the young state's political stability. The election was conducted in a thoroughly orderly manner, and without rancour. In terms of local elections being a springboard for Dáil aspirants, only one successful candidate, William Desmond of the Businessmen's Party, managed to win a Dáil seat in 1932 as a Cumann na nGaedhael candidate.[17] He had also been elected in the 1920 local election as a Nationalist representative.

Surprisingly enough, at the inaugural meeting of the new Council, Seán French was unanimously re-elected Lord Mayor, being proposed and seconded by two Independent councillors, Jack O'Sullivan and Daniel

Gamble respectively. Obviously, the fact that he had topped the poll was an important consideration here. In addition, he had been Lord Mayor since 1924 and was generally considered to have prioritised the affairs of the city on his political agenda.[18]

The *Cork Examiner* welcomed the results as clear evidence that the electors of Cork had paid little attention to electoral tags:

> The only group that can be said to have scored in the election is the Business Party. They succeeded in returning as many candidates as the two political groups put together. This, taken with the success of the 'Independents', is an indication that the people are not so engrossed in politics as the politicians think they ought to be. Certainly the Local Government electors of Cork have given a decisive indication that they want no more politics in the Municipal Council.

It did not occur to the *Examiner* that the particularly low-key campaigns of the two major parties may have influenced the vote. In its analysis of the results, the paper displayed its continuing hostility towards Fianna Fáil:

> The one group that kept themselves free to introduce general politics into the Council fared very badly. One man belonging to it headed the poll, but the redistribution of his surplus votes showed that a great many of those who voted for him did not do so from political motives, and though he obtained more than two quotas of first preference votes, the next of his party to be elected fell short of a full quota, while the third obtained a place by fluke.

Commenting on the failure of Labour to win more than two seats, the paper argued that the party had run too many candidates. In addition, it considered that the electorate was 'sick of sectional, party and political wrangling, and desire a purely business management of the city's affairs'. Finally, the editorial raised the question of what would happen if a general election was held on the same basis with no reference to 'treaties' or 'republics'. The editorial speculated on whether a Businessmen's Party would defeat the two main political parties and advanced the view that the electorate would welcome such a development.[19]

The intriguing question posed by the *Cork Examiner* in 1929 was clearly answered in the 1932 general election which was dominated by the two main political parties, Fianna Fáil and Cumann na nGaedhael. Non-party political interests did not figure prominently at all in that contest. Given the particular social and economic climate, circumstances were not at their most favourable for Cumann na nGaedhael when President Cosgrave announced on 29 January 1932 that a general election would be held on 16 February. Cumann na nGaedhael decided to form an alliance with William Redmond's National League, a move which inevitably antagonised the Irish-Ireland element of the party. Another incident which further alienated this group was the revelation in the *Irish Press* of a 'private and confidential circular' indicating that prominent Unionists were funding Cumann na nGaedhael. The Farmers' Party also had a tactical electoral alliance with Cumann na nGaedhael.[20]

On the other side, Fianna Fáil did not receive official support from either Sinn Féin or the IRA. However, despite being somewhat bitter about the 'split' in 1925 and Fianna Fáil's participation in the Free State Dáil, the overriding desire of these bodies was to see Cumann na nGaedhael ousted. The rank-and-file of these organisations voted accordingly.[21] Labour had a troublesome campaign, though its difficulties were to some extent overshadowed by the battle between the two bigger parties. Labour also suffered from internal splits. In Cork, for example, the party's outgoing Deputy, Richard Anthony, had been expelled from the party for breaking a whip to vote for the draconian 1931 Public Safety Act.[22] He stood as Independent Labour and was successful.

The Cumann na nGaedhael selection convention in Cork was an interesting affair, with outgoing TD Barry Egan failing to secure a nomination. The *Cork Examiner* reported on 22 January 1932 that five names had been placed before the convention: President Cosgrave, Barry Egan, Alexander Healy, William Desmond and Alderman John J. Horgan, formerly of the National League. Both Cosgrave and Horgan were unanimously selected and on a ballot between the remaining three, Healy and Desmond were successful. Unfortunately, de Róiste's diaries do not cover the 1932 general election, so we have no detailed reasons for Egan's omission, although it may be significant that several years earlier, de Róiste had identified him with the Irish-Ireland element of the party.[23] The *Cork Examiner* had very little to say about the background to the convention and expressed no surprise on the matter. Horgan's unanimous selection represented the fusion of National League and Cumann na nGaedhael interests in the city. Horgan told the convention:

> that nothing that had happened in public life for the past few years had pleased him more than the unity between the constitutionalists and nationalists and the Government party. It was because of that unity that he had consented to become a candidate.[24]

Recently, there had been an increase in Republican violence (including fatal shootings) and a growth in the far-Left which included a new Republican–Left organisation, Saor Éire. The government sought to connect Fianna Fáil with the IRA, Saor Éire and similar groups. In Cork, as in the rest of the country, the Cumann na nGaedhael campaign thus concentrated on portraying Fianna Fáil as the party of choice for communists and gunmen and claimed that chaos and anarchy would follow its rise to power. One of the strongest attacks came from P. J. Hogan, the Minister for Agriculture, when he described Fianna Fáil as being 'acknowedged perjurers and liars', a message driven home in Cumann na nGaedhael's posters and leaflets. One such poster showed three men playing cards. One is an upright *Saorstát* citizen playing cards with a de Valera-like figure (labelled 'Fianna Fáil'), who is slipping the joker to a murky-looking Saor Éire individual. The caption reads:

Fianna Fáil's game
Don't let them
Cheat you
Vote for Cumann na nGaedhael

Another poster featured de Valera riding a worn-out donkey, endeavouring to keep it moving by dangling a carrot (with 'Empty Formula') in front of him. Labour and the National League are hanging on at the back. The caption reads:

A carrot a day won't
Keep failure away
Plump for Cumann na nGaedhael[25]

Some posters were particularly hard-hitting, laying blame for the entire Civil War on de Valera's shoulders.

One depicted de Valera being led by Mother Erin to a graveyard dotted with crosses inscribed with the names of prominent individuals who had died during the war: Michael Collins, Rory O'Connor, Cathal Brugha, Seán Hales and so on. Mother Erin points in a disapproving manner to these crosses, and the caption reads:

> The dead who died for an 'empty formula'
> Was it worth it?
> Vote for Cumann na nGaedhael.

The government also put across a more subtle message to the electorate, suggesting that while Fianna Fáil's time would come one day, they could not be trusted yet. However, as Dermot Keogh notes, 'Cumann na nGaedhael went to the hustings not realising that de Valera had long since come out from the shadow of the gunman as far as many of the key sectors in Irish society were concerned.'[26] It attacked Fianna Fáil's economic policies, particularly on protectionism, and argued that they would result in an increase in the cost of living. On the land annuities, Cumann na nGaedhael speakers argued that refusal to pay them would result in a breakdown in economic relations with Britain and a consequent increase in unemployment. Cumann na nGaedhael defended its economic performance in government and once again resurrected the Civil War, claiming that it had proved a major hindrance to economic development.

On the question of Fianna Fáil and communism, Cumann na nGaedhael ministers pulled no punches. Ernest Blythe, Minister for Finance, speaking in Monaghan, declared:

> If Fianna Fáil are returned at this election they will not hold power for a year. Control will be in the

hands of the gun bullies and of the small group calling themselves the IRA. There was only one way of dealing with Communists and that was to put them in gaol and shoot them if necessary.

Desmond FitzGerald argued that the election was about:

the maintenance of ordered society and of a civilised state and the chaos following the overthrow of the existing state, out of which anarchy revolutionists hoped would emerge a Communist Republic . . . Fianna Fáil was receiving the support of the people who are pro-Russia in this country for the very good reason that these people knew that if Fianna Fáil was returned to power they would be much nearer their goal – a Communist Republic in Ireland.

This message was reinforced in the party's advertisements. In the week before polling day, Cumann na nGaedhael took out front-page advertisements in the *Cork Examiner*. The advertisement appearing on the day before polling, told the electorate: 'The Gunmen are voting for Fianna Fáil. The Communists are voting for Fianna Fáil'.[27]

Not all government ministers concentrated on this theme. Patrick Hogan, Minister for Agriculture, launched a major attack on Fianna Fáil's economic policies, particularly protectionism. He believed that agricultural tariffs were detrimental to the farmer and militated against increased agricultural production and the capacity of the country to export its surplus dairy produce to the English market. On industrial tariffs, he argued that their effect was to raise the price of consumer goods, something which the Irish people could not afford: 'The position in this country was that while agricultural tariffs would not raise the price of what the farmer had to sell, industrial tariffs would permanently increase the price of what he had to buy'. Hogan also stressed that economic issues should dominate the campaign and berated Fianna Fáil for raising the issue of the oath.[28]

The highlight of Cumann na nGaedhael's campaign in Cork was a major public meeting that was held on 31 January. The meeting was addressed by both President Cosgrave and Captain William Redmond. Cosgrave gave a comprehensive speech covering the restoration of peace and order, unemployment, the boundary question, land distribution, the necessity for the Public Safety Act of 1931 and the government's record on housing and rural infrastructure. Captain Redmond concentrated on the Anglo-Irish Treaty saying that:

> The Treaty had once more been challenged by a certain section of their people, when it should be past history for Irishmen to-day and if the paramount issue at this election was support for the Treaty or not, it was the fault of the Fianna Fáil party.

These sentiments were echoed by the other Cumann na nGaedhael candidates in Cork. Alexander Healy, at a meeting in Passage West, questioned Fianna Fáil's capacity to increase employment, given the party's policy of 'non-co-operation with England'. He also spoke out against 'overloading the country with tariffs'. Speaking at the same meeting, John J. Horgan raised doubts about Fianna Fáil's ability to maintain the country's credit rating, arguing that the confidence of financiers would be eroded following a Fianna Fáil victory.[29]

Cumann na nGaedhael in Cork received the support of a number of prominent businessmen who, at a specially convened meeting, passed the following resolution:

This meeting of Cork city business men, desiring the development of the Free State on sane national lines, which will safeguard the welfare and interest of every class in the community, are of opinion (especially in view of the world economic crisis) that the best policy for the Irish people at this election is to return the present Government to power by a decisive majority.

Among those attending the meeting were Alderman F. J. Daly, Sir Stanley Harrington, Dr J. C. Foley, W. Dinan and Richard Cudmore. All these individuals, together with others present, were prominent members of the Businessmen's Party which had contested the 1929 local government elections.[30]

Fianna Fáil selected four candidates to contest the election: Deputy Hugo Flinn, T. P. Dowdall, Alderman Seán O'Leary and Dr Humphrey Kelleher. It is difficult to ascertain why the outgoing Seán French did not contest the election. The Fianna Fáil parliamentary party minutes indicate that French was a frequent absentee from party meetings and on 26 March 1931, a 'notice of motion' was submitted to the parliamentary party proposing 'that the case of Mr. Seán French should be considered at the second next Party meeting'. At a subsequent meeting, it was reported that Gerry Boland, the honorary party secretary, had been sent to interview French and had obtained from him a letter stating 'that he does not intend to be a candidate at the next Dáil Election, but will give all the assistance in his power to the Fianna Fáil candidates'. According to the minutes of the meeting, French's letter was later published in that week's issue of *The Nation*, Fianna Fáil's weekly newspaper before the *Irish Press* was established in 1931. That French's decision not to go forward for election was voluntary is confirmed by the fact that he acted as election agent for the four candidates.[31]

Fianna Fáil countered Cumann na nGaedhael's allegations that communism and chaos would ensue if the party was elected. It claimed in its advertisements (which were on the inside pages of the *Cork Examiner*) that Cumann na nGaedhael was being financed by the Masonic Order in Ireland. The party also highlighted the position of a number of former Cumann na nGaedhael supporters in Cork who had switched their loyalties to Fianna Fáil. On the day before polling, an advertisement in the *Cork Examiner* drew these two themes together:

> Men who stood shoulder to shoulder in pre-Treaty days have come together again rejoicing at the prospect of National Unity. Men who supported Cumann na nGaedhael 'til it became insufferable, men who were T.D.s for this city – Professor Alfred O'Rahilly, J. J. Walsh, Andrew O'Shaughnessy and Senator Lenihan, have given us a lead. Let us close our ranks . . . If a well-entrenched Mason-financed clique can by clever tricks and dishonest propaganda manage to maintain a permanent grip on the country, there is bound to be a reaction. And the next time neither we nor you may be able to control it. Let Spain be an object lesson to us.

Indeed, Fianna Fáil was particularly pleased to publish O'Rahilly's comments on the electoral tactics of Cumann na nGaedhael. The professor had been particularly irked by Cumann na nGaedhael's vision of the 'Godless communism' of Fianna Fáil:

> Everyone who has the temerity to disagree with the present Ministers is declared to be an indifferent

Catholic, a dishonest lawyer, an indiscriminate economist . . . Well, even at the risk of excommunication, I declare publicly that unless President Cosgrave and the fellow members of his new-fangled Synod give up their attempt to intimidate us with Lenten Pastorals, unless they proceed to argue fairly and squarely against the perfectly legitimate alternative policy put forward by their opponents, I for one am going for the first time, to vote for Fianna Fáil as the only hope of securing political peace and progress in this country.[32]

The *Cork Examiner*, in a number of editorials during the campaign, clearly sided with Cumann na nGaedhael. The paper believed that Fianna Fáil's policy of refusing to pay the land annuities, in addition to its overall protectionist policy, would lead to an economic war with Britain in which Ireland would be the loser. On 22 January the paper's editorial declared:

Never in the history of Ireland was there more urgent necessity for stability and for avoidance of any bickerings with our neighbours not to say 'another round' with them. Five more years of settled government would give the Free State a chance of improving on the steady progress which it has been making.[33]

In a further editorial on 29 January, the paper warned its readers about the consequences of following de Valera's advice on breaking away from the Commonwealth:

Let us start a serious dispute with England over the annuities, or some other matter and this develops into a trade war, and what happens? England loses, let us say, the Free State market for her manufactures. It amounts, all told, to about 5 per cent of her export trade. The Free State loses the British market, which amounts to about 90 or 95 per cent of our whole export trade. Which of the two countries would stand to lose most in six or twelve months?[34]

Fianna Fáil tried to counteract this argument by portraying itself as a moderate and reasonable party. Throughout the campaign in Cork, its candidates concentrated on economic matters. At a meeting in Passage West, Alderman Seán O'Leary attacked the government's record on employment, blaming the dumping of foreign goods on the Irish market. At the same meeting, T. P. Dowdall spoke in a similar vein while Hugo Flinn stressed Fianna Fáil's view that the state had a role in the creation of employment. He made no bones about what the party stood for. 'The business of Fianna Fáil', he said, 'was to build up the economic strength of the people and make them self-controlled'. At subsequent meetings, the Fianna Fáil candidates reiterated these sentiments, concentrating mostly on economic issues and countering allegations of communism. At a meeting in Blackrock, Hugo Flinn declared that 'he personally could not find one Communist in the country. The Dean of Cork had said that there was no communism in the country'.[35] Towards the close of the campaign, T. P. Dowdall also endeavoured to portray Fianna Fáil as a responsible party of law and order:

> As a responsible businessman he had no use for disorder or trouble and would not be on the platform of a party whose policy would lead to breaches of the peace and failure to maintain law and order. Fianna Fáil would guarantee that the law of the Free State would be the law of the majority

and that every man would be guaranteed the possession of his person and property.

At the party's major rally in Cork, held on 11 February, de Valera guaranteed the rights of private property:

> We solemnly pledge ourselves that the person and property of every citizen in this country will be safeguarded as well by a Fianna Fáil Government as by a Government of Cumann na nGaedhael.

Earlier in the speech, de Valera had argued that the major factor which was responsible for Ireland's high level of unemployment was the country's low level of industrialisation. Towards the close of his speech, de Valera reiterated Fianna Fáil's belief in 'private ownership'. Peace and stability were required, he asserted, to ensure the implementation of the Fianna Fáil programme. Finally, in an advertisement in the *Cork Examiner* on 13 February, Fianna Fáil promised:

> that if elected in a majority we shall not exceed the mandate here asked for without again consulting the people . . . We shall strive also to bring British statesmen to realise that the interests of Britain are best secured by an understanding and settlement which will permit the people of the two islands to live side by side as independent friendly nations each respecting the rights of the other and co-operating freely in matters of common concern.[36]

Clearly therefore, Fianna Fáil strove very hard during the campaign to present itself as a totally responsible party with no desire to engage in 'another round' with Britain, a party committed to the upholding of law and order and the rights of private property, as well as promoting a coherent economic programme. Again the party was assisted in this task by Professor Alfred O'Rahilly, who outlined his position in a lengthy letter to the *Cork Examiner*:

> I am intensely interested in trying to show that in this election Fianna Fáil is standing as a Constitutional Party capable of securing its immediate aim by peaceful legitimate means. I was under the delusion that all peace-loving citizens would unite with me in trying to bring this about and to end the panic and uncertainty which are strangling us. But apparently this would not suit those who, by picturing their opponents as anarchists and revolutionaries, hope to secure for their own party an indefinitely continued monopoly of political power. If they succeed, they and all of us may live to rue it.[37]

The *Cork Examiner*, conscious of this effort by Fianna Fáil, warned the electorate in its editorial on the day before the election that:

> [Fianna Fáil] candidates and speechmakers seem to have purposely relegated their republican programme to the background and their diehardism towards the 'ould enemy' has been toned down in the South . . . the evident object being to lull the people into a false sense of security that after all, the Fianna Fáil party may be trusted not to make trouble if elected . . . But the electors should not allow themselves to be led this way into a false position. The existence of the Treaty is as much at stake in the present election as it was in the election of 1922.[38]

The Labour candidate, Councillor Jeremiah Hurley concentrated on the unemployment question. At the launch of the party's campaign in Cork, he declared that:

> The pressing problems of the moment are unemployment and houses, and these should be first attended to. The undoing of the Cumann na nGaedhael Party would be their statement that it was not the duty of a Government to find employment for the people. They had had the result of that policy in Cork, where they had the largest number of unemployed in proportion to their population.

Hurley also attacked the government's record on housing and committed the Labour Party to providing adequate housing for the working classes. He believed that Labour would hold the balance of power and consequently, would be able to implement its programme. Speaking at the same meeting, the Wicklow deputy, James Everett, defended Labour's stance on the Public Safety Act of 1931, thanking God that the Labour party would not be 'a party to the coercion of their fellow Irishmen'. On the land annuities, Labour adopted an ambiguous position. In an official statement the party declared:

> On the matter of land annuities the Labour Party affirms that there is no difference between responsible political parties in respect to the liability of the tenant purchasers of the land. Fianna Fáil, Cumann na nGaedhael and the Labour Party agree in saying that the purchaser is under both moral and legal obligation to pay annuities. The Labour Party blames both Fianna Fáil and Cumann na nGaedhael for treating as a subject of party controversy what is essentially a national issue and one which if good

results for the country are looked for must be dealt with by friendly diplomatic negotiation.[39]

Therefore, the party dodged the issue of whether the annuities should be paid to the British government. Labour's campaign was a low-profile one and did not receive the same media attention as those of the two big parties. It was also damaged by the split in its ranks caused by the expulsion of Richard Anthony who ran a strong campaign as Independent Labour.

In the course of his campaign, Anthony defended his decision to vote for the Public Safety Act of 1931 on the grounds that it safeguarded the lives and property 'of the common people and even the state itself against armed attack'. He committed himself to furthering the policies of Labour while avoiding any outright attacks on the government – obviously hoping to benefit from transfers from government party candidates. He clearly saw his expulsion from the Labour Party as a temporary phenomenon:

> He would not utter a derogatory word about old comrades and friends with whom he had worked so long, and he regretted that they had differed on this question; but he would continue to act as he had acted in the past on all matters of labour policy, notwithstanding his temporary separation from their councils.[40]

In other speeches, Anthony condemned Fianna Fáil and 'certain of their Labour allies whose policy was dictated by the forces of the IRA and Saor Éire', on one occasion concluding with the plea:

> In God's name vote for the Labour Party, that is myself . . . but do not vote for the people who will

release the prisoners, who have held up banks or farmers or have gone round the country with masks, or who were out to murder Civic Guards.

He argued that unemployment was due to the worldwide recession and that the opposition parties were exploiting the unemployed by claiming that they could solve the problem.[41]

In Cork, the result of the 1932 general election brought little change in the parties' fortunes: Cumann na nGaedhael retained its two seats as did Fianna Fáil and Richard Anthony as 'Independent Labour'. The first count saw President Cosgrave elected, having polled almost two quotas with a first preference vote of 18,125, followed by T. P. Dowdall who also exceeded the quota. Significantly, 2,593 of Cosgrave's surplus transferred to Anthony which enabled him to snatch back his seat from the official Labour candidate, Jeremiah Hurley, who had received the third highest first preference vote. William Desmond received 3,296 votes from Cosgrave's surplus which put him ahead of his Cumann na nGaedhael rivals. He eventually took the fifth seat. Hugo Flinn took the third seat after the other Fianna Fáil party candidates, O'Leary and Kelleher, were eliminated.[42]

Nationally, the turnout was the highest in the history of the Free State – 77 per cent. Fianna Fáil received a substantial increase in popular support, raising its share from 35.2 per cent in 1927 to 44.5 per cent in 1932. Cumann na nGaedhael dropped a little over 3 per cent, from 38.7 per cent to 35.7 per cent. Labour's national vote dropped to an alarming 7.7 per cent. Fianna Fáil did not win an overall majority. However, it managed to form a government with the support of the Labour Party and three Independents. The defeated Republicans of 1923 had, by peaceful and constitutional means, attained power, an event which in the words of John A. Murphy, 'demonstrated the political maturity and stability of the young state'.[43] Certainly, Cumann na nGaedhael's efforts to generate fear that Fianna Fáil had been taken over by gunmen and communists were unrealistic to the point of absurdity.

To suggest that a margarine manufacturer like T. P. Dowdall, who was a prominent supporter of Cumann na nGaedhael until 1927 and whose brother, J. C. Dowdall, had been a member of the Free State Senate since its inception, was soft on communism and violence was stretching credulity to the limit. Dowdall had been a prominent member of the Cork Industrial Association and the Cork Businessmen's Association. Ironically, T. P. Dowdall seconded the nomination of William Desmond to contest the 1929 local government elections on behalf of the Businessmen's Party, thereby helping him along the road to higher political office. Equally, to suggest links between Hugo Flinn and communism was ridiculous. Flinn was a very wealthy businessman with considerable financial interests in England. Indeed, during the campaign he was forced to defend this aspect of his life. Responding to jibes that he was an Englishman, he gave at one political meeting the following account of his origins:

> His father came from County Down and his mother from Wicklow. His father carried on a big fish trade at Kinsale, and then went to the Isle of Man for no other reason than that there was no opening for the fishing fleets in Ireland. He himself was born in the Isle of Man, and he was unable to trace one drop of blood in his family which was not Irish. Himself and his brothers were now living in Ireland, and the specific and only reason why he himself was in

Ireland was that his children should be born and brought up here. Another complaint was that he had a banking account in England. The banking account in England was belonging to his father, and it was through this account that his father carried on the Irish side of his trade in England and through which large sums of money were paid to fishermen in Ireland.[44]

Such a background did not suggest communist leanings, and indeed, it is significant that Flinn and Dowdall only became publicly identified with Fianna Fáil after the party's entry into Dáil Éireann.

Another unlikely communist was the third Fianna Fáil candidate, Alderman Seán O'Leary, who actually attacked Cumann na nGaedhael for failing, during its term of office, to act as a Catholic Christian government.[45] Finally, it must be stressed that people like John J. Horgan, William Desmond, Barry Egan, T. P. Dowdall, Hugo Flinn, Seán O'Leary and Seán French all knew each other having worked together for many years on bodies such as the Cork Industrial Association, the Cork Businessmen's Association, Cork Corporation and the Cork Harbour Commissioners and must have been privately amused by their national leaders' choice of insults. Significantly, it was the respective front-bench personnel of the two main parties who engaged in the various allegations relating to communism and fascism. The local candidates in Cork (apart from Cosgrave) refrained from labelling their opponents in the same terms as their party leaders.

Fianna Fáil's warning in one official advertisement that victory for Cumann na nGaedhael would lead to the emergence in Ireland of a militaristic regime was also far-fetched. It was an unfair jibe at President Cosgrave and his party, whose behaviour in ten years' government had been thoroughly democratic (except, perhaps, in the exceptional circumstances of the Civil War). Every election since 1922, whether local or general, was held in a free, open and democratic manner and conducted without corruption. Joseph Lee fittingly concludes:

> Cosgrave would do the ship of state one final service, by the manner in which he quietly left the bridge and handed over the wheel to the rival captain. Bitter though it was in party terms – indeed precisely because it was so bitter in party terms – it was his finest hour.

The peaceful change of office after the election belied Fianna Fáil allegations that Cumann na nGaedhael would refuse to yield power. Brian Reynolds mistakenly suggests that these were merely the accusations of a few individuals peddling their own propaganda.[46] In Cork, this was the stuff of official party advertisements which appeared regularly in the *Cork Examiner*. However, Fianna Fáil candidates in the city concentrated on economic issues rather than on negative campaigning.

Fianna Fáil benefited considerably from the active support of public figures who had previously been members of Cumann na nGaedhael. The endorsement of Fianna Fáil by well-known politicians such as J. J. Walsh, a former minister, and Professor O'Rahilly, one of the leading intellectuals in the city and a former deputy, and Andrew O'Shaughnessy, a successful businessman and former TD, provided a powerful answer to the allegations that the party bore a revolutionary and communistic character. Their shift of allegiance was also a public manifestation of a political realignment. These individuals had long been part of the Irish-Ireland group of Cumann na nGaedhael in Cork and their public support for Fianna Fáil was a clear signal to voters who shared their views to switch allegiance. The results reflect this. Cumann na nGaedhael comfortably achieved two quotas but it did so only in an alliance with the National League: at the general election of June 1927 the two parties had more than three quotas between them (although the National League lost its seat in September 1927), while Fianna Fáil had less than two and Labour had one.

Of the ten candidates who contested the 1932 general election only four stood in the local government elections in 1929, and of these only William Desmond, John J. Horgan and Seán O'Leary were successful. Apart from Desmond, the other four successful Dáil candidates had never experienced a local government contest although each had a considerable public profile. Indeed, local government as an issue did not figure at all in the 1932 election in Cork. Viewed in the longer term, the general election of 1932 consolidated the emerging 'two-and-a-half-party' system in Ireland. This was clearly the case in Cork where the pattern did not significantly change for a considerable time thereafter.

6
BROKERAGE & THE ROLE OF THE BACKBENCH DEPUTY

Many political scientists and historians have commented on the role of 'brokerage' in Irish politics. According to Mart Bax, the Dáil deputy's 'first and foremost task is that of intermediary'; he or she is 'the link between the electorate and the various offices of local and central government'. In his illuminating analysis of the Irish political system, Bax paints a picture of a public representative who has to deliver (and be seen to do so), as he puts it, 'prizes' such as jobs, contracts, new roads, footpaths, grants and sewerage systems, very often in competition not merely with representatives of other parties, but with those of his or her own. Before the election, Bax's politician has time and money at his or her disposal, often uses local council elections as a springboard for advancement, and has a team of 'prize producers', or a team of advisers to help satisfy the constituent or 'prize-consumer'. The TD can also draw on a 'machine' although for this, Bax cannot ascribe an 'exact moment of origin' on the grounds that complex social forms, like political machines, do not materialise overnight'.[1]

It is interesting to study the period between 1918 and 1932 in the context of Bax's analysis. Without engaging in the type of field study undertaken by Bax, it is still possible to identify traces of brokerage-style politics, which can help to illustrate the role of a backbench TD in the early years of the modern Irish state. By studying the minutes of the parliamentary parties of Cumann na nGaedhael and Fianna Fáil, the ard-fheiseanna programmes of both and the private papers of some deputies, one can build a reasonable profile of political brokerage in the early years of the system. However, it is important to stress also that the type of political leader who emerged from the War of Independence was more accessible to the voter than at any time in the past. These new leaders came from the same classes as the majority of the people and did not control votes like the old landed ascendancy had done prior to the Secret Ballot Act of 1872. As a result, the bargaining power of the voters *vis-à-vis* the political elite increased considerably.[2]

For the most part after 1922, this political elite was elected on reputations that had been built up during the War of Independence. However, more often than not, these politicians were also well known in their localities and were members of various local bodies in their constituencies before their selection in 1918 as parliamentary candidates for Sinn Féin. J. J. Walsh, for example, was a former chairman of the Cork County Board of the GAA and a founding member of the Irish Volunteers in Cork.[3] De Róiste was a founding member of the Cork Industrial Development Association in 1903, the Celtic Literary Society, Conradh na Gaeilge, the Irish Volunteers, the International Trading Company and the Moore McCormack Shipping Line between Cork and America. Terence MacSwiney and Tomás MacCurtain were also members of either these or similar cultural or political bodies.[4] By 1918, therefore, these people were already known to their future constituents and were actively involved in their communities. However, it should be stressed that it was the constitutional question rather than ordinary local concerns which were dominant in the run-up to the 1918 general election and the electorate voted accordingly.

Despite the importance of political and constitutional issues in the public mind, we learn from de Róiste's diary that the TD of the time had other matters with which to deal. Indeed, it is clear that the workload of a Sinn Féin TD during this period was similar in nature and intensity to that of a modern TD. For example, in an entry dated 11 July 1919, de Róiste summarises the type of work in which he was engaged as a TD in the First Dáil:

> Very busy – interviewing builders, painters, removers, etc.; doing Coláiste na Mumhan work, the sessions having opened last Monday; keeping up with Sinn Féin work, attending Industrial Association meetings; trying to avoid opening Bazaars and callers who want to get positions in Ford factory; answering correspondence; judging Oireachtas compositions *agus a lán nithe eile* [and a lot of other things].

De Róiste's own problem was lack of income because since he was elected to Dáil Éireann, he had given up regular employment. The Sinn Féin Executive did promise him £200 a year but apparently the money was slow in coming. De Róiste was also involved in the administration of Dáil Courts and the organisation of the Dáil Loan.[5]

On 13 October 1920, de Róiste indicated that he had become tired of dealing with a myriad of 'small things' and wrote of his desire to get away from:

> persons coming to one wanting a job at Fords, wanting information regarding rents of houses,

wanting advice on investments, wanting money, wanting even to use influence to get a supply of coal! Then there are innumerable committees, meetings, conferences one is supposed to attend.[6]

Furthermore, it should be remembered that during this period, de Róiste was on the run, constantly moving from one house to another.

In the 1920 local government elections, the two sitting Dáil deputies for the Cork City Borough constituency had stood for Sinn Féin, as did Terence MacSwiney, who was already the Dáil deputy for the Mid-Cork constituency. This reliance on familiar figures is explained by de Róiste's comment that there was a difficulty 'in getting men nationally sound' to stand.[7] Clearly, Sinn Féin wanted an overwhelming endorsement of its national policy as this had evolved since 1918 and it sought to ensure this by putting its leading figures into the ring. The wisdom of Dáil deputies becoming involved in municipal administration was not questioned. Mart Bax's study of the Irish party-political system dates the entry of TDs into local politics to the early 1930s when deputies with national records began to realise that 'ideology and regional hero worship were no longer enough for a safe seat'.[8] However, it would appear from an examination of the politics of Cork City Borough constituency that this development occurred at an earlier date there.

In the 1923 general election, for instance, only Walsh could claim to have had the requisite 'national record', having fought in the GPO in Dublin in 1916. Mary MacSwiney was, of course, sister of the deceased Lord Mayor of Cork, Terence MacSwiney, whose popular reputation was of obvious electoral benefit to her. On the other hand, her running mate, Dr Con

Lucey, had been medical officer of the 1st Southern Division of the IRA and later, of the Republicans in Cork during the Civil War. Yet he failed to gain a seat. Professor Alfred O'Rahilly, although elected to Cork Corporation in 1920, was not a 'fighting man'. He contested the election only after being asked to do so by President Cosgrave. For his part, de Róiste agreed to stand (after a good deal of persuasion) only because of the difficulty in finding a candidate with an 'Irish-Ireland' outlook. The Progressive Association managed to get its two candidates, Richard Beamish and Andrew O'Shaughnessy, elected even though neither had any 'national record'.[9] Indeed, Beamish was an opponent of Sinn Féin in the 1920 local elections, standing for the Commercial Party.[10] Furthermore, at the first meeting of the new Council, he spoke against breaking from Westminster and in favour of making nominations for the office of sheriff of the city. (Sinn Féin had opposed nominating anybody on the grounds that the process reflected the legacy of a foreign power.) Yet he was put forward by an organisation of which T. P. Dowdall was chairman and which also had members of Cumann na nGaedheal involved in its deliberations.

The point here is that from a very early stage in the new Free State, to have fought in the War of Independence or indeed, even to have been on the Sinn Féin side during the period, was not an essential ingredient for electoral success. The 1924 by-election, for instance, resulted in the election of Councillor Michael Egan to Dáil Éireann. Egan had stood for Labour in the 1920 local elections and as late as January 1924 was still proclaiming his Labour affiliations. In 1920, he had been an opponent of Sinn Féin. Yet within two years of the signing of the Anglo-Irish Treaty, he was a Dáil deputy on behalf of Cumann na nGaedheal.

In June 1927, John J. Horgan of the National League and Richard Anthony of Labour were elected. The National League was the successor of the old Irish Parliamentary Party, the party which was effectively wiped out in the 1918 general election by Sinn Féin. Richard Anthony, while a popular candidate, had not been an active participant during the War of Independence. Seán French was elected for Fianna Fáil in this election, defeating Mary MacSwiney of the Sinn Féin party. French, who owned a chemist's business, was elected Lord Mayor of Cork in 1924, having been a successful candidate in the 1920 local government elections. Yet he had no record of military involvement during the War of Independence. Neither had Barry Egan, the second Cumann na nGaedhael TD elected. He was a member of Cork Corporation and of various bodies in the city such as the Industrial Development Association and the Harbour Commissioners.

This trend was continued in the general election of September 1927 when J. J. Walsh bowed out of electoral politics. Egan and Cosgrave were elected for Cumann na nGaedhael, with Anthony again securing a seat for Labour. Seán French was again elected for Fianna Fáil but this time, he was joined by a wealthy businessman, Hugo Flinn, who was elected with the help of Horgan's transfers. Flinn was yet another successful candidate who had not been prominent in public life during the War of Independence but this did not in any way hinder his political progress. Incidentally, de Róiste was not even considered by Cumann na nGaedhael as a candidate in this election and was quite bitter as a result. In the 1932 general election Barry Egan, outgoing Cumann na nGaedhael TD, failed to get a nomination. John J. Horgan, the defeated National League candidate in the previous election, was nominated, as was William

Desmond, who stood for the Commercial Party in the 1920 local elections and the Businessmen's Party in 1929. President Cosgrave was again nominated along with Alexander Healy. Of the four Cumann na nGaedhael candidates, Cosgrave and Desmond were elected. On the Fianna Fáil side, T. P. Dowdall replaced Seán French who did not go forward, and was elected along with Hugo Flinn. Dowdall, of course, was very active behind the scenes throughout the entire period and was a committed Irish-Irelander. However he had never been a military man.

Quite clearly, therefore, the possession of a 'national record' was not the determining factor in the selection of candidates in the early 1920s in Cork politics. Interestingly, within Cumann na nGaedhael, there appears to have been an ongoing power struggle throughout the decade between members with an Irish-Ireland outlook and those who adhered to the old Nationalist school of politics, with the latter group emerging victorious in 1932. The fact that Cumann na nGaedhael was formed within a year of the Anglo-Irish Treaty was mainly responsible for this, as people with different political perceptions united around upholding the Treaty and securing the stability of the new state. As time went on, the Treaty issue receded in importance and 'normal' politics resumed.

The often-repeated assertion that membership of local councils can serve as a springboard to success in parliamentary elections is certainly borne out by the Cork city experience. The municipal elections of 1920 produced ten councillors who were to stand in future general elections. Of these, eight were successful.[11] In addition, Bax's finding that the War of Independence ushered in a new breed of 'approachable' public representative, owing to a marked shift in the class backgrounds of those becoming involved in political activity, is confirmed by an analysis of the occupations of the successful Sinn Féin and Transport Union candidates in the 1920 local elections. Of the Sinn Féin and Transport Union candidates elected, three were TDs, four were self-employed, two were university professors, two were accountants, four were clerks, three were described as organisers (possibly trade unionists) and the remainder, tradesmen or manual workers. It could be said that the voters watched their neighbours and fellow-workers become the new political elite both at national and local level.

One important question that arises concerns the role of the backbench TD in the early years of the party political system. Was the TD a legislator or an intermediary for his constituency? In his diaries, de Róiste frequently complained about the lack of consultation between 1918 and 1922 and was very critical of Ernest Blythe and Patrick Hogan, who resented the independent stance taken by de Róiste in the Dáil during the Civil War.[12] O'Rahilly's experience in the Dáil would seem to indicate that the Cumann na nGaedhael Executive felt that backbench TDs were there primarily to support the government and not to determine policy. President Cosgrave's attitude to O'Rahilly's complaints was one of annoyance, as is demonstrated by his caustic comment that the parliamentary party would want an executive of its own 'if it goes on demanding the same show'.[13] At an Ard Chomhairle meeting held on 30 May 1925, Pádraic Ó Máille, TD, claimed that the parliamentary party had very little say in the formulation of government policy and that permanent officials in the civil service had too much influence.[14] This theme recurs with noticeable regularity throughout the decade. J. J. Walsh had come to many of the same conclusions. His was simply a more prominent route.

The type of work undertaken by TDs is also glossed by the regular absences from the Dáil. Both Cumann na nGaedhael and Fianna Fáil had ongoing problems in relation to their deputies' attendance at the Dáil. Fortunately the minutes of the Fianna Fáil parliamentary party are available from 1927 and these reveal that attendance problems were discussed frequently. At a parliamentary party meeting held on 12 July 1928, Lemass proposed that members who were absent for two days from the Dáil through illness should furnish a medical certificate before being excused and it was also agreed that a meeting of deputies who were also members of county councils should be called in order to work out arrangements for these deputies to attend the Dáil without, if possible, neglecting their duties as councillors.[15] On 22 November 1928, Gerry Boland, TD, reported that three members of the party had absented themselves without permission from the Dáil to attend county council meetings.[16] On 18 April 1929, the party whips were asked to make arrangements to secure a better attendance of members of the party in the Dáil Chamber during sittings.[17]

At a parliamentary party meeting held on 31 October 1929, it was noted that permission for leave of absence from the Dáil for the purpose of attending county council meetings should be refused[18] and at a further meeting on 14 November, three notices of motions relating to the issue were given. The first was from Martin Corry:

That the two Cork City TDs be fined £1 each for not asking permission of the party to attend Cork Harbour Board on Wednesday 7th inst.

The second was from Tommy Mullins, asking that before any report of a deputy's absence from the Dáil be circulated to the constituency, 'a copy of same be sent to the individual concerned for his explanation and that within five days from date of receipt, the report and excuse be sent out'. The third notice of motion was again from Martin Corry, demanding that no further reports of deputies' absences from the Dáil be sent to the Comhairle Ceanntair. The party had decided to report a TD's absence to the local constituency committee and obviously this did not suit certain deputies.[19] At a meeting held on 9 July 1931, the matter was again raised although this time in relation to selection of candidates for the impending election. The issue was discussed and the following resolution was read from the National Executive:

> That the National Executive request the Party to inform the Executive of the names of those members of the Party whose conduct or attendance at Dáil Divisions is considered unsatisfactory by the party.

In a response to this, the parliamentary party decided that the following system of reporting to the National Executive be discussed at the next meeting:

> Members whose attendance at Dáil is unsatisfactory to be reported to the National Executive with a request that they be not ratified as candidates in future.[20]

Although the Cumann na nGaedhael parliamentary party minutes are available only from 1930, it is clear that the party had similar problems in relation to attendances. At a meeting held on 6 March 1930, it was agreed that members of the party who were absent from a number of divisions should be written to by the chief whip and that the monthly list should be sent to the general secretary of the party. A suggestion that the list of monthly attendances should be published in the press was deferred for future consideration.[21] And at a meeting held on 28 March 1930, following the government's defeat in the Dáil on the second reading of the Old Age Pensions Bill, it was unanimously decided that any member of the party who 'absents himself in future without just cause shall render himself to expulsion'.[22] In general, the Cumann na nGaedhael party was worried about the number of absentees from Dáil divisions, and a weekly record of such absences was kept. It was always the first item on the agenda at meetings of the parliamentary party.[23]

What were the TDs doing if they were not attending Dáil divisions? From the evidence of the Fianna Fáil parliamentary party minutes, it appears that meetings of the municipal bodies frequently clashed with Dáil sessions and that on these occasions, Dáil deputies opted to attend the former in preference to the latter.[24] As Bax has pointed out, up to the 1940s, county councils had immense powers and local councillors in particular had tremendous influence over a wide range of issues from the allocation of council houses to major road improvements.[25] One could speculate that deputies were consolidating their local electoral bases by attending local bodies of which they were members and by avoiding too many absences from their constituencies.

We know from a number of sources that Dáil deputies during this period acted as intermediaries for their constituents and that the followers of the two main parties expected rewards for their allegiances. Many of the problems experienced by Cumann na nGaedhael in its early years, already discussed in Chapter 3, were partially caused by the unrealised expectations of its members and supporters in relation to appointments and contracts. For example, on 10 October 1924, the Coiste Gnótha of Cumann na nGaedhael prepared a statement relating to the political situation at that time. As to whether the government was looking after its members and supporters, the statement had this to say:

> The power of this Organisation to hold the people's loyalty and, by gaining their support for its nominees, to secure the stability of the State, depends upon its efficiency, through the Government of its election, in giving reasonable satisfaction to the needs and hopes of its supporters. The question imposes itself whether it has been able to give them much satisfaction. The answer is undoubtedly no. The organisation's influence on Government policy and its power to affect patronage has been negligible, if not nil. In parts of the country it is openly recognised that to be connected with Cumann na nGaedhael is in most cases a handicap and in many cases a complete bar to appointments, preferments or even a fair deal in Land or Compensations.[26]

In relation to the Land Commission, the Coiste Gnótha reported continuing dissatisfaction among party members with its operation. It stated that a deputation from the organisation would shortly be seeing the Minister for Agriculture in order to lodge complaints concerning specific cases where his subordinates seemed to have discriminated in their operations against members of Cumann na nGaedhael. The report revealed that one Cumann na nGaedhael TD described the Land Commission in the following terms:

It is impossible to make the people believe that there is not some 'old gang' running the Land Commission and in league with the old gang left in the country.[27]

On the question of appointments, the Coiste Gnótha felt that this was the 'sorest question of all'. Cumann na nGaedhael party members were complaining that those 'who won the fight have not done well out of the victory, whereas the pro-British ascendancy who lost the fight have done disproportionately well and got a new lease of life from the Free State'.[28]

The significance of this statement from the Coiste Gnótha is the revelation that Cumann na nGaedhael members and supporters expected rewards in the form of jobs, land and favours of various kinds from the Free State government. Obviously, it was through their local TDs that these requests were made.

Although source material for this subject is somewhat scarce, a memo prepared by General Eoin O'Duffy for the government in 1931 objecting to its decision to cut Garda pay for the third time in a decade gives a revealing picture of the role played by the Garda Síochána as 'prize-producers' for the Cumann na nGaedhael TDs:

> And what I am about to say now I would prefer to leave unsaid if I could avoid it. The Garda, individually and collectively, has been for the past nine years more loyal and faithful and constant in its support of the present Government than any other state service. It has been recruited 99% from supporters of Cumann na nGaedhael, and up to date Cumann na nGaedhael organisers rely upon the local Sergeants for hints and advice to enable them to carry out their organising work.[29]

During general elections, O'Duffy continued, it was the local sergeant who was the power behind the scenes, having an intimate knowledge of the people who could bring the most influence to bear on others for the purpose of securing their votes for the government. He added that the TDs were fully aware of this situation because over the previous few weeks, every post had brought him appeals from deputies to cancel transfers of gardaí until after the coming election, which he duly did. O'Duffy then recounted an incident that had occurred in County Leitrim where a garda found it necessary on one or two occasions to engage cars from garages owned by Fianna Fáil supporters. A complaint was made to O'Duffy concerning the loyalty of the garda and on investigation and examination of the official records, it was found that the garda concerned consistently engaged cars from government supporters. On the occasions referred to, no cars other than from Fianna Fáil garages were available, the others being also on Garda duty. In addition, prosecutions of publicans who were supporters of the government, left the local gardaí open to allegations of disloyalty and O'Duffy had to investigate hundreds of such cases. O'Duffy noted that 'Gardaí grew up in the belief, because of circumstances, that they were servants of the Government Party rather the State itself, and felt very badly discriminated against'.[30] Finally, in the Mulcahy and Blythe papers, there are occasional letters requesting the minister to use his influence to procure a job for someone, or (as in the case of Barrry Egan, TD) trying to secure another opportunity for a client to pass an oral Irish examination so as to maintain her position in the public service.[31]

However, this type of 'brokerage' activity was by no means confined to the Cumann na nGaedhael party. The minutes of the Fianna Fáil parliamentary party contain plenty of examples of TDs acting as intermediaries for their constituents. The papers of Fianna Fáil's Séamus Fitzgerald tell similar tales.[32] At a meeting of the parliamentary party held on 1 May 1930, Deputy Ben Maguire proposed a motion calling on Dáil Éireann to disapprove of the action of the Minister for Local Government in refusing to allow deputies make personal representations to the deciding officer on behalf of old-age pensions claimants whose cases had been appealed by the pension officer.[33] When Fianna Fáil assumed power in 1932, its members and supporters expected increased rewards and services, just like their Cumann na nGaedhael counterparts had ten years previously. For example, at a meeting held on 9 June 1932, Deputies Maguire and Allen put forward the following motion: 'That a dependable person be put in charge of each department of Government to deal with all inquiries submitted by TDs'.[34]

The motion was discussed at length and was eventually withdrawn. However, the fact that it had been tabled at all reveals the trend that was developing and also perhaps the volume of inquiries being processed by TDs. At a meeting held on 7 July 1932, Deputy Seán Moylan proposed a motion asking the ministry to define its position with regard to the employment of ex-IRA men and how far it was possible for ministers to proceed in placing such men in and under their various departments. He also asked how far they were prepared to involve members of the party in apportioning work and filling vacancies in the various constituencies. It was decided to send a copy of the motion to the Executive Council for reply by the next party meeting.[35] It was eventually agreed on 3 November, again in response to a motion by Moylan, that in the event of positions becoming vacant in government departments or under the local authorities in the constituencies, no deputy from an outside constituency ought to interfere without first discussing the case with the local deputy.[36] At a meeting of the party on 9 December, Deputy Murphy complained of the manner in which he had been received by Dr Conn Ward, Minister for Local Government and Public Health, when he asked him to meet a deputation. At the same meeting, Dr Ward was authorised to form a committee to make recommendations with regard to the system of making public appointments.[37]

The Fianna Fáil grass roots also felt that they would be 'looked after' once Fianna Fáil had attained power and this is reflected in motions to the 1933 Ard-Fheis. Motion 5 put it quite bluntly:

> That as the provision of employment for the idle members of the organisation, with particular reference to those who took an active part in the national fight, is of paramount importance, this Ard-Fheis requests the Government to lend its energies to this very urgent problem with a view to its early solution. (Wolfe Tone Cumann, Dublin North)[38]

A number of *cumainn* also called for the abolition of the Local Appointments Commission and the restoration to local authorities of the powers which had been taken from them by the Commission. This, of course, would have put local councillors at the helm in relation to deciding appointments to local authorities. The government was also called upon to make provision for a special scheme of cottages to be let out at a minimum rent to members of the Old IRA. This, according to the proposers, would defeat victimisation by hostile majorities on local boards. Finally, a motion from *cumainn* in Dundalk and Dublin called on the government to give the same degree of preference to those who had served in the IRA during the War of Independence as the 'Cosgrave government' had accorded to those who had served in the Free State army.[39]

It is quite clear, therefore, that brokerage-style politics were practised from the very beginning of the modern Irish party political system. Dáil deputies were expected to act as intermediaries for their constituents and did so.

POSTSCRIPT

This study of the politics of the period between 1918 and 1932 has traced the milestones of the development of 'party' in Cork city. Inevitably, as has been shown, these have been marked by elections and the ways in which various political interests competed with one another for the public trust. As we move from election to election, it can be seen how these interests came to define themselves in much clearer ways even if a considerable amount of crossover continued. We have also seen how this process of defining party politics was informed by a wide menu of policies. While the 'national issue' remained central to the politics of the day, party leaders, or at least those who realised the new climate of post-1922 Ireland, sought to broaden their political rhetoric to include socio-economic as well as political matters. This sense of pragmatism and realism was important in developing Fianna Fáil into a durable political party and ensured that it would develop a heterogenous base from the time of its establishment.

My study has also shown that the TDs who represented Cork at this time were expected to see voters as 'clients' as well as constituents. TDs were expected to act as intermediaries for their constituents. The supporters of both Cumann na nGaedhael and Fianna Fáil expected rewards for their services and many of the internal difficulties in Cumann na nGaedhael during the 1920s had their origin in the perception among its supporters that they were not receiving their due rewards. Nonetheless, it ensured the success of these parties and the demise of those who clung to the policy of abstentionism. In the process, Dáil Éireann came to be established not only as the legislative focus of the country but as the forum that would decide on concerns much nearer home. These last, the perception of the TD as someone who could address issues of more personal concern to his or her constituents was underlined by the fact that most TDs were also anxious to serve as local authority representatives. While this situation no longer exists, many would argue that the role of the TD as intermediary between constituent and decision maker has not. In any event, the parties of our early republic saw this intermediary role of the TD as being as important as that of the legislator and it proved to be crucial to their success.

The TDs who represented Cork were no different from colleagues who represented other parts of the country. However, what was different was the political context in which they were elected, a flavour of which I hope I have conveyed here. In doing so, I hope that I have also highlighted the importance and integrity with which men and women in democratic societies can, in honour and freedom, express an opinion on the issues of the day. In the crucial years before 1932, Ireland's political system both reflected and was driven by this sense of democracy. This essential liberty that whatever the issue, the people of Ireland can choose their destiny by democratic means is one which I hold very dear. That it was a liberty that was consolidated by the ways in which the leaders of our early republic stood, irrespective of party, establishes not only its historical worth but the enduring legacy of free speech. This book is a comment on this legacy.

NOTES

1. R. K. Carty, *Parish and Parish Pump: Electoral Politics in Ireland* (Canada, 1981); Richard Rose and Derek Unwin, 'Social Cohesion, Political Parties and Strains in Regimes' in *Comparative Political Studies* (1969) and 'Persistance and Change in Western Party Systems since 1945' in *ibid.* (1970).
2. Carty, *Parish and Parish Pump*, p. 3.
3. Peter Pyne, 'The Third Sinn Féin Party 1923–1926, Part II' in *Economic and Social Review* i (1969–70), pp. 235–37; Tom Garvin, 'Nationalist Elites, Irish Voters and Irish Political Development' in *ibid.* viii (1977), pp. 170–2; Erhard Rumpf and A. C. Hepburn, *Nationalism and Socialism in Twentieth-Century Ireland* (Liverpool, 1977).
4. Basil Chubb, *The Government and Politics of Ireland* (London, 1970).
5. Brian Farrell, *The First Dáil and After in the Irish Parliamentary Tradition* (Dublin, 1973), p. 212.
6. Cornelius O'Leary, *Irish Elections, 1918–1977: Parties, Voters and Proportional Representation* (Dublin, 1979), p. 7.
7. Basil Chubb, 'Society and the Political System' in Howard B. Penniman, ed., *Ireland at the Polls: The Dáil Elections of 1977* (Washington, DC, 1978) p. 10.
8. *Ibid.*, p. 11.

Chapter 1
1. O'Leary, *Irish Elections*, 1918–1977, p. 7.
2. Brian M. Walker (ed.), *Parliamentary Election Results in*

Ireland 1801–1922 (Dublin, 1978), p. xii.

3. Michael Laffan, *The Resurrection of Ireland: The Sinn Féin Party 1916–1923* (Cambridge, 1999), p.118.

4. De Róiste Diaries, Vol. 20, 28 May 1918. De Róiste's second quotation is cited from his letter to the Mansion House Committee, 2 June 1917, as in Laffan, *Resurrection of Ireland*, p.105. For biographical information, see the entry on de Róiste in the Royal Irish Academy's *Dictionary of Irish Biography* (forthcoming, 2009). I am grateful to the editor-in-chief, James McGuire, for allowing me to consult this information.

5. Sinn Féin. Tenth Convention. Thursday, 25 October 1917 (Dublin, 1917), p. 9.

6. Laffan, *Resurrection of Ireland*, p. 118.

7. For Labour's withdrawal, see Michael Laffan, 'Labour Must Wait: Ireland's Conservative Revolution', in Patrick J. Corish (ed.), *Radicals, Rebels and Establishments* (Belfast, 1985), pp. 214–6; Laffan, *Resurrection of Ireland*, p. 159.

8. *Cork Examiner (CE)*, 2 November 1918.

9. De Róiste Diaries, Vol. 20, 21 August 1918.

10. *CE*, 14 September 1918.

11. De Róiste Diaries, Vol. 20, 4, 5 September 1918.

12. *Ibid.*, 6 September 1918; Laffan, *Resurrection of Ireland*, p. 158. For the views of the Standing Committee, see Sinn Féin Standing Committee Minutes, 23 July 1918.

13. De Róiste Diaries, Vol. 20, 8 September, 28 October 1918.

14. Brian Farrell, 'Labour and the Irish Political Party System: A Suggested Approach to Analysis', *Economic and Social Review* i (1970), pp 489–502.

15. Dáil Éireann. Minutes of proceedings of the first parliament of the Republic of Ireland, pp. 22–3 (21 January 1919).

16. It could be argued that the Programme had been designed more as an appeal to Labour than a genuine exposition of intention. For example, see Brian Farrell, *The Founding of Dáil Éireann* (Dublin, 1971), pp. 57–8.

17. De Róiste Diaries,Vol. 22, 5 November 1918.

18. *CE*, 23 October 1918. Bishop Cohalan said that 'it was of vast importance to Ireland to have together a national gathering that resisted and broke conscription . . . to present our case to the Peace Conference'.

19. De Róiste Diaries, Vol. 22, 11 November 1918.

20. *Ibid.*, Vol. 23, 1 December 1918.

21. *CE*, 2 November 1918.

22. *Ibid.*, 21 November 1918.

23. J. J. Walsh, *Recollections of a Rebel* (Tralee, 1944), pp. 9, 28.

24. De Róiste Diaries, Vol. 21, 15 September 1918.

25. Peter Hart, *The IRA and its Enemies: Violence and Community Life in Cork, 1916–1923* (Oxford, 1998), p. 236.

26. *CE*, 13 December 1918.

27. *Ibid.*, 13, 14 December 1918.

28. F. S. L. Lyons, *Ireland since the Famine* (London, 1971), p. 399. However, Hart notes that 'intimidation of fathers by their children continued unabated through to the general election of December 1918; see Hart, *The IRA and its Enemies*, p. 166. See also Joost Augusteijn, *From Public Defiance to Guerrilla Warfare: The Experience of Ordinary Volunteers in the Irish War of Independence, 1916–1921* (Dublin, 1996), p. 260, concerning the impact of the young voter in 1918.

29. *CE*, 13 December 1918; Peter Hart, 'Class, Community and the Irish Republican Army in Cork, 1917–1923' in P. O'Flanagan (eds.), *Cork: History and Society* (Dublin, 1993), p. 971.

30. De Róiste Diaries, Vol. 23, 15 December 1918.

31. Laffan, *Resurrection of Ireland*, p. 162.
32. De Róiste, Diaries, Vol. 23, 8 December 1918.
33. Hart, *The IRA and its Enemies*, pp. 154–5; Walker, *Parliamentary Election Results*, p. 5.
34. Dáil Éireann. Minutes of proceedings of the first parliament of the Republic of Ireland, pp. 22–3 (21 January 1919), pp. 7–24 (21 January 1919); Arthur Mitchell, *Revolutionary Government in Ireland: Dáil Éireann, 1919–1922* (Dublin, 1995), pp. 16–17.
35. Tim Pat Coogan, *De Valera: Long Fellow, Long Shadow* (London, 1995), pp. 157–60; Laffan, *Resurrection of Ireland*, p.319.
36. Mary Koutsonouris, *Retreat from Revolution: the Dáil Courts, 1910–24* (Dublin, 1994); James Casey, 'Republican Courts in Ireland, 1919–22', *Irish Jurist*, 5 (1970) and 'The Genesis of the Dáil Courts' in *ibid.*, 9 (1974); Francis Costello, 'The Republican Courts and the Decline of British Rule in Ireland, 1919–1921' in *Éire-Ireland*, 25, 2 (1990).
37. Charles Townshend, *Political Violence in Ireland: Government and Resistance Since 1848* (Oxford, 1983), pp. 334–5.38. De Róiste Diaries, Vol. 29, 2 December 1919.
38. De Róiste Diaries, Vol. 29, 2 December 1919.
39. De Róiste Diaries, Vol. 28, 21 December 1919.
40. Hart, *The IRA and its Enemies*, pp. 237.
41. Mart Bax, *Harpstrings and Confessions: Machine-style Politics in the Irish Republic* (Essen & Amsterdam, 1976) p. 3; Chubb, Government and Politics of Ireland.
42. Tim Pat Coogan, *The IRA* (London, 1970), pp 24–5; J. Bowyer Bell, *The Secret Army: A History of the IRA 1916–1971* (Dublin, 1980; revised ed., Dublin, 1989); Hart, The IRA and its Enemies, pp. 237–8; Laffan, *Resurrection of Ireland*, pp. 193–8; David Fitzpatrick, *Politics and Irish Life, 1913–1921: Provincial Experience*

of War and Revolution (Cork, 1998), pp. 173–5;
Augusteijn, *From Public Defiance to Guerrilla Warfare.*

43. According to Desmond Greaves, Cork city was the only
    place where this electoral alliance took place; see
    C. Desmond Greaves, *The Irish Transport and General
    Workers' Union: The Formative Years* (Dublin, 1982), p.
    259.
44. *CE*, 6 January 1920 (full details of all nominations are
    given in this issue). See also Micheál Martin, 'The
    Formation and Evolution of the Irish Party Political
    System with Particular Reference to the Cork City
    Borough Constituency, 1918–1932' (MA thesis, UCC.,
    1988), pp 321–38.
45. *CE*, 12 January 1920.
46. *Ibid.*
47. De Róiste Diaries, Vol. 29, 3 January 1920.
48. *CE*, 6, 14 January 1920.
49. *Ibid.*, Laffan, *Resurrection of Ireland*, p. 328.
50. *CE*, 1, 6 January 1920. For the introduction of PR, see
    O'Leary, *Irish Elections*, p. 8.
51. *CE*, 13 January 1920.
52. *Ibid.*, 15 January 1920.
53. *Ibid.*, 19 January 1920. Full details of the election results
    are given in this issue. The percentages were calculated
    by myself.
54. These figures are approximates, calculated from figures
    given in the *CE*, 19 January 1920.
55. De Róiste Diaries, Vol. 50, 1 Febuary 1924.
56. *CE*, 21 January 1924. Only three candidates were
    elected on the official Labour Party ticket in 1920.
57. For the election results see Martin, 'Irish Party Political
    System', Appendix I, pt 2, pp 339–50.
58. De Róiste Diaries, Vol. 29, 18 January 1920.
59. This figure includes the estimated six Transport Union
    candidates who stood on the Sinn Féin platform. The ten

who stood in later Dáil elections were: J. J. Walsh, Richard Beamish, Professor Alfred O'Rahilly, Seán French, Michael Egan, John Horgan, William Desmond, Liam de Róiste, Seán O'Leary and Edward Fitzgerald. The last two were unsuccessful in their attempts.

60. De Róiste Diaries, Vol. 29, 17 January 1920.
61. *CE*, 19 January 1920.
62. *Ibid.*, 20 January 1920.
63. *Ibid.*, 31 January 1920. A detailed account of the meeting is given on p. 7.
64. *Ibid.*, 20 March 1920.
65. *Ibid.*, 20, 22 March 1920.
66. Hart, *The IRA and its Enemies*, p. 79.
67. Móirín Chavasse, *Terence McSweeney* (Dublin, 1961), p.132, p. 145. UCD, Mary MacSwiney Papers, P48b/ 400; Francis J. Costello, *Enduring the Most: The Life and Death of Terence MacSweeney* (Dingle, 1995), pp. 139–56.
68. Dorothy MacArdle, *The Irish Republic* (repr. London, 1968), p. 360; Hart, *The IRA and its Enemies*, p. 85. Details of interviews given by de Róiste to foreign pressmen at this time are given in his diary.
69. *CE*, 20 October1920.
70. *Ibid.*, 26 October 1920.
71. *Ibid.*, 26 October 1920.
72. *Ibid.*, 30 October 1920; Dermot Keogh, *The Vatican, the Bishops and Irish Politics 1919–1939* (Cambridge, 1986), p. 49, p. 58. While in Brixton, MacSwiney had also been visited by the Bishop O'Sullivan of Kerry and Bishop Browne of Cloyne.
73. *CE*, 20 October 1920.
74. Townshend, *Political Violence in Ireland*, p. 359; *The Burning of Cork City* (Cork, 1978).
75. British Labour Party, *Report of the Labour Commission to Ireland* (London, 1921), pp. 35, 38.

76. Keogh, *The Vatican, the Bishops and Irish Politics*, p. 61. Professor Keogh argues convincingly that Bishop Cohalan's decree on 12 December was very much misunderstood by Republicans at the time and that many saw it as a justification of English rule in Ireland. However, de Róiste was not among these.

77. Rumpf and Hepburn, *Nationalism and Socialism in Twentieth-Century Ireland*, p. 57. See also David Fitzpatrick, 'The Geography of Irish Nationalism' in C. E. H. Philpin (ed.), *Nationalism and Popular Protest in Ireland* (Cambridge, 1987), pp. 403–39; Michael Hopkinson, *Green Against Green: The Irish Civil War* (Dublin, 1988), pp. 40–6; and for comparative purposes, Marie Coleman, 'County Longford, 1910–1923: A Regional Study of the Irish Revolution' (PhD dissertation, UCD, 1998).

78. *CE*, 9 May 1921.

79. O'Leary, *Irish Elections, 1918–1977*, p. 9.

80. Laffan, *Resurrection of Ireland*, p.338.

81. De Róiste Diaries, Vol. 36, 5 May 1921.

82. *Ibid.*, 9 May 1921; Éamon de Valera to Austin Stack, 7 May 1921, as in UCD, Éamon de Valera Papers, as quoted in Laffan, *Resurrection of Ireland*, p. 338.

83. De Róiste Diaries, 20 October 1917, as in National Library of Ireland (NLI), Florence O'Donoghue Papers, MS 31, 146 (1).

84. De Róiste Diaries, Vol. 36, 3, 15, 20 May 1921.

85. Tom Garvin, *1922: The Birth of Democracy* (Dublin, 1996), p.42.

86. *CE*, 9 May 1921.

87. *Ibid.*, 14 May 1921.

Chapter 2

1. Iris Dháil Éireann: Official Report. Debate on the Treaty between Great Britain and Ireland signed in London on 6 December 1921 (19 December 1921), p. 32.

2. The oath which technically swore 'true faith and allegiance to the Constitution of the Irish Free State as by law established and that ___ will be faithful to HM George V, his heirs and successors', was repeatedly portrayed by the anti-Treatyites as an oath of allegiance to the British king. Nonetheless, the anti-Treatyites used the mistake, or deliberate misrepresentation, to good effect; see Treaty between Great Britain and Ireland signed in London on 6 December 1921; MacArdle, *Irish Republic*, p. 574.
3. Iris Dháil Éireann: Official Report. Debate on the Treaty between Great Britain and Ireland signed in London on 6 December 1921 (3 January 1922), p. 190.
4. Walsh, *Recollections of a Rebel* p. 56.
5. De Róiste Diaries,Vol. 41, 26 December 1921.
6. Iris Dháil Éireann: Official Report. Debate on the Treaty Between Great Britain and Ireland Signed in London on 6 December 1921 (21 December 1921), p. 110.
7. De Róiste Diaries, Vol. 41, 12 December 1921.
8. As Hart has pointed out, de Róiste was in a position to make such reports as 'he watched Cork hasten to divide'; see Hart, *The IRA and its Enemies*, pp. 112–6.
9. De Róiste Diaries, Vol. 41, 30 December 1921.
10. *Ibid.*, Vol. 42, 2 January 1922.
11. *Ibid.*, Vol. 41, 26, 27 December 1921.
12. *Ibid.*, 29, 30, 31 December 1921.
13. *Ibid.*, Vol. 42, 2–30 January 1922; Hart, *The IRA and its Enemies*, pp. 237–8.
14. De Róiste Diaries, Vol. 42, 26 January 1922.
15. *Ibid.*, 28 January 1922.
16. *Ibid.*, 30 January 1922.
17. *Ibid.*, 1 Febuary1922.
18. *Ibid.*
19. *Ibid.*
20. *Ibid.*, 14 Febuary 1922.
21. John A. Murphy, *Ireland in the Twentieth Century*

(Dublin, 1975), p. 47.

22. Hart, *The IRA and its Enemies*, pp. 112–3.
23. Garvin, *1922*, p. 126.
24. Michael Gallagher, 'The pact general election of 1922' in *Irish Historical Studies* (IHS), 21 (September 1979), pp. 404–21; Garvin, *1922*, pp. 127–40
25. De Róiste Diaries, Vol. 44, 29 May 1922.
26. *Ibid.*, 16 June 1922.
27. *Ibid.*, 10 June 1922.
28. *CE*, 12 June 1922.
29. *Ibid.*
30. *CE*, 12 June 1922.
31. De Róiste Diaries, Vol. 44, 12 June 1922.
32. *Ibid.*, 6 June 1922.
33. *CE*, 12 June 1922.
34. *Ibid.*, 16 June 1922.
35. *Ibid.*, 10 June 1922.
36. *Ibid.*, 14 June 1922.
37. *Ibid*, 14 June 1922.
38. *Ibid.*, 14 .June 1922.
39. *Ibid.*, 8 June 1922.
40. *Ibid.*, 15 June l922.
41. De Róiste Diaries, Vol. 44, 3 June 1922.
42. *CE*, 15 June 1922, where a full account of the meeting is given.
43. For an assessment of Collins' speech, see Gallagher, 'The pact general election of 1922', pp. 412–3.
44. *CE*, 15 June 1922
45. *Ibid.*, 12 June 1922.
46. *Ibid.*, 17 June 1922.
47. Walker, *Parliamentary Election Results*, pp. 104–8.
48. *CE*, 19 June 1922. See also appendix to Martin, 'Formation and Evolution of the Irish Party Political System', pp. 353–6.
49. *CE*, 19 June 1922.

50. Hart, *The IRA and its Enemies*, pp. 113–4.
51. Rumpf and Hepburn, *Nationalism and Socialism in Twentieth-Century Ireland*, p. 32
52. Murphy, *Ireland in the Twentieth Century*; Richard Sinnott, *Irish Voters Decide: Voting Behaviour in Elections and Referendums Since 1918* (Manchester, 1995); Laffan, *Resurrection of Ireland*, p. 64, pp. 406–7.
53. De Róiste Diaries, Vol. 44, 18 June 1922.
54. De Róiste Diaries, Vol. 44, 10 June 1922.
55. Hopkinson, *Green Against Green*, pp. 124–5, 132, 189–91.
56. Moss Twomey to Robert Brennan as quoted in Robert Brennan, *Allegiance* (Dublin, 1950), p. 351.
57. De Róiste Diaries, Vol. 46 (July–October 1922) gives a detailed account of the behind-the-scenes activities of the period.
58. De Róiste Diaries, Vol. 46, 26 September 1922.
59. UCD, Mulcahy Papers, P7 A/81), Lynch to O'Malley, 1 October 1922. 60. De Róiste Diaries, Vol. 46, 15 July 1922.

Chapter 3
1. UCD, Cumann na nGaedhael Papers, p. 39; Minutes of General Election Committee, 7 September 1922.
2. *Ibid.*, 7 September, 27 October, 3 November 1922.
3. *Ibid.*, Cumann na nGaedhael Party Minute Books, p. 39/1/1; Minutes of Preliminary Conference of Cumann na nGaedhael, 7 December 1922.
4. John M. Regan, *The Irish Counter-Revolution 1921–1936* (Dublin, 1999), p. 141.
5. Séamas O hAodha, secretary of the General Election Committee, to General Mulcahy, 21 December 1922. There is also an account of the meeting in UCD, Mulcahy Papers, P7/B/325, Minutes of Preliminary Conference, 7 December 1922.

6. UCD, Cumann na nGaedhael Papers p. 39; Minutes of meeting of Provisional General Council, 2 Febuary 1923.

7. *Ibid.*, Minutes of Drafting Subcommittee, 30 September 1922.

8. *Ibid.*, Minutes, 15 June 1923; Regan, *Irish Counter-Revolution*, pp. 129–44.

9. UCD, Cumann na nGaedhael Papers, Minutes of Drafting Subcommittee, Secretary's statement on finance for special meeting of Coiste Gnótha, 26 September 1924.

10. *Ibid.*, Report of Convention, 27 May 1923.

11. Peter Pyne, 'The Third Sinn Féin Party, 1923–1926', Part I, in *The Economic and Social Review*, i (1969) p. 32; Laffan, *Resurrection of Ireland*, p. 428.

12. Pyne, 'The Third Sinn Féin Party', p. 33; Laffan, *Resurrection of Ireland*, p. 436; Keogh, *The Vatican, the Bishops*, p. 123.

13. Murphy, *Ireland in the Twentieth Century*, p. 59; Laffan, *Resurrection of Ireland*, p. 437; Walker, *Parliamentary Election Results*, pp. 108–15; Richard Sinnott, *Irish Voters Decide*, pp. 96–7.

14. *CE*, 31 August 1923; Walker, *Parliamentary Election Results*, p. 109.

15. De Róiste Diaries, Vol. 48, 2, 7 and 16 July 1923. T. P. Dowdall was to join Fianna Fáil in September 1927 and was elected a TD in the 1932 general election.

16. *CE*, 9 July 1923.

17. *Ibid.*

18. De Róiste Diaries, Vol. 48, 16 July 1923.

19. *Ibid.*, 19 July 1923

20. *Ibid.*, 22, 26 June and 2 July 1923.

21. *Ibid.*, 30 July 1923.

22. *Ibid.*

23. *Ibid.*, 3 August 1923.

24. *Ibid.*, Vol. 49, 18 August 1923.

25. J. Anthony Gaughan, *Alfred O'Rahilly Vol. II Public Figure* (Dublin, 1989), pp. 198–200.
26. UCD, Mulcahy Papers, P7a/182, Cosgrave to O'Rahilly, 17 August 1923.
27. UCD, Cumann na nGaedhael Papers, Minutes of National Standing Committee 9 August 1923.
28. *Ibid.*, 22 August 1923.
29. *CE*, 16 August 1923. At this convention T. P. Dowdall was appointed with others to make collections for the national funds.
30. *Ibid.*, 20, 21 August 1923.
31. *Ibid.*, 25, 27 August 1923.
32. *Ibid.*, 15 August 1923.
33. *Ibid.*, 20 August 1923.
34. *Ibid.*
35. *Ibid.*, 25 August 1923.
36. The Provisional Government had been replaced by the Free State Government in December 1922.
37. *CE*, 21 August 1923.
38. *Ibid.*, 22 August 1923.
39. Walsh, *Recollections of a Rebel*, p. 32.
40. *CE*, 24 August 1923.
41. *Ibid.*, 22 August 1923.
42. *Ibid.*, 20 August 1923.
43. *Ibid.*
44. *Ibid.*, 13 August 1923.
45. *Ibid.*
46. *Ibid.*, 25 August 1923.
47. *Ibid.*, 20 August 1923.
48. *Ibid.*, 18 August 1923. A Comprehensive account of the meeting is given.
49. *Ibid.*, 22 August 1923.
50. Dáil Debates iii, cols. 1700–1, 8 June 1923.
51. *CE*, 24 August 1923.
52. *Ibid.*, 25 August 1923.

53. *Ibid.*

54. *Ibid.*, 30 August 1923; Walker, *Parliamentary Election Results*, p. 109. Walker's figure for Corcoran is slightly different from what I have listed here (1,616 instead of 1,618). For full details and analysis of the election results see Martin, 'Irish Party Political System', Appendix II, pp 357–66.

55. Cumann na nGaedhael meetings were always reviewed on p.7 of the Cork Examiner with very large headlines and considerable allocation of space.

56. *CE*, 31 August 1923.

57. Laffan, *Resurrection of Ireland*, p. 436; Pyne, '*The Third Sinn Féin Party*', pp 33–4, p. 35.

58. Pyne, '*The Third Sinn Féin Party*', pp 41, 42. (There were no Elections in Cork city in 1925 owing to the abolition of Cork Corporation in 1924).

59. De Róiste Diaries, Vol. 50, 1 Febuary 1924; Richard Dunphy, *The Making of Fianna Fáil Power in Ireland* (Oxford, 1995), p. 65.

60. *CE*, 31 January 1924. A comprehensive account of the mayoral election is given in this issue.

61. *Ibid.*

62. *Ibid.*

63. *Ibid.*

64. *Ibid.*

65. UCD, Mulcahy Papers, P7 A/182, O'Rahilly to Mulcahy, 3 January 1924.

66. Regan, *Irish Counter-Revolution*, pp. 221–2; Gaughan, *Alfred O'Rahilly*, pp. 210–5.

67. UCD, Mulcahy Papers, P7 A/182, O'Rahilly to Mulcahy, 3 January 1924.

68. O'Rahilly is quoted in Regan, *Irish Counter-Revolution*, p. 222.

69. UCD, Mulcahy Papers, P7 A/182, 3 January 1924.

70. De Róiste Diaries, Vols. 48–55.

71. Minutes of Ard Chomhairle, 13 May 1924. See also Regan, *Irish Counter-Revolution*, pp. 199–200 and 'The Politics of Reaction: The Dynamics of Treatyite Government and Policy 1922–23' I *IHS* 30 (November, 1997), pp. 556
72. Minutes of Coiste Gnótha, 13 May 1924.
73. Maryann G. Valiulis, *Almost A Rebellion: The Irish Army Mutiny of 1924* (Cork, 1985) and 'The "Army Mutiny" of 1924 and the Assertion of Civilian Authority in Independent Ireland' in *IHS*, 32, 92 (November 1923); J. P. Duggan, *A History of the Irish Army* (Dublin, 1991), pp. 130–7; and Ronan Fanning, *Independent Ireland* (Dublin, 1983), pp. 49–52.
74. UCD, Blythe Papers, Séamus Dolan, secretary of Cumann na nGaedhael, to Ernest Blythe, 17 September 1924.
75. *Ibid.*
76. *Ibid.*, Coiste Gnótha to Ernest Blythe, September 1924
77. *Ibid.*
78. Regan, *Irish Counter-Revolution*, p. 222.
79. De Róiste Diaries, Vol. 52, 28 October 1924.
80. Mrs Collins-Powell's comments were recorded in de Róiste's diary on 30 October 1924.
81. De Róiste Diaries, Vol. 52, 3 November 1924.
82. Minutes of Coiste Gnótha, 24 October 1924 (Cumann na nGaedhael Papers, p. 39).
83. Minutes of Coiste Gnótha 31 October 1924.
84. De Róiste Diaries, Vol. 52, 18 November 1924
85. *Ibid.*, 16 March 1925.
86. *Ibid.* Vol. 54. 20 November l925.
87. *Ibid.*, 30 November 1925.
88. Patrick Maume, *'Life That is Exile': Daniel Corkery and the Search for Irish Ireland* (Belfast, 1993), p. 91.
89. *Ibid.*, 2 May 1925.
90. *The Irish Tribune*, 12 March 1926 (copy in NLI).

91. *Ibid.*, 12 March – 31 December 1926.
92. Pyne, '*The Third Sinn Féin Party*', p. 43; Thomas P. O'Neill, 'In Search of a Political Path: Irish Republicanism, 1922 to 1927' in G. A. Hayes-McCoy, *Historical Studies X* (Galway, 1976), pp. 163–4.
93. Confidential police reports 3 August 1924, 20 September 1924, as in UCD, Blythe Papers, P24/223.
94. Pyne, '*The Third Sinn Féin Party*', p. 44; John Horgan, *Seán Lemass: The Enigmatic Patriot* (Dublin, 1997), pp. 42–3; Peter Pyne, 'The New Irish State and the Decline of the Republican Sinn Féin Party, 1923–26' in *Éire-Ireland*, 11 (Autumn, 1976), p. 53; Dunphy, *The Making of Fianna Fáil Power*, p.68.
95. Michael Laffan, *The Partition of Ireland 1911–1925* (Dundalk, 1987), pp. 91–105; J. J. Lee, *Ireland 1912–1985. Politics and Society* (Cambridge, 1995), pp. 140–51; G. J. Hand (ed.), Report of the Irish Boundary Commission 1925 (Shannon, 1965) and 'MacNeill and the Boundary Commission' in F. X. Martin & F. J. Byrne (eds.), *The Scholar Revolutionary* (Shannon, 1973).
96. Pyne, 'Freedom to Choose', p. 44; Dunphy, *The Making of Fianna Fáil Power*, pp. 69–70.
97. Report of Sinn Féin Ard-Fheis, 10 March 1926 (Dublin, 1926); Sinn Féin Funds Case, Book 49, Minute 11, p.16, as quoted in Pyne, '*The Third Sinn Féin Party*', pp. 45–6.
98. Pyne, '*The Third Sinn Féin Party*', pp. 45–6.
99. *Ibid.*, pp. 47–9; O'Neill, 'In Search of a Political Path', pp. 169–71.
100. Minutes of Ard Chomhairle, December 1925 (Cumann na nGaedhael Papers, p. 39).
101. *Ibid.*
102. *Ibid.*
103. *Ibid.*
104. De Róiste Diaries, Vol. 54, 6 December1925.
105. *Ibid.*, 3 December 1925.

106. *Ibid.*, 6 December 1925.
107. Pyne, '*The Third Sinn Féin Party*', pp. 245–6.
108. *Ibid.*, p. 252; Dunphy, *The Making of Fianna Fáil Power*, pp. 96–7.
109. Pyne, '*The Third Sinn Féin Party*', pp. 248–51.
110. John Whyte, *Dáil Deputies: Their Work, Its Difficulties, Possible Remedies* (Tuairim Pamphlet No. 15, Dublin,) pp. 9, 12; Laffan, *Resurrection of Ireland*, p. 446; Pyne, 'The New Irish State and the Decline of the Republican Sinn Féin Party', pp. 64–5.
111. Bax, *Harpstrings and Confessions*, p. 71.
112. Pyne, '*The Third Sinn Féin Party*', p. 244.
113. *Ibid.*, p. 252; Dunphy, *The Making of Fianna Fáil Power*, pp. 84–5.
114. Sinnott, *Irish Voters*, pp. 96–100.
115. Garvin, 'Nationalist Elites, Irish Voters and Irish Political Development', p. 169.
116. Peter Mair, 'Labour and the Irish Party System Revisited. Party Competition in the 1920s', *Economic and Social Review*, 9, 1, (1977), p. 64.

Chapter 4

1. B. A. Reynolds, 'The Formation and Development of Fianna Fáil, 1926–1932' (PhD dissertation, TCD, 1976).
2. *Ibid.*; Dunphy, *The Making of Fianna Fáil Power*, p.74.
3. Robert Briscoe, *For the Life of Me* (London, 1959), p. 228.
4. UCD, Fianna Fáil Papers.
5. *Ibid.*
6. Michael McInerney, interview with Seán MacEntee, *The Irish Times* 23 July 1974.
7. UCD, Fianna Fáil Papers, FF/702, Hon. Secretary's report, 1928.
8. Reynolds, 'Formation and Development of Fianna Fáil'. The National League was founded by Captain William

Redmond in 1926. It wanted to move beyond the Civil War and urged that the country be governed by those who had taken no part in that war. Clann Éireann, or the People's Party, was founded in the wake of the Boundary Commission by disgruntled former members of Cumann na nGaedhael. Its policies were very vague and included the removal of the oath. See Warner Moss, *Political Parties in the Irish Free State* (New York, 1933), pp. 25–7, p. 141.

9. Extract from an interview given by Éamon de Valera to the representative of the United Press, 17 April 1926, reprinted in *Éamon de Valera, A National Policy Outlined: Speech Delivered at the Inaugural Meeting of Fianna Fáil* (Dublin, 1926), p. 18.
10. Reynolds, 'Formation and Development of Fianna Fáil'.
11. Lyons, *Ireland Since the Famine*, p. 481.
12. Michael McInerney, *Peadar O'Donnell: Irish Social Rebel* (Dublin, 1974), pp. 113–14.
13. UCD, Fianna Fáil Papers Ard-Fheis *clár*, 1926.
14. *Ibid.*
15. Ard-Fheis *clár*, 1927.
16. Ard-Fheis Report, 1928.
17. Reynolds, 'Formation and Development of Fianna Fáil'.
18. *Ibid.*
19. Walsh, *Recollections of a Rebel,* pp. 72, 90.
20. UCD, MacSwiney Papers, P48a/43. Eamon Donnelly to Mary MacSwiney, 2 April 1927.
21. *Ibid.*
22. *Ibid.* MacSwiney to Donnelly, 2 April 1927.
23. *Ibid.*, 10 April 1927.
24. *Ibid.*, MacSwiney to Standing Committee of Sinn Féin, 9 April 1927
25. *Ibid.*
26. *Ibid.*, Michael O'Donnell to MacSwiney, 21 April 1927.
27. *Ibid.*, Donnelly to MacSwiney, n.d.

28. Peadar O'Donnell to secretary, Sinn Féin, 27 April (*ibid.*, P48a/43). Those present at the meeting were: Tom Maguire, Dr John A. Madden, Seán Buckley, John Joe Sheehy, Ernie O'Malley, P. J. Ruttledge, Seán Lemass, Dr James Ryan, Eamon Donnelly, Michael Kilroy and Tom Derrig. Also present on behalf of the IRA were Andy Cooney, Moss Twomey, Seán MacBride, Tom Daly and Peadar O Donnell.
29. UCD, MacSwiney Papers, P48a/43, MacSwiney to de Valera, 11 May 1927.
30. *Ibid.*, de Valera to MacSwiney, P48a/43 (50).
31. Pyne, '*The Third Sinn Féin Party*', p. 245.
32. UCD, Blythe Papers, P24/453, Speech by Cosgrave to Cumann na nGaedhael Ard-Fheis, 1927.
33. Murphy, *Ireland in the Twentieth Century*, p. 69.
34. Reynolds, 'Formation and Development of Fianna Fáil'.
35. De Róiste Diaries, Vol. 54, 16 April 1927.
36. *Ibid.*, 1–2 May 1927.
37. O'Leary, *Irish Elections*, p. 37.
38. CE, 2 May 1927.
39. *Ibid.*, 11 May 1927.
40. *Ibid.*
41. *Ibid.*
42. *Ibid.*, 8 June 1927.
43. *Ibid.*
44. *Ibid.*
45. *Ibid.*, 10 May 1927.
46. *Ibid.*
47. *Ibid.*
48. *Ibid.*
49. *Ibid.*
50. *Ibid.*, 11 May 1927.
51. *Ibid.*, 9 June 1927.
52. *Ibid.*, 7 June 1927.
53. *Ibid.*

54. *Ibid.*, 2 May 1927.

55. *Ibid.*, 7 June 1927.

58. *Ibid.*, 2 May 1927.

60. *Ibid.*, 8 June 1927.

62. *Ibid.*, 7 June 1927.

63. *Ibid.*, 10 June 1927; Regan, *Irish Counter-Revolution*, p. 270.

64. De Róiste Diaries, Vol. 54, 17 May 1927.

65. Walsh, *Recollections of a Rebel*, p. 67.

66. *CE*, 13 June 1927.

68. *Ibid.*, 14 June 1927.

69. Sinnott, *Irish Voters*, p. 98.

70. UCD, Fianna Fáil Papers. Minutes of the first meeting of Fianna Fáil parliamentary party, 22 June 1927.

71. *Ibid.*, Minutes of second meeting, 23 June 1927.

72. *Ibid.*, Minutes of third meeting, 18 July 1927.

73. Terence de Vere White, *Kevin O'Higgins* (London, 1948); Regan, *Irish Counter-Revolution*, pp. 83–7; Lee, *Ireland 1912–1985*, pp. 152–3.

74. Lyons, *Ireland Since the Famine*, p. 498.

75. UCD, Fianna Fáil Papers, Minutes of fourth meeting, 26 July 1927.

76. *Ibid.*, Minutes of fifth meeting, 5 August 1927.

77. Dunphy, *The Making of Fianna Fáil Power*, pp. 119–22.

78. UCD, Fianna Fáil Papers, 6 August 1927. Information of this meeting is available on loose pages attached to the party minute book. The members of the committee were: Éamon de de Valera (Chairman), Seán T. O'Kelly, Seán Lemass, Seán MacEntee, Gerald Boland, and Frank Aiken.

79. NLI, William O'Brien Papers, MS 17168, O'Kelly,

1927.8 August

FREEDOM TO CHOOSE

Boland and Aiken to Johnson and O'Brien, 8 August
1927.
80. *Ibid.*
81. UCD, Fianna Fáil Papers, Minutes of sixth meeting, 11
August 1927.
82. *Ibid.*, Minutes of meetings, 12 August 1927.
83. NLI, William O'Brien Papers, MS 17168. The Public
Safety Act was passed in 1927 after the assassination of
Kevin O'Higgins. Among other provisions, it listed new
and draconian powers of detention as well as the
suspension of habeas corpus.
84. Tim Pat Coogan, *Ireland since the Rising* (London,
1966) pp. 65–6; Dermot Keogh, *Twentieth-Century
Ireland.* (Dublin, 1944), p. 48; Coogan, *De Valera*, p.
406.
85. For Jinks, see Frank Pakenham Lonford and Thomas P.
O'Neill, *Éamon de Valera* (Dublin, 1970), p. 260.
86. UCD, Fianna Fáil Papers, Minutes of ninth meeting, 13
August 1927.
87. *Ibid.*, Minutes of fifth meeting, 5 August 1927.
88. Lee, *Ireland, 1912–1985*, pp. 154–5. According to
Regan, the act was designed 'to divide Fianna Fáil on the
issue of taking the oath'; Regan, *Irish Counter-
Revolution*, p. 274.
89. Reynolds, 'Formation and Development of Fianna Fáil'.
90. O'Kennedy-Brindley Advertising Ltd., *Making History:
The Story of Remarkable Campaign* (Dublin, 1927).
91. *CE*, 3 September 1927.
92. De Róiste Diaries, Vol. 54, 14 May 1927.
93. Regan, *Irish Counter-Revolution*, p. 275. In *Recollections
of a Rebel*, Walsh admits that he had been urged by
Dennis McCullogh and others to form a government.
However, the initiatives broke down over disagreements
concerning the Labour Party; see Walsh, *Recollections of
a Rebel*, p. 70.

254

94. De Róiste Diaries, Vol. 54, 22 Febuary 1927..
95. *CE*, 3 September 1927.
96. Regan, *Irish Counter-Revolution*, p. 275.
97. De Róiste Diaries, Vol. 54, May 1927.
98. *Ibid.*, Vol. 55, 30 August 1927.
99. *Ibid.*, 13 September 1927.
100. De Róiste is quoted from Regan, *Irish Counter-Revolution*, p.275.
101. Walsh, *Recollections of a Rebel*, p. 71.
102. *Ibid.*, p. 72.
103. Moss, *Political Parties in the Irish Free State*, p. 114.
104. De Róiste Diaries, Vol. 54, 13 September 1927.
105. *Ibid.*
106. *CE*, 10 September 1927.
107. *Ibid.*, 2 September 1927.
108. Dunphy, *The Making of Fianna Fáil Power*, p.128; Reynolds, 'Formation and Development of Fianna Fáil', p. 90.
109. *CE*, 15 September 1927.
110. *Ibid.*, 12 September 1927.
111. See William Murphy, 'In Pursuit of Popularity and Legitimacy: The Rhetoric of Fianna Fáil's Social and Economic Policy, 1926–34' (MA dissertation, UCD, 1998).
112. *CE*, 10 September 1927.
113. *Ibid.*, 10, 14 September 1927. See also P. J. McGilligan, Dáil Éireann, lx, Col. 551, 30 October 1924.
114. *CE*, 14 September 1927
115. *Ibid.*
116. *Ibid.*, 12 September 1927.
117. *Ibid.*
118. *Ibid.*, 3 September 1927.
119. *Catholic Bulletin*, 9, 17 September 1927.
120. *CE*, 10 September 1927.
121. *Ibid.*

122. *Ibid.*, 14 September 1927.
123. *Ibid.*, 13 September 1927.
124. *Ibid.*, 10 September 1927.
125. *Ibid.*, 14 September 1927.
126. *Ibid.*, 19 September 1927; Walker, *Parliamentary Election Results*, p. 126.
127. Sinnott, *Irish Voters*, pp. 98–100.

Chapter 5
1. Bax, *Harpstrings and Confessions*, p. 40; Dunphy, *Making of Fianna Fáil Power*, pp. 74–83.
2. Bax, *Harpstring and Confessions*, pp. 45–67; Dunphy, *Making of Fianna Fáil Power*, p. 72.
3. Dunphy, *Making of Fianna Fáil Power*, p. 211.
4. Dáil Debates xxx, col. 1360, 13 June 1929.
5. Reynolds, 'The Formation and Development of Fianna Fáil', p. 81.
6. *Ibid.*
7. Sinnott, *Irish Voters*, pp. 98–100.
8. Reynolds, 'The Formation and Development of Fianna Fáil', p. 81.
9. *CE*, 23 Febuary 1929.
10. *Ibid.*, 6 March 1929.
11. *Ibid.*, 16 March 1929.
12. *Ibid.*, 16, 20 March 1929.
13. *Ibid.*, 9, 16, 18 March 1929.
14. *Ibid.*, 11 March 1929.
15. *Ibid.*, 8 March 1929. For the election results, see Martin, 'Irish Party Political System', Appendix III, pp 383–6.
16. *CE*, 8 March 1929.
17. Councillor John Horgan also stood for Cumann na nGaedhael in 1932 while Jeremiah Hurley stood for Labour.
18. *CE*, 31 March 1929.
19. *Ibid.*, 25 March 1929.

20. For a more detailed discussion of these alliances, see Reynolds, 'The Formation and Development of Fianna Fáil' and Regan, *Irish Counter-Revolution.*

21. J. Bowyer Bell, *The History of the IRA, 1916–1979* (Dublin, 1980), pp 92–3; *Secret Army: Ireland Since the Rising,* p. 61; and Coogan, *De Valera,* p. 61.

22. In October 1931, the government had introduced the Constitution (Amendment No. 17) Bill which established a military tribunal to deal with political crime and to punish it with the death penalty, if necessary. In the Dáil, the Labour Party opposed the Act. However, Anthony defied the party whip and voted for the Act and was expelled for doing so.

23. De Róiste Diaries, Vol. 54, November 1925.

24. *CE,* 22 January 1932.

25. Copy in UCD, Mulcahy Papers, P7A/172

26. *Ibid*; Dermot Keogh, 'De Valera, the Catholic Church and the "Red Scare", 1931–1032' in John A. Murphy and J. O'Carroll (eds.), *De Valera and his Times* (Cork, 1983), p. 135.

27. *CE,* 22, 25 January, 15 Febuary 1932 .

28. *Ibid.,* 29 January 1932.

29. *Ibid.,* 29 January, 1 Febuary 1932.

30. *Ibid.,* 6 Febuary 1932.

31. UCD, Fianna Fáil Papers, minutes of meeting, 26 March, 7 May 1931; *CE,* 15 Febuary 1932. See also Eunan Ó hAilpín, 'Parliamentary Party Discipline and Tactics: The Fianna Fáil Archives, 1926–32' in *Irish Historical Studies* 30, 120 (November 1997), pp. 581–90.

32. *Irish Press,* 1 Febuary 1932.

33. *CE,* 22 January 1932.

34. *Ibid.,* 29 January 1932 .

35. *Ibid.,* 25 January, 9 Febuary 1932.

36. *Ibid.,* 11, 12, 13 Febuary 1932.

37. *Ibid.,* 4 Febuary 1932.

38. *Ibid.*, 15 Febuary 1932.
39. *Ibid.*, 21, 29 January 1932.
40. *Ibid.*, 2 Febuary 1932.
41. *Ibid.*, 9 Febuary 1932; *Irish Press*, 1 Febuary 1932.
42. *CE*, 20 Febuary 1932.
43. Sinnott, *Irish Voters*, pp. 100–2; Murphy, *Ireland in the Twentieth Century*, p. 75.
44. *CE*, 8 March, 9 Febuary 1929.
45. *Ibid.*, 4 Febuary 1932.
46. Lee, *Ireland 1912–1985*, p. 174; Reynolds, 'The Formation and Development of Fianna Fáil'.

Chapter 6
1. Bax, *Harpstring and Confessions*, p. 40.
2. *Ibid.*, pp. 45–67, 186.
3. Walsh, *Recollections of a Rebel*, pp. 9, 22.
4. De Róiste Diaries, Vol. 1, January and Febuary 1903.
5. *Ibid.*, Vol. 27, 11 July 1919.
6. *Ibid.*, Vol. 34, 13 October 1920.
7. *Ibid.*
8. Bax, *Harpstring and Confessions*, p.186.
9. See Chapter 3.
10. See Chapter 1.
11. These ten were J. J. Walsh, Richard Beamish, Professor Alfred O'Rahilly, Seán French, Michael Egan, John Horgan, William Desmond, Liam de Róiste, Seán O'Leary and Edward Fitzgerald – the last two being unsuccessful in their attempts to win Dáil seats during the period.
12. De Róiste Diaries, Vols 46–7.
13. UCD Mulcahy Papers, P7A/182, Cosgrave to Mulcahy, 3 January 1924.
14. UCD, Cumann na nGaedheal Papers, Minutes of the Ard Comhairle, 30 May 1925.
15. UCD, Fianna Fáil Papers, papers of the parliamentary

party, 12 July 1928; O Halpin, 'Parliamentary Party Discipline and Tactics', pp. 581–90.

16. UCD, Fianna Fáil Papers, Minutes, 22 November 1928.
17. *Ibid.*, 18 April 1929.
18. *Ibid.*, 31 October 1929.
19. *Ibid.*, 14 November 1929.
20. *Ibid.*, 9 July 1931.
21. UCD, Minutes of Cumann na nGaedhael parliamentary party, 6 March 1930, p. 39.
22. *Ibid.*, 28 March 1930.
23. *Ibid.*
24. At one Fianna Fáil parliamentary party meeting, Dr P. J. Dowd, TD, gave the organisation of a local feis [a concert of Irish dancing and singing] as his excuse for missing a Dáil division.
25. Bax, *Harpstring and Confessions*, pp 3, 187.
26. UCD, Cumann na nGaedhael Papers, Statement attached to minutes of Coiste Gnótha 10 October 1924.
27. *Ibid.*
28. *Ibid.*
29. UCD Archives, Blythe Papers, P24/488, Memo from General Eoin O'Duffy, Commissioner of the Garda Síochána to the government, 1931.
30. *Ibid.*
31. *Ibid.*, P24/388.
32. Cork Archives Institute, Séamus Fitzgerald Papers, PR/6/417–455.
33. UCD, Fianna Fáil Papers, Minutes, 1 May 1930.
34. *Ibid.*, 9 June 1932.
35. *Ibid.*, 7 July 1932.
36. *Ibid.*, 3 November 1932.
37. *Ibid.*, 9 December 1932.
38. *Ibid.*, Ard-Fheis *clár*, 1933.
39. *Ibid.*

SOURCES & SELECTED BIBLIOGRAPHY

Primary Sources: Manuscripts

Dublin: The Archives Department, UCD
Ernest Blythe Papers
Caitlín Brugha Papers
Cumann na nGaedhael Papers
Fianna Fáil Parliamentary Party: Minutes
Fianna Fáil National Executive: Minutes
Tim Healy Papers
Hugh Kennedy Papers
Patrick McGilligan Papers
Thomas McPartlin Papers
Mary MacSwiney Papers
Terence MacSwiney Papers
Richard Mulcahy Papers
Ernie O'Malley Papers

Dublin: National Library of Ireland
Piaras Béaslaí Papers
Thomas Johnson Papers
Tommy Mullins Papers
William O'Brien Papers
Florence O'Donoghue Papers
Seán T. Ó Ceallaigh
Austin Stack Papers

Cork: The Archives Institute
Seamus Fitzgerald Papers
Liam de Róiste Diaries

Primary Sources: Printed

Newspapers:
Catholic Bulletin
Cork Examiner
Cork Weekly Tribune, 1926
Irish Press
Irish Times
The Nation
An Phoblacht

Dáil Reports
Minutes of Proceedings of the First Parliament of the Republic of Ireland, 1919–21: Official Record (Dublin, 1921)
Official Report: Debate on the Treaty between Great Britain and Ireland (Dublin, [1922])
Official Report for periods 16 August 1921 to 26 August 1921, and 28 February 1922 to 8 June 1922 (Dublin, 1922)
Private Sessions of Second Dáil: Minutes of Proceedings 18 August 1921 to 14 September and Report of Debates 14 December 1921 to 6 January 1922, ed. T. P. O'Neill (Dublin, 1972)
Dáil Debates (Dublin, 1922–)

Primary Sources: Interviews

Seán MacEntee, founding member of Fianna Fáil, and the party's first Minister for Finance.
Bridie Mullins, wife of Tommy Mullins, former General Secretary of Fianna Fáil.
Mr Thomas Dowdall, Dunslands, Glanmire, son of Senator J. C. Dowdall and nephew of T. P. Dowdall, TD for Cork during the period.

Selected Secondary Sources

Andrews, C. S., *Man of No Property* (Cork, 1982)

Augusteijn, Joost, *From Public Defiance to Guerrilla Warfare: The Experience of Ordinary Volunteers in the War of Independence, 1916–1921* (Dublin, 1996)

Ayearst, M., *The Republic of Ireland: Its Government and Politics* (New York & London, 1970)

Barrington, T. J., *From Big Government to Local Government* (Dublin, 1975)

The Irish Administrative System (Dublin, 1980)

Barry, Tom, *Guerilla Days in Ireland* (9th ed., Tralee, 1981)

The Reality of the Anglo-Irish War 1920–21 in West Cork: Refutations, Corrections and Comments on Liam Deasy's Towards Ireland Free (Dublin, 1974)

Bax, Mart, 'Patronage Irish Style: Irish Politicians as Brokers', *Sociologische Geds*, 17, 3 (1970)

'Integration, Forms of Communication and Development: Centre-Periphery Relations in Ireland in Past and Present', *Sociologische Geds*, 19, 2 (1972)

'The Political Machine and its Importance in the Irish Republic', *Political Anthropology*, 1, 1 (1975)

Harpstring and Confessions: Machine Style Politics in the Irish Republic (Assen & Amsterdam, 1976)

Béaslaí, Piaras, *Michael Collins and the Making of a New Ireland* (New York, 1925)

Bell, J. Bowyer, *The Secret Army: A History of the IRA, 1916–1979* (Dublin, 1980; revised ed., Dublin, 1989)

Blondel, J., 'Party Systems and Patterns of Government in Western Democracies', *Canadian Journal of Political Science*, 1, 2 (1968)

Boissevain, J., 'Patrons as Brokers', *Sociologische Geds*, 16, 6 (1969)

Boland, Kevin, *Up Dev!* (Dublin, 1977)

The Rise and Decline of Fianna Fáil (Dublin, 1982)

Boyce, D. G., *Englishmen and Irish Troubles: British Opinion and the Making of Irish Policy, 1918–1922* (London, 1922)
Nationalism in Ireland (Dublin, 1982)
Boylan, Tom, Curtin, Chris, and O'Dowd, Liam, 'Politics and Society in Post-Independence Ireland' in Thomas Bartlett *et al.* (eds.), *Irish Studies: A General Introduction* (Dublin, 1978)
Briscoe, Robert, *For the Life of Me* (London, 1959)
Brown, Terence, *Ireland: A Social and Cultural History 1922–79* (London, 1981)
Butler, Ewan, *Barry's Flying Column* (London, 1971)
Butler, Hugh, *The Irish Free State: An Economic Survey* (Washington, 1928)
Campbell, Colum, *Emergency Law in Ireland 1918–1925* (Oxford, 1925)
Carroll, J. P. and Murphy, John A. (eds.), *Éamon de Valera and his Times* (Cork, 1983)
Carty, R. K., 'Social Cleavages and Party Systems: A Reconsideration of the Irish Case', *European Journal of Political Research* (1976)
'Politicians and Electoral Laws: An Anthropology of Party Competition in Ireland', *Political Studies*, 28, 4 (1988)
Electoral Politics and Ireland: Party and Parish Pump (Waterloo, 1981).
Chavasse, Móirín, *Terence MacSwiney* (Dublin, 1961)
Chubb, Basil, 'Cabinet Government in Ireland', *Political Studies*, 3 (1955)
'The Independent Member in Ireland', *Political Studies*, 5, 2 (1957)
'Going Around Persecuting Civil Servants: The Role of the Irish Parliamentary Representative', *Political Studies*, 11 (1963)
A Source Book of Irish Government (Dublin, 1964)

The Government: An Introduction to the Cabinet System (revised ed., Dublin, 1968)

The Government and Politics of Ireland (London, 1970; 3rd ed., London, 1992)

The Constitution and Constitutional Change in Ireland (Dublin, 1978)

'The Republic of Ireland' in S. Hening (ed.), *Political Parties in the European Community* (London, 1979)

Clarkson, J. D., *Labour and Nationalism in Ireland* (New York, 1925)

Coakley, John, and Gallagher, Michael (eds.), *Politics in the Republic of Ireland* (Dublin, 1992; 2nd ed., Dublin, 1993)

Cohan, A. S.,'The Open Coalition in the Closed Society: The Strange Pattern of Government Formation in Ireland' in *Comparative Politics* 11, 3 (1979)

Comerford, Máire, *The First Dáil* (New Haven, 1966)

Coogan, Tim Pat, *Ireland since the Rising* (London, 1966)

The IRA (London, 1970)

Michael Collins (London, 1990)

De Valera: Long Fellow, Long Shadow (London, 1993)

Cosgrave, W. T., *Policies of Cumann na nGaedhael* (Dublin, 1927) (election leaflet; copy in Ernest Blythe Papers, P24/617 (Archives Department, UCD)

Costello, Francis J., *Enduring the Most: The Life and Death of Terence MacSwiney* (Dingle, 1995)

Curran, J. M., *The Birth of the Irish Free State, 1921–1923* (London, 1980)

Cutright, P., 'National Political Development' in N. W. Palsley, R. A. Dentler and P. A. Smith (eds.), *Politics and Social Life* (Boston, 1963)

Dahl, Robert A., *Political Oppositions in Western Democracies* (New Haven, 1966)

Davis, Richard, *Arthur Griffith and Non-Violent Sinn Féin* (Dublin, 1974)

Deasy, Liam, *Towards Ireland Free: The West Cork Brigade in the War of Independence, 1917–1921* (Dublin, 1973)
   Brother against Brother (Dublin & Cork, 1982)

de Róiste, Liam, 'Mar is Cuimhin Liom', *Evening Echo*, 19 August To 6 November 1954.

De Valera, Éamon, A National Policy Outlined: Speech Delivered at the Inaugural Meting of Fianna Fáil (Dublin, 1926)
   Speeches and Statements, 1917–73, ed. Maurice Moynihan (Dublin, 1980)

De Vere White, Terence, *Kevin O'Higgins* (London, 1948)

Doherty, Gabriel, and Keogh, Dermot (eds.), *Michael Collins and the Making of the Irish State* (Cork, 1998)

Dooney, Seán, *The Irish Civil Service* (Dublin, 1976)

Dunphy, Richard, *The Making of Fianna Fáil in Ireland, 1923–1948* (Oxford, 1995)

Duverger, Maurice, *Political Parties* (London, 1959)

Dwyer, T. Ryle, *De Valera's Darkest Hour, 1919–1932* (Cork, 1982)
   De Valera's Finest Hour, 1932–1959 (Dublin & Cork, 1982)

Eason, J. C. M., 'An Analysis of showing the Objects of Expenditure and Revenue and the Source of Revenue of the Irish Free State during the Financial Years 1924–25 to 1929–30', *Journal of the Statistical and Social Inquiry Society of Ireland* (1930)

Eckstein, H., *Division and Cohesion in Democracy* (Princeton, 1966)

Edmonds, Seán, *The Gun, the Law and the Irish People* (Tralee, 1971)

Elliot-Bateman, Michael, Ellis, John, and Bawdren, Tom, *Revolt to Revolution: Studies in the Nineteenth European Experience* (Manchester, 1974)

English, Richard, *Radicals and the Republic: Socialist Republicanism in the Free State 1925–1937* (Oxford, 1994)

Ernie O'Malley: IRA Intellectual (Oxford, 1998)

Fahy, A. M., 'Place and Class in Cork' in O'Flanagan, P. & Buttimer, C. G. (eds.), *Cork: History and Society* (Dublin, 1993)

Fallon, Charlotte H., *Soul of Fire: A Biography of Mary MacSwiney* (Dublin & Cork, 1986)

Fanning, Ronan, *Independent Ireland* (Dublin, 1983)
'"The Rule of Order": Éamon de Valera and the IRA, 1923–1940' in J.P. O'Carroll and John A. Murphy (eds.), *De Valera and his Times* (Cork, 1983)

Farrell, Brian, 'Irish Political Culture and the New State', *Administration*, 1, 3 (1968)
'A Note on the Dáil Constitution, 1919', *Irish Jurist*, new series, 4 (1969)
'Labour and the Irish Political Party System: A Suggested Approach to Analysis', *Economic and Social Review*, 1, 3 (1970)
'The Drafting of the Irish Free State Constitution' (4 parts), *Irish Jurist*, new series, 6 (1970) and 7 (1971)
Chairman or Chief? The Role of Taoiseach in Irish Government (Dublin, 1971)
The Founding of Dáil Éireann: Parliament and Nation-Building (Dublin, 1971)
(ed.), *The Irish Parliamentary Tradition* (Dublin, 1973)
'Irish Government Re-observed' in *Economic and Social Review*, 6, 4 (1975)
Seán Lemass (Dublin, 1983)
'Coalitions and Political Institutions: The Irish Experience' in Vernon Bogdanor (ed.), *Coalition Government in Western Europe* (London, 1983)
'Ireland: From Friends and Neighbours to Clients and Partisans: Some Dimensions of Parliamentary Representation under PR-STV' in Vernon Bogdanor (ed.), *Representatives of the People? Parliamentarians and Constituents in Western Democracies* (London, 1985)

'From First Dáil through Irish Free State' in Brian Farrell (ed.), *De Valera's Constitution and Ours* (Dublin, 1988)

Feeney, P. J., *Glory O, Glory O, Ye Bold Fenian Men: A History of the Sixth Battalion Cork First Brigade, 1913–1921* (Dripsey, 1996)

Fennell, Desmond, 'The Failure of the Irish Revolution and its Success', *Capuchin Annual* (1964)

Fitzgerald, Seamus, 'East Cork Activities – 1920', *Capuchin Annual* (1967)

Fitzgerald, William (ed.), *Voices of Ireland* (Dublin, 1924)

Fitzpatrick David, *Politics and Irish Life 1913–1921: Provincial Experience of War and Revolution* (Dublin, 1977; repr., Cork, 1998)

'The Geography of Irish Nationalism, 1910–1921' in C. E. H. Philpin (ed.), *Nationalism and Popular Protest in Ireland* (Cambridge, 1987)

(ed.), *Revolution? Ireland 1917–1923* (Dublin, 1990)

The Two Irelands, 1912–1939 (Oxford, 1998)

Forester, Margery, *Michael Collins: The Lost Leader* (London, 1971)

Foster, R. F., *Modern Ireland, 1600–1972* (London, 1988)

Fox, R. M., *Rebel Irishwomen* (Dublin, 1935)

Friedrich, C. J., 'The Political Theory of New Democratic Institutions', *Review of Politics*, 12.

Gallagher, Frank, *The Indivisible Island* (London, 1957)

The Anglo-Irish Treaty (London, 1965)

Gallagher, Michael, 'Disproportionality in a Proportional Representation System: The Irish Experience', *Political Studies*, 23 (1975)

'Electoral Support for Irish Political Parties, 1927–1973' (Contemporary Political Sociology Series, London, 1976)

'Socialism and the Nationalist Tradition in Ireland, 1798–1918', *Éire-Ireland*, 12, 2 (Summer 1977)

'Party Solidarity, Exclusivity and Inter-Party Relationships in Ireland, 1922–1977: The Evidence of

Transfers', *Economic and Social Review*, 10, 1 (1978)
'The Impact of Lower-Preference Votes on Irish Parliamentary Elections, 1922–1977', *Economic and Social Review*, 11 (1978)
'The Pact General Election of 1922', *Irish Historical Studies*, 21, 84 (1979)
The Irish Labour Party in Transition, 1957–82 (Manchester & Dublin, 1982)
Political Parties in the Republic of Ireland (Dublin, 1985)
(with Komito, Lee), 'Dáil Deputies and their Constituency Work' in John Coakley and Michael Gallagher (eds.), *Politics in the Republic of Ireland* (Dublin, 1992; 2nd ed., Dublin, 1993)
'The Impact of Lower-Preference Votes on Irish Parliamentary Elections, 1922–1977', *Economic and Social Review* 11, 1 (1978)
Garvin, Tom, 'Continuity and Change in Irish Electoral Politics, 1923–1969', *Economic and Social Review*, 3 (1971–72)
'Political Cleavages, Party Politics and Urbanization in Ireland: The Case of the Periphery-Dominated Centre', *European Journal of Political Research*, 2, 4 (1974)
'Nationalist Elites, Irish Voters and Irish Political Development: A Comparative Perspective', *Economic and Social Review*, 8, 3 (1977)
'The Destiny of the Soldiers: Tradition and Modernity in the Politics of de Valera's Ireland', *Political Studies*, 26 (1978)
'Decolonisation, Nationalism and Electoral Politics in Ireland, 1832–1945' in O. Büsch (ed.), *Wählerbewegung in der Europäischen Geshichte* (Berlin, 1980)
The Evolution of Irish Nationalist Politics (Dublin, 1981)
'The Anatomy of a Nationalist Revolution: Ireland, 1858–1928', *Comparative Studies in Society and History*, 28 (1986)

Nationalist Revolutionaries in Ireland (Oxford, 1987)
'Democracy in Ireland: Collective Somnambulance and Public Policy', Administration, 39 (1991)
1922: The Birth of Irish Democracy (Dublin, 1996)
Gaughan, J. Anthony, *Thomas Johnson* (Dublin, 1980)
Alfred O'Rahilly (3 vols, Dublin, 1986–92)
Geary, R. C., 'Irish Economic Development since the Treaty', *Social Studies*, 40 (1951)
Gellner, Ernest, *Nations and Nationalism* (Ithaca, 1982)
Glandon, Virginia, *Arthur Griffith and the Advanced Nationalist Press. Ireland 1900–1922* (New York, 1985)
Gogan, Vincent, 'Irish Constitutional Development', Studies 40 (1951)
Gwynn, Denis, *Éamon de Valera* (London, 1933)
The History of Partition, 1912–1925 (Dublin, 1950)
The Irish Free State, 1922–27 (Dublin, 1928)
Gwynn, Stephen, *Éamon de Valera, Irish Statesman and Rebel: The Two Lives of Éamon de Valera* (London, 1933)
The Irish Free State, 1922–27 (Dublin, 1928)
Hand, G. J. (ed.), *Report of the Irish Boundary Commission 1925* (Shannon, 1969)
'Ireland' in J. Georgel and C. Sasse (eds.), *European Electoral Systems Handbook* (London, 1979)
Hanley, Joseph, *The National Ideal* (Dublin, 1931)
Harkness, D. W., *The Restless Dominion: The Irish Free State and the British Commonwealth of Nations, 1921–31* (London & Dublin, 1969)
Hart, Ian, 'Public Opinion on Civil Servants and the Role and Power of the Individual in the Local Community', *Administration* (1970)
Hart, Peter, 'Youth Culture and the Cork IRA' in David Firzpatrick (ed.), *Revolution? Ireland, 1917–23* (Dublin, 1990)
The IRA and its Enemies: Violence and Community in Cork, 1916–1923 (Oxford, 1998)

'Class, Community and the Irish Republican Army in Cork, 1917–23' in O'Flanagan, P. & Buttimer, C. G. (eds.), *Cork: History and Society* (Dublin, 1993)

Hays, S. P., 'Political Parties and the Community-Society Continuum' in W. N. Chambers and W. N. Chambers and W. D. Burnham (eds.), *The American Party Systems* (New York 1967)

Henry, Robert Mitchell, *The Evolution of Sinn Féin* (Dublin, 1920)

Hermens, F. A., 'The Dynamics of Proportional Representation' in H. Eckstein and R. Apter (eds.), *Comparative Politics: A Reader* (New York, 1963)

Hogan, James, *Could Ireland Become Communist?* (Dublin, 1934)

Election and Representation (Cork, 1945)

Hopkinson, Michael, *Green against Green: The Irish Civil War* (Dublin, 1988)

Hoppen, K. Theodore, *Ireland Since 1800: Conflict and Conformity* (London, 1989)

Horgan, John, *Seán Lemass: The Enigmatic Patriot* (Dublin, 1997)

Jackson, T. Alvin, *Ireland 1798–1998* (Oxford, 1999)

Jones, Thomas, *Whitehall Diary, Vol. III: Ireland, 1918–1925*, Keith Middlemas (ed.) (London, 1971)

Kee, Robert, *The Green Flag: A History of Irish Nationalism* (London, 1972)

Ireland: A History (London, 1982)

Kennedy, Brian P., 'The Failure of the Cultural Republic: Ireland, 1922–39', *Studies*, 81 (1992)

Keogh, Dermot, *The Rise of the Irish Working Class* (Belfast, 1982)

The Vatican, the Bishops and Irish Politics, 1919–1939 (Cambridge, 1986)

Ireland and Europe, 1919–1948 (Dublin, 1988)

Twentieth-Century Ireland: Nation and State (Dublin, 1994)

'De Valera, the Catholic Church and the "Red Scare", 1931–1932' in Carroll, John P. and Murphy, John A. (eds.), *De Valera and his Times* (Cork, 1983)

Komito, Lee, 'Irish Clientelism: A Reappraisal', *Economic and Social Review*, 15 (1984)

'Voters, Politicians and Clientelism', *Administration*, 36 (1989)

'Brokerage or Friendship? Politics and Networks in Ireland', *Economic and Social Review*, 22 (1992)

Kostick, Conor, *Revolution in Ireland: Popular Militancy 1917 to 1923* (London, 1996)

Laffan, Michael, 'The Sinn Féin Party, 1916–1921', *Capuchin Annual* (1970)

'The Unification of Sinn Féin in 1917', *Irish Historical Studies*, 17, 67 (1971)

The Partition of Ireland, 1911–1925 (Dundalk, 1983)

'"Labour Must Wait": Ireland's Conservative Revolution' in P. J. Corish (ed.)

Radicals, Rebels and Establishments: Historical Studies XV (Belfast, 1985)

The Resurrection of Ireland: The Sinn Féin Party 1916–1923 (Cambridge, 1999)

Lakeman, Enid, *How Democracies Vote: A Study of Majority and Proportional Electoral Systems* (London, 1970)

Lankford, Siobhán, *The Hope and the Sadness: Personal Recollections of Troubled Times in Ireland* (Cork, 1980)

Lapalombara, J., and Weiner, M., (eds.), *Political Parties and Political Development* (Princeton, 1966)

Laver, Michael, 'How To Be Sophisticated, Lie, Cheat, Bluff and Win at Politics', *Political Studies*, 25, 4 (1978)

'Are Irish Parties Peculiar?' in J. H. Goldthorpe and C. T. Whelan (eds.), *The Development of Industrial Society in Ireland* (Oxford, 1992)

Law, H. A., 'The Irish Elections and Plebiscite', *Contemporary Review*, 3 (1937)

Lawless, M., 'The Dáil Electoral System', *Administration*, 5 (1957)

Lawlor, Sheila, *Britain and Ireland, 1914–1923* (London, 1983)

Lee, Joseph, *1917–23: Politics and Society* (Dublin, 1990)
The Modernisation of Irish Society, 1848–1918 (Dublin, 1973)
'Irish Nationalism and Socialism: Rumpf Reconsidered', *Saothar*, 6 (1980)
Ireland 1912–1985: Politics and Society (Cambridge, 1989)
(and Ó Túaithaigh, Gearóid), *The Age of de Valera* (Dublin, 1982)

Lemarchand, R. and Legg, K., 'Political Clientelism and Development: A Preliminary Analysis', *Comparative Politics*, 4, 2 (1972)

Leonard, Jane, 'Getting Them At Last: The IRA and Ex-Servicemen' in David Fitzpatrick (ed.), *Revolution? Ireland 1917–23* (Dublin, 1990)

Leys, C., 'Models, Theories and the Theory of Political Parties' in H. Eckstein and R. Apter, *Comparative Politics: A Reader* (New York, 1963)

Longford, Earl of, and O'Neill, T. P., *Éamon de Valera* (London, 1970)

Lynch, Diarmuid, *The IRB and the 1916 Insurrection* (Cork, 1957)

Lynch, Patrick, 'The Social Revolution That Never Was' in T. D. Williams (ed.), *The Irish Struggle, 1916–26* (London, 1966)
(and Carter, C.F.), *Planning for Economic Development* (Dublin, 1959)

Lyons, F. S. L., *The Fall of Parnell* (London, 1960)
John Dillon: A Biography (London, 1968)
Ireland since the Famine (London, 1971)
Culture and Anarchy in Ireland (Oxford, 1979)

MacArdle, Dorothy, *The Irish Republic* (London, 1937; repr. London 1968)

MacCartan, Patrick, *With de Valera in America* (Dubllin, 1932)

MacDonagh, Oliver, *Ireland* (Englewood Cliffs, 1968)

McDonnell, Kathleen Keyes, *There is a Bridge at Bandon* (Cork, 1972)

MacEntee, Seán, *Episode at Easter* (Dublin, 1966)
'De Valera: The Man I Knew', *Iris: Fianna Fáil Party Journal* (winter 1975)

McInerney, Michael, *Peadar O'Donnell, Irish Social Rebel* (Dublin, 1971)

MacManus, Francis (ed.), *The Years of the Great Test, 1926–1939* (Cork, 1967)

McNamara, T., 'Pressure Groups and the Public Service', *Administration*, 25
'Parliamentary Party Discipline and Tactics: The Fianna Fáil Archives, 1926–32', *Irish Historical Studies*, 30, 120 (1997)

MacSwiney, Terence, *Principles of Freedom* (New York, 1970)

Maguire, M., 'Pressure Groups in Ireland', *Administration*, 25 (1977)

Mair, Peter, 'Labour and the Irish Party System Revisited: Party Competition in the 1920s', *Economic and Social Review* 8 (1977)
The Changing Party System (London, 1987)
(and Michael Laver), 'Proportionality, PR and STV in Ireland', *Political Studies*, 23 (1975)

Malone, Andrew E., 'The Development of Party Government in the Irish Free State', *Political Science Quarterly* 11, 4 (1929)

Manning, Maurice, *Irish Political Parties: An Introduction* (Dublin, 1971)

Mansergh, Nicholas, *The Irish Free State: Its Government and Politics* (London, 1934)

The Unresolved Question: The Anglo-Irish Settlement and its Undoing, 1912–72 (New Haven & London, 1991)

Marsh, M. A., 'Ireland' in I. Crewe and D. Denver (eds.), *Electoral Change in Western Democracies: Patterns and Sources of Electoral Volatility* (London, 1985)

Maume, Patrick, *'Life that is Exile': Daniel Corkery and the Search for Irish Ireland* (Belfast, 1993)

Meagher, P. J., *Local Government in Ireland* (5th ed., Dublin, 1975)

Meenan, James, 'From Free Trade to Self-Sufficiency' in Francis MacManus (ed.), *The Years of the Great of the Great Test, 1926–1939* (Cork, 1967)
The Irish Economy since 1922 (Liverpool, 1970)

Miller, David, *Church, State and Nation in Ireland, 1898–21* (Dublin, 1973)

Mitchell, Arthur, *Labour in Irish Politics 1890–1930* (Shannon, 1974)
Revolutionary Government in Ireland: Dáil Éireann, 1919–22 (Dublin, 1955)

Moody, T. W. (ed.), *Nationality and the Pursuit of National Independence* (Dublin, 1980)

Moss, Warner, *Political Parties in the Irish Free State* (New York, 1933)

Munger, Frank, *The Legitimacy of Opposition: The Change of Government in Ireland in 1932* (Beverly Hills & London, 1969)

Murphy, John A., 'The Irish Party System, 1938–51' in K. B. Nowlan and T. D. Williams (eds.), *Ireland in the War Years and After, 1939–51* (London, 1969)
Ireland in the Twentieth Century (Dublin, 1975)

Murray, P., 'Irish Elections: A Changing Pattern', *Studies*, 65 (1976)

Neeson, Eoin, *The Civil War in Ireland* (Cork, 1966; revised ed., Dublin, 1989)
The Life and Death of Michael Collins (Cork, 1968)

Nevin, Donal, 'Labour and the Political Revolution' in Francis MacManus (ed.), *The Years of the Great Test, 1926–1939* (Cork, 1967)
    'Radical Movements in the Twenties and Thirties' in T. D. Williams (ed.), *The Irish Struggle, 1916–26* (London, 1966)

Norman, Edward, R., *The Catholic Church and Ireland in the Age of Rebellion* (London, 1965)

Nowlan, K. B., 'President Cosgrave's Last Administration' in Francis MacManus (ed.), *The Years of the Great Test, 1926–1939* (Dublin, 1973)

O'Beirne-Ranelagh, John, 'The IRB from the Treaty to 1924', *Irish Historical Studies*, 20, 77 (1976)

O'Brien, John V., *William O'Brien and the Course of Irish Politics 1881–1918* (Berkeley, Calif., 1976).

O'Carroll, J. P., and Murphy, John A., (eds.), *De Valera and his Times* (Cork, 1983)

O'Connor, Frank, *The Big Fellow: Michael Colllins and the Irish Revolution* (London,1961)

O'Connor Lysaght, D. R., *The Republic of Ireland* (Cork, 1970)

O'Donoghue, Florence, *No Other Law* (Dublin, 1986)
    Tomás Mac Curtain: Soldier and Patriot (Tralee, 1971)
    'The Irish Volunteers in Cork 1913–1916', *Journal of the Cork Historical and Archaeological Society* (1996)

Ó Faoláin, Seán, *De Valera* (London, 1939)

O'Farrell, Padraic, *Who's Who in the Irish War of Independence and the Civil War, 1916–1923* (Dublin, 1997)

O'Flanagan, P. & Buttimer, C. G. (eds.), *Cork: History and Society* (Dublin, 1993)

O'Halloran, Clare, *Partition and the Limits of Irish Nationalism: an Ideology Under Stress* (Dublin, 1987)

O'Halpin, Eunan, 'Army, Politics and Society in Independent Ireland, 1923–1945' in T. G. Fraser and Keith Jeffery

(eds.), *Men, Women and War: Historical Studies* 17
'Parliamentary Party Discipline and Tactics: The Fianna Fáil Archives, 1926–32', *Irish Historical Studies*, 30, 120, (1997).
O'Hegarty, P. S., *The Victory of Sinn Féin* (Dublin, 1924)
A History of Ireland Under the Union, 1801–1922 (London, 1952)
O'Leary, Cornelius, I*rish Elections, 1918–1977: Parties, Voters and Proportional Representation* (Dublin, 1979)
O'Mahony, T. P., *The Politics of Dishonour: Ireland, 1916–1977* (Dublin, 1977)
O'Malley, Ernie, *On Another Man's Wound* (Dublin, 1936)
Ó Fiach, Tomás, 'The Catholic Clergy and the Independence Movement', *Capuchin Annual* (1970)
O'Hegarty, P. S., *The Victory of Sinn Féin* (Dublin, 1924)
O Murchadha, Diarmuid, *Liam de Róiste* (Dublin, 1976)
O'Rahilly, Alfred, *Thoughts on the Constitution* (Dublin, 1938)
The Case for the Treaty (Dublin, 1922)
Orridge, A., 'Explanations of Irish Nationalism: A Review and Some Suggestions', *Journal of the Conflict Research Society*, 1, 1 (1977)
O'Sullivan, Donal, *The Irish Free State and its Senate* (London, 1940)
Phillips, W. Allison, *The Revolution in Ireland, 1906–1923* (London, 1923)
Philpin, C. E. H. (ed.), *Nationalism and Popular Protest in Ireland* (Cambridge, 1987)
Powell, J. P., 'Peasant Society and Clientelist Politics', *American Political Science Review*, 64, 2 (1970)
Praeger, Jeffrey, *Building Democracy in Ireland: Political Order and Cultural Integration in a Newly Independent Nation* (Cambridge, 1986)
Pyne, Peter, 'The Freedom to Choose: The Third Sinn Féin Party, 1923–1926', *Economic and Social Review*, 1 & 2 1969–70)

(and Urwin, D.), 'Social Cohesion, Political Parties and Strains in Regimes', *Comparative Political Studies*, 2, 1 (1969)

Regional Differentiation and Political Unity in Western Nations (London, 1975)

'The New Irish State and the Decline of the Republican Sinn Féin Party, 1923–1926', *Éire-Ireland* 11, 3 (1976)

Rae, Douglas W., *The Political Consequences of Electoral Laws* (New Haven & London, 1971)

Regan, John M., ''The Politics of Reaction: The Dynamics of Treatyite Government and Policy, 1922–33', *Irish Historical Studies*, 30, 120 (1997)

The Irish Counter-Revolution 1921–1936 (Dublin, 1999)

Roche, D., *Local Government in Ireland* (Dublin, 1982)

Ross, J. F. 'Persistence and Change in Western Party Systems since 1945', *Political Studies*, 8, 3 (1970)

Regional Differentiation and Political Unity in Western Nations (London, 1975)

Rumpf, E. And Hepburn, A. C., *Nationalism and Socialism in Twentieth Century Ireland* (Liverpool, 1977)

Rustow, D., 'Transitions to Democracy: Towards a Dynamic Model', *Comparative Politics*, 2, 3 (1970)

Ryan, Meda, *The Tom Barry Story* (Cork, 1982)

The Real Chief: The Story of Liam Lynch (Cork, 1986)

Sacks, Paul M., *The Donegal Mafia* (New Haven and London, 1976)

Saorstát Éireann, *Official Handbook* (1932)

Schmitt, D. E., *The Irony of Irish Democracy* (Lexington, 1973)

Sinnott, Richard, *Irish Voters Decide: Voting Behaviour in Elections and Referendums Since 1918* (Manchester, 1995)

Taylor, Rex, *Michael Collins (*London, 1958)

Towey, Thomas, 'The Reaction of the British Government to the 1922 Collins–de Valera Pact', *Irish Historical Studies*, 22, 85 (1980)

Townshend, Charles, *The British Campaign in Ireland, 1919–1921* (Oxford, 1975)

Travers, Pauric, *Settlements and Divisions: Ireland 1870–1922* (Dublin, 1992)

Valiulis, Maryann G., 'After the Revolution: The Formative Years of Cumann na nGaedhael' in A. Eyler and R. F. Garnatt (eds.), *Portrait of a Revolutionary: General Richard Mulcahy and the Founding of the Irish Free State* (Dublin, 1992)

Walker, Brian M. (ed.), *Parliamentary Election Results in Ireland, 1801–1922* (Dublin, 1978)

Walsh, J. J., *Recollections of a Rebel* (Tralee, 1949)

Ward, A. J., 'Parliamentary Procedures and the Machinery of Government in Ireland', *Irish University Review*, 4, 2 (1974)

Whyte, John H., *Church and State in Modern Ireland, 1923–1979* (Dublin, 1980)

Williams, T. Desmond (ed.), *The Irish Struggle, 1916–1926* (London, 1966)

Woodman, K., *Media Control in Ireland, 1923–1983* (Galway, 1986)

Younger, Calton, *Ireland's Civil War* (London, 1968)
A State of Disunion (London, 1972)

Unpublished Dissertations

Martin, Micheál, 'The Formation and Evolution of the Irish Party Political System, with particular emphasis on the Cork City Borough Constituency, 1918–1932' (MA dissertation, UCC, 1988)

Murphy, Brian S., 'Politics and Ideology: Mary MacSwiney and Irish Republicanism, 1872–1942' (PhD dissertation, UCC, 1994).

Reynolds, Brian A., 'The Formation and Development of Fianna Fáil, 1926–1932' (PhD dissertation, Trinity College Dublin, 1976).

INDEX

Civil War, 75–79, 83, 179
Clann Éireann, 161, 168–169
Cohalan, Bishop, 8, 9, 10, 37,
40–41, 86–87, 157–158
Coiste Gnótha, 117, 118, 120,
122–123
Collins, Jeremiah, 90, 105–106,
107
Collins, Michael, 18, 51, 58, 60,
69–70, 76, 78
Collins-Powell, Mary, Mrs, 88,
89, 90, 122, 131, 171, 172
Comerford, Mary, 99
Commercial Party (or Ratepayers),
22, 25, 29, 31, 33, 87
communism, 200–201
Corcoran, Timothy, 90, 106, 148,
155
Cork and District United Trades
and Labour Council, 22
Cork City Management Bill, 189
Cork Corporation, 1920 election,
21–22, 24, 29, 31, 57, 111,
113, 195, 220
Cork Examiner
on 1918 general election, 14
on 1920 local election, 26, 30
on 1922 election, 65
on 1923 election, 104–105,
108–110
on 1929 local election, 190,
196–197
on 1932 election, 205
on abolition of Cork City
Council, 189
on behaviour of Republicans
during Civil War, 104
on the death of T. MacSwiney,
40
on election of Seán French,
113
on Fianna Fáil, 153–154, 208

political advertisements for
1920 elections, 27
support for Cumann na
nGaedhael, September
1927, 182–183
on the Treaty, 158–159
Cork Progressive Association,
91–93, 105, 108, 180
Cork, violence in 1920 and
1921, 42–43
Corry, Martin, 224, 225
Cosgrave, W. T., 51, 79, 83,
85–86, 147, 151, 167, 169,
173–174, 178, 183, 197,
202, 221, 222, 223
and A. O'Rahilly, 89, 115, 116
campaign for 1923 election,
97–98
performance in 1932 election,
211
at 'Preliminary Conference' of
Cumann na nGaedhael,
81, 82
Craig, Sir James, 130
Cronin, John, 30
Crosbie, George, 40
Crowley, Con, 55, 89, 90
Crowley, Patrick, 191
Cudmore, Richard, 203
Cumann na mBan, 13
Cumann na nGaedhael, 79, 80,
84, 85, 86, 110, 118, 122,
138, 142, 147, 169
1923 election campaign, 91,
93–94, 108
1924 by-election, 113–114
1927 June election campaign,
149, 151
1927 September election
campaign, 176, 178–179
1929 local election campaign,
193–194

O'Brien, William, 6, 165
O'Callaghan, Donal, 4, 45, 48,
 56, 57, 58, 60, 63, 69
 on Anglo-Irish Treaty, 52, 53
 performance in 1922 election,
 71
O'Callaghan, Fr, 47
O'Connell, Jeremiah, 129
O'Connor, Batt, 122
O'Connor, Rory, 76
O'Connor, William F., 23, 25, 94
O'Donnell, Michael, 145
O'Donnell, Peadar, 140
O'Duffy, Eoin, 58, 126, 228–229
O'Flanagan, Fr, 15, 128
Ó hAodha, Séamas, 81
O'Hegarty, Seán, 59
O'Higgins, Kevin, 51, 77, 85, 86,
 117, 142, 151, 152, 162
O'Kelly, Seán T., 6, 152, 162,
 165
old-age pension, 118, 119–121
Old Age Pensions Act, 119, 121
O'Leary, Seán, 148, 154, 194,
 203, 206, 211, 213, 215
Ó Máille, Pádraic, 117, 223
O'Malley, Ernie, 77
O'Rahilly, Alfred, 54, 55, 56, 77,
 88, 89, 90, 116, 124, 125,
 186, 187, 204, 208, 220
 1923 election, 96–97, 106
 letter to Richard Mulcahy,
 114–115
 resignation of, 122
 support for Fianna Fáil in
 1932, 214
O'Regan, Thomas, 194
O'Shannon, Cathal, 4
O'Shaughnessy, Andrew, 88, 92,
 93, 106, 107, 129, 204,
 214, 220
O'Sullivan, Gearóid, 58

O'Sullivan, Jack, 195
O'Sullivan, R. L., 12, 13, 17

partition, 49
Peace Conference, 8, 9, 10, 18
Phoblacht, An 126
Plunkett, Count, 18
politicians, elected after 1922,
 217
Price, Michael, 128
pro-Treaty group, performance
 in 1922 election, 74
Progressive Association, 87,
 91–93, 106, 220
proportional representation, 27,
 28, 34
protectionism, 142, 150, 170,
 171, 186, 187
Provisional Committee, 82
Public Safety Act, 175, 177, 179,
 198, 202, 209, 210
Punch, John, 131
Pyne, Peter, 110, 127, 128, 132,
 133, 135

Redistribution of Seats (Ireland)
 Act (1918), 1
Redmond, William Archer,
 148–149, 155, 197, 202
Regan, John, 122, 170
Representation of the People Act
 (1918), 1, 13
Reynolds, Brian, 139, 187, 214
Routledge, Patrick, 140
Rumpf, Erhard, 43, 73

Saor Éire, 199
Senate, 185, 186
Sinn Féin, 1, 2–3, 5, 13, 23–24,
 32, 34, 125, 126–127, 140,
 145, 168